Preface

Dea...er,

Sinc...ng *Body Language Basics* (Adams Media, 2005), I've been besieged with
que...rom family, friends and friends-of-friends about the meanings behind
part...ody movements. I've also been asked on more than a few occasions to
dem...te the best ways of getting – and keeping – someone's attention. I'm
happ...are what I've learned, because it isn't difficult to teach: confidence and
frien...will open more doors for you than you ever thought possible.

He...most important thing that I tell my friends: knowing what people
are s...with their gestures involves careful observation and putting those
beh...nto context. Focusing on one lone non-verbal cue while ignoring
ten...ill only lead you to the wrong conclusions time and time again. For
exar...a man is invading your personal space, that could definitely be a sign
of in...unless you're in a crowded bar, he has his back turned to you, and
he h...ed your way just once – when he accidentally stepped on your foot.
You...pend your night wondering if that was his way of getting to know
you,...could take the reins, show your interest in him through your body
lang...nd see what happens.

Us...nformation in this book wisely; use it well; use it to your advantage.

Be...ck,

Shelly *agen*

THE ONLY BOOK YOU'LL EVER NEED
Body Language

THE ONLY BOOK YOU'LL EVER NEED
Body Language

David and Charles

A DAVID & CHARLES BOOK
© F&W Media International, LTD 2011

David & Charles is an imprint of F&W Media International, LTD
Brunel House, Forde Close, Newton Abbot, TQ12 4PU, UK

F&W Media International, LTD is a subsidiary of F+W Media, Inc.
4700 East Galbraith Road, Cincinnati, OH 45236

First published in the UK in 2011

Text copyright © F+W Media Inc. 2011

The material in this book has been previously published in *The Everything Body Language Book*, published by Adams Media, 2008.

F+W Media Inc. has asserted the right to be identified as author of this work in accordance with the Copyright, Designs and Patents Act, 1988.

A catalogue record for this book is available from the British Library.

ISBN-13: 978-1-4463-0141-8 paperback
ISBN-10: 1-4463-0141-9 paperback

Printed in China by RR Donnelley
for F&W Media International LTD,
Brunel House, Forde Close, Newton Abbot, TQ12 4PU, UK

10 9 8 7 6 5 4 3 2 1

Senior Acquisitions Editor: Freya Dangerfield
Assistant Editor: Felicity Barr
Project Editor: Ame Verso
Design Manager: Sarah Clark
Senior Production Controller: Kelly Smith

F+W Media publish high quality books on a wide range of subjects.

For more great book ideas visit: www.rubooks.co.uk

Contents

Top Ten Situations for Using and Decoding Body Language /10
Introduction /11

1 The Evolution of Body Language /13
Survival of the Fittest 14 • Modern Body Language 17 • What da Vinci Knew 18 •
Judge Not? 20 • Hey, New Best Friend! 22 • Learn It, Know It, Use It! 24

2 What You're Saying Without Saying a Word /25
What Body Language Tells People About You 26 • Contradicting Yourself 28 •
Body Parts and Body Language 29 • Personalities in Disguise 30 • Check Your
Body Language Skills 33 • Correcting Errant Body Language 37

3 The Language of Hands /41
Hand Motions 42 • Talk to the Hand 43 • Hyped-Up Hands 46 • Shake It Like You
Mean It 48 • Politicians and the Perfect Hand Positioning 52 • Signing 54

4 Straight Talk: What Your Posture Tells the World /55
Perilous Posture 56 • Perfecting Your Posture 58 • Head and Shoulders Above
the Crowds 62 • Arm Awareness 63 • What's Your Angle? 65 • The Position of
Authority 66

5 The Remarkable Head /69
Is Beauty All in Your Head? 70 • Heads Up 71 • Hair Basics 74 • Hair Twirls and
Flicks 77 • Yes, No and Everything in Between 79

6 The Mighty Mouth /81
Let Your Mouth Do the Non-Verbal Talkin' 82 • Lip Behaviours 83 • Tongue
Twisters 85 • The Law of the Jaw 87 • Happy at Last 90

7 The Eyes Have It /93

Looking Awful? 94 • Eye Awareness 94 • Those Mysterious Brows 95 • Eyelashes 96 • Open Wide 96 • Look at Me!100 • Emotional Eyes 104

8 Nosing Around /107

A Flare for Emotion 108 • Read My Nose 110 • Crinkle, Crinkle, Little Nose 112 • Sneezing and Snorting 113

9 Can't Stop Moving /117

Movers and Shakers 118 • Nervous Hands 118 • Shifting Seats 122 • Happy Feet? 123 • Jumping for Joy 125 • Redirecting Nervous Energy 127

10 Children and Body Language /129

Nature or Nurture? 130 • Live and Learn 134 • Exclusion Zone 135 • Little Liars 136 • Emotional Overdrive 138

11 Business Body Language /141

Talk the Talk, Walk the Walk 142 • Listen to Your Grandmother! 143 • Some Handy Tips 145 • Face the Interview 147 • Win or Lose 148 • Turning the Tables150 • Inside the Office 151

12 Gestures Around the World /155

Once More, From the Top 156 • Eyeing International Body Language 157 • Worldwide Noses 160 • Slip of the Lip 160 • The Messages of the Upper Appendages 162 • The Lower Appendages 165

13 Dress Up Your Body Language /167

Clothing and Common Sense 168 • Dressing the Part 169 • Common Errors in Judgment 173 • Looking for Love in All the Wrong Places 176 • A Trip Around the Colour Wheel 177

14 Physique and Body Language /179

The Incredible Shrinking Woman 180 • The Ideal Attitude 183 • Mr Perfect 184 • Weight and Body Language 185 • Does Fitness Improve Body Language? 187 • Sheldon's Somatypes 188

15 Trust Me: How to Spot a Liar /191

Eye Spy 192 • It's Written All Over Your Face 194 • Under- and Overstatements 196 • Suspicious Positioning 198 • Is Everyone Dishonest? 199

16 Love at First Eye Contact? /201

Beauty Is in the Eye of the Beholder 202 • Beauty and the Beast Within 202 • Playing the Confidence Card 203 • The Purpose Behind the Pick-Up 205 • Signals for Singles 206 • Things to Avoid 208 • He Loves Me, He Loves Me Not 210

17 Skills for Single Girls /215

Eye Love You 216 • Lips Don't Lie … or Do They? 220 • Move Over 223 • Play Up Your Assets 225 • Full of Grace 226 • Move On 227

18 Guidance for Guys /229

Eye Saw You First 230 • The Best You 233 • Getting Friendly 234 • Turn, Turn, Turn 235 • Bust a Move, Not Your Ankle 238 • When to Give It Up 238 •

19 Body Language Online /241

The Talkative Type 242 • Keyboard Cronies 244 • Picture Perfect 246 • Reading Minds Online 249

20 Minimizing Body Language Mistakes /251

Content and Context 252 • Duelling Gestures 253 • Voyages of Discovery 256 • Non-Verbal Tricks 257 • Patterns of Behaviour 259 • Symptoms of Illness 260 • It's All Human Nature 262

Appendix: Some Important Body-language signs /263

Index /265

Top Ten Situations for Using and Decoding Body Language

1. First dates.

2. Job interviews.

3. Public speaking.

4. Looking for the truth.

5. Negotiating the purchase of a car.

6. Shopping in a commission-based boutique.

7. Responding to a domineering man or woman.

8. Determining if the cute guy over there is into you.

9. Determining if the cute girl over there is into you.

10. Not offending the locals when you're travelling the world.

Introduction

Imagine a world where you're never misunderstood, where you never send mixed messages, where you never have to backtrack and say, 'That's not what I meant!' The way you hold your hands, position your eyebrows and turn your body can all have a major impact on how well your intended message comes across to others. Getting your body language right can land you a long-term relationship, whether it's business or personal; getting it all wrong might ruin your chances.

Some men and women view learning body language as a sort of luxury, something they'll look into when they have some extra time on their hands. It may come as a surprise to these people to learn that some experts estimate non-verbal communication accounts for well over half of all face-to-face interactions. (This makes learning body language seem more like a necessity than a luxury, doesn't it?) The experts go on to say that even if you don't openly acknowledge those silent gestures and movements, your brain is still registering them subconsciously, an occurrence that has the potential to cause all sorts of confusion. When you can't separate the spoken message from its accompanying non-verbal cues, the likelihood of misinterpretation is high.

Most people want to learn about body language so that they can do well at a job interview, win over the object of their affection or catch a liar in the act. But what you learn about non-verbal communication can be used in all kinds of situations, from work to school to interacting with your neighbours. It's one thing to know how to charm people with your words; fortifying your spoken words with the correct unspoken cues really sells you and your personality to the people around you.

Reading body language can help you navigate your way around almost any situation where you feel you need some sort of key to understand the other person's intention. Think of this knowledge as your own personal Rosetta Stone for decoding your interpersonal relationships. This book will take you over the different areas of the body and help you understand what their various movements mean. Along with this information, you'll look at different scenarios where having an intimate knowledge of the meaning behind the gestures will give you a definite advantage and make your life significantly less stressful.

Be prepared: friends and family members will marvel at your newfound confidence and your ability to defuse the people who frustrate you the most. (Sounds good, doesn't it?) Tempting as it may be, don't keep the secret to yourself – let them know that anyone can get an inside scoop on human behaviour by simply reading up on non-verbal cues. Don't stand there wearing a frown and pursed lips (two signs of confusion or disbelief) – not only is this true, it's very possible. So get going and learn this incredibly useful skill. You'll kick yourself (an indication of anger) if you don't.

Chapter 1

The Evolution of Body Language

You hear about body language all the time, and from diverse sources. Women's magazines, for example, claim to hold the secrets of communicating with men without saying a word. Business websites offer tips for wowing potential employers or clients. Scientific journals, meanwhile, try to crack the codes of body language and separate fact from fiction. So, are any of these points of view valid? And where did this notion of non-verbal communication begin, anyway? This chapter will take a look at the origins of, and reasons for, studying body language.

Survival of the Fittest

Not surprisingly, people have used body language since the beginning of time; however, centuries ago, few men and women understood the power of the unspoken message. Body language was an intangible part of the communication process. Spouses and lovers may have suspected that there was more to a story than what they were hearing from their mates, but they couldn't quite put their finger on what was adding to or detracting from their conversations.

Monkey See, Monkey Do

The person credited with discovering non-verbal communication cues was none other than Charles Darwin (1809–1882), who is, of course, also credited with a few other scientific discoveries, such as that little project he called the Theory of Evolution.

A recent study suggested that fear can be caused by reading others' non-verbal cues. Participants were shown pictures of people who appeared to be frightened; using MRI technology on the participants, researchers measured increases in activity in the part of the brain that registers fear.

Darwin was a brilliant scientist, but even so, it's fair to question how and why anyone would believe that gestures speak louder than words. Remember, back in the 19th century, this was a completely new concept. In addition, during that time period, people were generally more reserved and didn't express themselves as passionately and openly as people do today. So, why would anyone think that bodily motions were the key to understanding human behaviour?

The answer lies in Darwin's earlier work. Darwin was very interested in finding any lingering connections between humans and animals. He noted several similarities in the way humans and animals express their emotions through facial expressions. For example, when an animal is frightened, it almost freezes in place – its eyes are wide open, its nostrils are flared and its mouth is slightly open. These are all classic fight-or-flight reactions as the animal prepares to either defend

2/3 = non-verbal

Read body language or predators to survive

itself or flee the scene. Interestingly, humans have the same type of reaction to extreme fear – their own fight-or-flight mechanism kicks in.

After making his initial links between animal and human behaviour, it wasn't such a stretch for Darwin to theorise that by studying the actions of animals, he could learn a lot about human behaviour. And so the study of non-verbal cues was born.

Studying animals allows us to understand human behaviour – theoretically.

Who Cares About Animal Behaviour?

Talking

Animals obviously don't have the gift of gab. They're almost totally dependent on reading and interpreting the actions of potential predators and prey in order to survive. Humans, on the other hand, often believe that almost all communication takes place verbally. However, unlike animals, humans really do have two forms of communication going on during any interaction. You move your body as you speak, often without thinking about it, and those gestures often define the meaning behind the spoken message.

Some experts estimate that only one-third of human communication is verbal. If you ignore body language, then, you might be missing two-thirds of any given interaction! This doesn't matter all that much if a person's words and their gestures are in sync, but what if the verbal message contradicts the body language (or vice versa)? What if, for example:

- Your date is saying all the right things but avoids making eye contact with you? *Lying*
- Your accountant is tapping his feet under his desk while he tells you that your money is safe and sound? *Nervous*
- Your colleague calls you 'pal' but consistently shakes your hand in a palm-down fashion? *Dominating / power*

Perhaps you're thinking, 'These actions don't mean anything on their own. I'd have to hear more of the conversation.' Well, you've just overlooked some classic body language cues to human behaviour. By recognizing them as red flags, you might be able to save yourself a lot of grief in the long run. Which isn't to say that you should dump an inattentive date or a fidgety accountant straight away, but you might want to pay attention to how the rest of the relationship is faring.

Body language isn't always about sending an obvious message. People also use certain gestures to hide their true feelings. Lack of eye contact, turning the body away and hiding the hands are just a few cues that indicate there's something more to someone's story.

Learning the Lingo

Certain non-verbal communications are innate. They simply happen in a given situation, and anyone who's watching you will instantly be able to read your body language because he shares the same primal instincts.

Earlier, this chapter talked about the body's response to fear and the kinds of physical cues you might see in someone who's experiencing a moment of pure terror (like being chased by a dog, for example, or losing control of your car). These types of responses are pre-programmed in the brain; when you fear for your life, you don't have to stop and say to yourself, 'Wow, if I could just make my eyes wider, I might be able to see any potential danger around me, and if I start breathing a little faster, I'll put enough oxygen into my bloodstream so that I'm ready for any kind of fight!' (And if you do know someone who has to tell himself how to react to fear, maybe you should be a little afraid – of him).

Plenty of body language is learned, however, from interacting with other people and mimicking what you see on television and at the cinema. As you work these learned behaviours into your everyday life, they become second nature. At that point, you use them without consciously making an effort to do so. Some examples of learned body language include:

- Batting your eyelashes at a potential mate (makes you look innocent).
- The palm-down handshake (a domineering move).
- Tilting the head (makes you look non-threatening).
- Well-timed touches (make you seem friendly).
- Glaring at someone who's made you angry (another domineering move).
- Widening the eyes during conversation (makes you look interested).

If you find yourself regularly leaving meetings or coming home from dates with the unshakable feeling that things just did not go well, consider the messages you're silently sending. Depending on what you've been doing with your various body parts, your boss or your partner may think you're hostile or completely uninterested in what she's saying. Fortunately, even if you have been putting out the wrong message, you can learn to correct your body language; and if you're not putting out any message at all, you can learn to crank things up so that others will take notice of you.

Although there are some behaviours that are expressed almost universally by all humans in a given situation, body language also includes learned gestures that you pick up from friends, siblings, the media or even strangers on the street.

Modern Body Language

Darwin began the study of body language in the 1800s; in the 1970s, a ballet dancer-turned-anthropologist named Ray Birdwhistell (1918–1994) picked up the ball and ran with it.

Kinesics

Birdwhistell referred to the study of body language as kinesics. Although he coined a new phrase, his area of interest was the same as Darwin's – he observed and analysed facial expressions and body movements, looking for hidden meanings in them.

The study of kinesics is broken down into five main sections of interest, which you might think would make it easy to understand. Unfortunately, these cues vary from culture to culture, so understanding why a Japanese person behaves in a certain way won't help you determine the meaning behind a Brazilian's gestures. However, it's interesting to know that anthropologists have found a way to reduce sometimes confusing human behaviour to just a few categories. These include:

- Emblems: non-verbal cues that clearly represent a verbal message, like a 'thumbs-up' gesture or the hand signal for 'OK'.
- Illustrators: gestures that underscore the meaning of the verbal message

     (think about someone who talks with his hands).

- Affect displays: facial gestures that convey a non-verbal message (a grimace, a smile, a frown).
- Regulators: non-verbal cues that determine how well the verbal communication is going. Basically, these are body-language cues that indicate the person has heard and/or understands what you've said (head nods or shakes, for example). Whether you go on talking or stop and repeat yourself depends on the regulators coming from the other person.
- Adaptors: relaxed movements (like shifting in your seat or shrugging your shoulders to loosen them) are a hot topic of debate. Some experts feel adaptors are the real clues to non-verbal messages; others say they're nothing more than comfort measures.

One of Birdwhistell's theories states that even if you don't make a conscious note of a person's gestures while you're talking to her, you still subconsciously register the meaning of her non-verbal cues.

While learning to read universal gestures isn't hard, applying your knowledge to everyday relationships isn't always easy. But with some practice, patience and a whole lot of perception, you can learn to separate the spoken word from non-verbal cues and get to the bottom of almost anyone's story.

What da Vinci Knew

Because Darwin was the first person to come up with a theory linking human expression to animals', the true study of body language didn't exist prior to the 19th century. However, there's evidence that suggests that at least one other man recognised the power of non-verbal communication – hundreds of years before Darwin made his discovery.

Mona Lisa Smile

Mona Lisa, painted by Leonardo da Vinci most likely in the early 1500s, is one of the most mysterious and debated images of all times. For centuries, scholars

Gestures can convey or disguise emotion - Da vinci

Leonardo da vinci - mona lisa

have argued over her smile – whether it's genuine or fake, whether this woman is happy or irritated about posing for the artist, whether that smile is an indication of love or if it's more of a patient smirk.

At first glance, her smile doesn't appear to be forced, but on closer inspection, you'll also note that although the corners of her mouth curve upwards as opposed to laterally (an upwards grin is an indication of a genuine smile), the rest of her face is rather unengaged. Her eyes, in particular, give her away, as their edges are still – they aren't crinkled or turned upwards, as they most likely would be in a smile that expressed great happiness or joy. So here is a lady who is patiently posing for a portrait, who may not be genuinely thrilled about it.

On Second Thoughts ...

Of course, this is hardly the definitive word on Mona Lisa's smile. As portraits took many days or weeks to complete, it's extremely likely that different parts of her face were painted at different times – and that might well explain the confusion over her smile. Perhaps the first time she sat for the portrait she was happy; the next time she was bored; the third time, she was ready for it to be finished.

Art historians will continue to debate the meaning behind her famous smirk, a project that would be much easier if they could also see her posture, her hand position and whether she crossed her legs or kept her feet flat on the ground. (Don't worry – all of these body-language cues will be explained in this book.)

Cultural Variation

Body language varies from culture to culture. Something that's appropriate in Britain (making eye contact with someone who walks past you, for example) may be completely unacceptable in other parts of the world. (If you find yourself in Japan, keep your eyes to yourself!)

For our purposes, the significant thing about Mona Lisa's smile isn't whether she's happy or sad or annoyed – it's that da Vinci knew back in the 16th century that a smile can convey – or disguise – different emotions.

Judge Not?

There are always those people who swear blind that they would never, ever judge a person based on his or her appearance. But the fact is, all people judge one another's 'look' at some time or another – some just do it more often (and more openly) than others.

Kids Will Be Kids

There's a classic sociology experiment where examiners present child-age test subjects with two pictures of other children – one picture of a slim child, the other of an overweight child. The children being tested are asked which child they'd rather be friends with. Most kids choose the slim child as their new friend. Their reasons include opinions that simply can't be derived as fact from a photo, such as the overweight child isn't as clever or as nice as his trim counterpart.

As noble as it is to claim that you never judge others' appearance, it's very difficult to carry through on that promise. Simply becoming aware of the ways you judge other people is a good first step towards minimizing the effects of your preconceptions.

Unfortunately, attitudes concerning appearance don't magically disappear as kids mature. Adults can be absolutely merciless when judging one another's appearances, and in some circles, picking apart friends and acquaintances is nothing less than an obsession. But what's the difference between judging a person's general appearance and judging his or her body language? Appearances are deceiving.

Let's go back to the experiments using the pictures of overweight children – but let's fast-forward 20 years. Research has shown that adults tend to view their overweight peers as being unintelligent, lazy and unhygienic.

'So what?' you ask. 'They must be lazy, otherwise they'd be thin. And anyone who can't work out how to lose weight must be stupid. I don't want to work on a project with anyone who's lazy and stupid because it'll make my life harder.' Do you see how these judgments create negative scenarios? Your heavy colleague

Stereotypes/perception get in the way of reading non-verbal cues.

might be the hardest-working and most intelligent person in your office, but because you've already judged his personality based on his appearance, it's going to be that much harder for you to read any of his non-verbal cues in a positive light.

You can't accurately evaluate someone's body language if you've already assigned him negative characteristics based on his appearance. That's like trying to look through a window after you've smeared it with dirt and grease. ✔✔

Shy Guys (and Girls)

If you're insecure about the way you look, it will definitely show in your body language. You'll avoid making eye contact, you won't stand tall, you won't smile at other people, you'll make sure never to touch others – in short you won't be putting out any sort of positive message. People may perceive your shyness as a lack of interest in them or as out-and-out snobbishness.

Case Study

Back in the 1990s, researchers at the College of New Rochelle in America conducted a study of nurses' attitudes towards their patients in the hope of uncovering hidden prejudice. The surprising result: attitudes were most negative towards white, obese patients. The not-so-surprising finding was that the nurses' beliefs negatively affected the care their obese patients received.

This chapter won't go any further into the psychology of how judging others' appearances affects you and them – but it does happen, it affects your daily interactions, and if you really want to know the people around you (and you want them to know you), you have to look below the surface. This is sometimes easier to do if you understand the difference between arrogant gestures, friendly overtures and insecure behaviour.

Don't Take It Personally

There are several medical conditions that can cause what's called a 'flat affect' of the face, which simply means that the facial muscles are impaired. You won't see joy, anger or surprise expressed in this person's face. What you will see is something of a blank stare with no emotion attached to it. There are other conditions that can cause a person's facial expressions to be distorted, so that he appears to be smiling even though he isn't happy.

Imagine that you're on your way into the supermarket and you accidentally walk straight into a customer who's walking out. He drops his bags and the contents come spilling out. You're mortified and spring into action, scooping up apples with one hand while juggling the loo rolls and eggs in the other. When you've placed all of the items back into their bags, you tell the person how sorry you are. This stranger just stares at you, mumbles a quick 'Thanks', and goes on his way. You feel angry that he wasn't more appreciative of your efforts to right your wrong. Some people would allow this kind of interaction to influence their future behaviour, by vowing not to help strangers anymore, for example.

Happened to me

Misunderstandings can occur when you come face to face with a stranger who's unable to express emotion, or does so in an inappropriate way. You might misinterpret his lack of emotion as indifference or even hostility.

As important as it is to know how to read non-verbal cues, it's as important to understand that what you see isn't always what you get – and even if you are on the receiving end of a blank stare or a frown, sometimes it's nothing personal. That's why it's also important to put non-verbal cues into some type of context before evaluating them – so that you avoid jumping to conclusions.

Hey, New Best Friend!

People who are well schooled in the finer points of body language know how to use it to their advantage – every day, in every situation. Despite your best intentions, you sometimes end up being the pawns in their little schemes. Is there a way to watch out for this kind of sketchy behaviour? Why, yes, there is! In fact, if you know the other person's motivation for being extra super nice to you, his body language not only becomes obvious, it becomes downright predictable.

You're Great! Sign Here, Please

Take, for example, the classic salesman. If he's any good at his job, you want to like him, even though you know you should take anything he says with a pinch of salt. You're wondering if he's the exception to the rule, the honest needle in the otherwise shady haystack. The answer: probably not. He might be a great bloke, but he has a job to do. Part of that job includes charming potential customers so that they'll drop their guard along with their hard-earned cash.

Someone who's working hard to win you over will:

- Smile. A lot.
- Use a firm handshake.
- Use eye contact in a way that makes you take notice. (He doesn't over- or underuse it).
- Widen his eyes and possibly raise his eyebrows as you speak.
- Nod when you speak.

Yes, this chap knows exactly how to reel you in, make you feel like his numero uno customer, and sell you an inferior product at a ridiculous mark-up. And what's more, you may be well aware that this guy isn't for real but you end up falling for his act anyway. Don't feel too badly about it; you aren't his first victim and you won't be his last.

Protecting Yourself Against False Charms

What is this power that body language has over people, and how can you defend yourself against it? Is there some sort of invisible shield available to those who are extremely gullible or should everyone simply adopt a completely cynical attitude?

While cynicism is certainly one way to protect against professional fibbers, it's also a really bad way to go through life. Yes, you'll end up blocking access to the undesirables, but you'll also end up shielding yourself from good, genuine people. No, the best way to fight back is to arm yourself with knowledge: what are the classic body-language signs that indicate lying? Which signs tell you that someone may not necessarily be lying, but may not be telling you the whole truth? In asking (and answering) these questions, what you're really looking for are the practical uses of an understanding of body language.

Learn It, Know It, Use It!

You've already read about a few situations that can be heavily impacted by body language. There are plenty of everyday situations where you'll find it helpful to know something about what someone's body is saying while she is talking, including:

- First (and last) dates.
- Job interviews.
- Meetings with clients.
- Interactions with salespeople.
- Dealings with children.
- Travelling abroad.
- Watching a politician speak.

In each of these situations, you need to know how to interpret the other person's non-verbal cues in order to understand what she's saying, but your part doesn't end there. In order to send your own message successfully, you need to get a handle on your own body language. Fortunately, you've come to the right place. Not only does this book give you advice for reading and sending non-verbal messages, it also reminds you – again and again – about putting those cues into an appropriate context so that you don't misread others' intentions.

You might be wondering how many body-language cues there are and how you'll ever keep them straight in your mind. The best place to begin is by studying yourself. Once you learn to recognise your own non-verbal behaviour, it's much easier to evaluate someone else's.

Chapter 2

What You're Saying Without Saying a Word

Chapter 1 talked about the study of body language –
where and when the concept began and how people
use it to evaluate perfect strangers on the street. This
chapter will turn the tables, so to speak, and take a
look at what you're saying to other people with your
gestures and movements. This isn't an attempt to
make you feel badly about yourself; it's a wake-up call
for you to realise that (almost) every move you make
can be interpreted as a message by someone else.
What kind of signals are you sending?

What Body Language Tells People About You

Even if you don't believe that gestures and motions contain a hidden language, plenty of other people do. Some of these people are intentionally searching for patterns in your behaviour; others are simply intuitive enough to know when there's something amiss (such as when your mouth is saying one thing but your body is telling a completely different story). Fair or not, people tend to look at one another as open books. When the book seems to be written in a language that you don't understand, body language is often brought in as the interpreter.

Right on Cue(s)

You can understand someone being interested in gestures if they happen to be a psychologist or an anthropologist (in other words, if they have a 'legitimate' reason to study human behaviour), but why does your friend analyse every piece of seemingly random data concerning her boyfriend's eye movements? How can she be so convinced that he's lying? (And why is he such a bad liar?)

In Chapter 1, you read that people learn certain body-language cues from each other. For example, you might learn from a mentor at work how to carry yourself in a professional manner in the office. People also find – and copy – examples of body language presented in the media. One celebrity exhibits a certain behaviour, such as fist-bumping or excessive pouting, fans mimic him, and before you know it you've got a whole new set of body-language cues to deal with on a personal basis. Real people might misuse these cues, though, which only confuses things further.

How a gesture is interpreted depends on who's using it and the setting he's using it in. Using current 'hip' hand motions in the pub makes you look like one of the lads, but displaying those same gestures in the office might make you look unprofessional.

User or Non-User

Even if you think you don't use body language, you do. Every single day, you move your hands, your head, your legs and your torso, probably without thinking about the messages attached to those movements.

Most people send off body-language signals because they don't know much about the study of physical gestures. They're relaxed and simply going about their business. These men and women are easy to observe and analyse, because they have no idea what their gestures are saying to the outside world.

Some people specifically study and perfect their body language to get ahead in life (salespeople and politicians, for example). Watch out for them – they're very skilled in matching their spoken word to their body movements, sending out a message that seems genuine but in many cases is anything but.

When you first start learning about body language and the ways you physically display the thoughts you believed were hidden safely in your head, it's natural to say to yourself, 'I'm going to sit on my hands and not make eye contact with people. I don't want anyone reading my behaviour!' But if you read far enough into any body language book, you'll know that sitting on the hands sends a message all its own, as does shifty eye contact.

Damned If You Do, Damned If You Don't

If all body language sends a message, does that mean you're trapped in a form of communication that you don't necessarily want to use? Perhaps you feel that there's no point in learning anything else on the topic because no matter what you do, people are going to analyse your moves and decide if what you're saying is genuine. Well, that's true (at least to some extent). And most of the time, this isn't a problem; it's just the way that life works. You might find yourself in quite the predicament, though, when the body language you're using is sending the wrong message.

For example, let's say you're rubbing your face while you tell your boss that your project is coming along terrifically. Maybe you have an itch; maybe your face is swollen; or maybe that facial rub just feels good to you. Trouble is, it's also a classic sign that someone's fibbing. And as many senior-level managers actually take classes in understanding body language, you might suddenly find yourself under a microscope at work without knowing why.

Many businesses offer courses in body language, for several reasons: salespeople need to know how to project a likeable persona; they also need to know how to spot a customer's weak points. Your boss, meanwhile, might study body language so that he knows the appropriate ways to deal with his international cohorts. Do an internet search for business-oriented body language websites and/or check out www.presentation-pointers.com.

Contradicting Yourself

Scientists, sociologists, psychologists and anthropologists all have their own reasons for studying body language. The average person also has a reason: to make sure that the messages he's sending with his body back up his verbal statements. Many studies have shown that when verbal and non-verbal messages are at odds, people tend to trust the non-verbal cues. This tends to lead to a lot of confusing situations. (For example, you may analyse a date and think, 'He said he likes me, but he was really stand-offish. So does he like me or not?' Classic verbal/non-verbal confusion.)

What Are You Doing Wrong?

Spot the flawed body language in these situations:

- You're out for dinner with your boyfriend, professing your love while staring intently – with raised eyebrows – at your water glass.
- You're arguing with a friend. You stand with your legs crossed at the ankles and your arms crossed tightly over your chest, flaring your nostrils as you insist that your point of view is right.
- Your colleague asks if you've finished the report you're working on; he needs it. You make direct eye contact, rub the back of your neck and say, 'It's just about done.'

In the first situation, the lack of eye contact detracts from your message. Eye contact is generally made during conversation and held during intense moments, such as this one. The eyebrow-raise (something you'll read about in Chapter 7) indicates that a person believes what he's saying, so that may save you here.

In the argument scenario, you've pulled your body in tightly, making yourself as small as possible, indicating that you're protecting yourself against your friend – but why would you need protection if you're right?

In the colleague situation, that neck-rub betrays the fact that your report is nowhere near complete. Self-touches are comforting measures, used to ease the stress of an uncomfortable situation (like when you're lying to someone's face). The hand to the back of the head or neck is a classic sign of anxiety and fibbing.

The point of learning body language isn't to help you become a better liar. Body language helps you to project a confident, genuine message and also helps to prevent misunderstandings, no matter what the situation.

Do Two Wrongs Make a Right?

If two gestures contradict each other, do they simply cancel each other out? This is the very question that confuses so many people. Take that first scenario again – maybe you are madly in love with this man, but if you continue to avoid eye contact with him, he's going to start to wonder about your intentions. The other two scenarios are similar. Regardless of whether you're telling the truth, the other person is picking up a non-verbal message from you. If that message happens to say, 'I don't believe what I'm saying,' the other person is going to run with it. It won't matter if you're 100 percent right in the argument with your friend, for example; she'll continue to argue her side of the issue because she sees the chink in your armour.

Body Parts and Body Language

This book will give you an overview of almost every body part (limited to those parts that are on display in polite company, of course) in an effort to shed some light on the messages emanating from these various areas. This section includes a brief overview of the regions of the body as they relate to body language.

- Head: used for affirming (nodding) or denying (headshake) information. Various angles of the head are also used to convey interest in what another person is saying.
- Face: conveys emotion, which will be discussed later in this chapter. The eyes are of particular interest, as you can snub someone simply by refusing to look their way.
- Shoulders: used for showing lack of interest (shrug; angling away from another person).
- Arms: can be used to express emotion; also used to make oneself look larger (hands-on-hips position). Arm crossing may indicate emotional discomfort, while flexing and extending the arms is a way to express strong emotion (positive or negative).
- Hands: can be used in a variety of ways: to express emotion; to show camaraderie (handshake); to show discomfort (self-touches).
- Legs: angling the legs is important. Pointing them towards the person you're speaking to shows interest; also, positioning of the legs can show power (wide stance) or fear (standing with legs crossed). Pigeon-toed people tend to look young, naïve and sloppy.

Personalities in Disguise

Is there anything more unsettling than realizing that someone isn't what you thought he was? Not finding out that your spouse has been leading a double life (though that might be a bit unsettling, too), but the realization that someone you thought was a real peach turns out to be a complete twerp, or vice versa.

Take a situation where you don't actually know a person very well but you see him often enough to draw certain conclusions about him – maybe he's a neighbour, a colleague or a friend of a friend. You've seen him in action from a distance and he appeared to be as grumpy as they come; now you've had the opportunity to talk to him and you can't believe how sweet he is! How could you have misjudged him so badly? You probably based your initial impressions on (drum roll, please) his body language.

Innocence Masked as Arrogance

Actually, this isn't an uncommon occurrence. Shy people are often perceived as being unfriendly and uppity. Think back to your days in secondary school and to all of those people you labelled as snobs. Of course, some of them did hold themselves in very high esteem, but were there a few who simply never spoke to anyone? Is it possible that they weren't stuck-up but were scared of other people?

How do these mistaken assignments of personality traits occur? Well, take the classic body-language cues that indicate someone is open and friendly, like:

- A broad smile.
- Good eye contact.
- Good posture.
- Physical touches (hugs, little touches on the arm).
- Angling his body to face you when you talk.

People who are very insecure (and/or painfully shy) often don't display these traits. They keep to themselves in the most literal sense, avoiding any kind of contact with others. It's not that they dislike people, exactly; they just don't have the social skills to deal with them.

Unfortunately, even the friendliest people – who are accepting of all sorts of behaviour – may not be able to differentiate between the body language of a person who's insecure and one who truly wants to be left alone. In the end, shy people end up isolated because of the way their behaviour is perceived by other people. It's almost as though their own behaviour holds them prisoner, socially speaking.

When Sweetness Turns Sour

The opposite can also happen: a nasty person can be mistaken for Mr Nice Guy. Finding a self-important person beneath a shy-seeming exterior is like getting a taste of vinegar when you were expecting honey (not nearly as nice a surprise as discovering that your 'cranky' neighbour is really just an insecure person).

You can understand how shyness can come across as arrogance, but how can the opposite happen? After all, arrogant people go out of their way to let everyone know how special they are. Classic signs of conceit include:

- The swaggering walk, which takes up more physical space than is necessary, a way of saying, 'Clear a path, I'm coming through!'
- The smirk – the smile with slightly pouty lips and squinty eyes – which says, 'Admit it: you think I'm amazing.'
- Minimal eye contact. When faced with saying hello to someone perceived as an underling, the arrogant person will pretend the other person simply isn't there. Refusing to look at the other person is the first step in establishing the arrogant person's imaginary world.
- Angling away from other people. When an arrogant person has to speak to people who aren't on his level, he won't bother to turn his upper body towards them (this goes along with not making eye contact – two gestures perceived as being very rude).

If you've somehow missed these body-language cues, you're thinking that maybe you should have your vision checked, especially if all of the signs were present but you were still drawn in by the sound of the person's voice and the curve of his face. But then again, maybe you shouldn't be so hard on yourself. Plenty of people know how to use body language to their advantage, even if it means (temporarily) suppressing their arrogant tendencies in the process.

Let's say that you're a man working in an office. Your desk is situated across the way from a woman who never says much, but only smiles sweetly when you look her way. When a big project lands on her desk (the impossible project – the one everyone is buzzing about, saying it'll never get done on time), you offer to help her. As you get to know her, you see her in situations that you weren't privy to before. You note, for example, that she's completely comfortable chit-chatting with the bosses and you watch other people hop out of her way when she does her power-walk through the office. You realise this woman has plenty of confidence – she's had no problem giving you orders and harshly criticizing your work. Slowly, it dawns on you that the reason she never speaks to her colleagues isn't because she's shy; it's because she thinks she's better than the rest of you.

And the sweet smile? Ooh, she's good: she's won you (and who knows who else?) over with an outward appearance of innocence. She's taken that old adage about catching flies with honey to heart and perfected it. Now ask yourself this: when was the last time you saw that precious grin? Was it directed at you – or at a new victim?

Check Your Body Language Skills

Let's put the manipulative colleagues aside and focus on someone far more interesting: you. More specifically, how others see you. Are you successful in your peer groups or are you constantly passed over when it's time for parties or promotions? Are you moving up in your career, being assigned projects that are at least on your level, or do you suspect someone thinks you're not capable of more difficult (and career-building) projects – even though your work has been more than adequate up to this point? At the same time, are you watching others shoot up that social or career ladder straight past you, even though you've been around for longer and you think you deserve some recognition?

These situations often go beyond what you're actually doing in your work or in your social situations – the trouble may be in how you're presenting yourself. You might very well be the most loyal friend who ever lived, but do you show an actual interest in others, or are you somewhat stand-offish, someone who's around but easily forgotten? Perhaps you should assess your body language skills with the following quiz:

1. You're talking with your friends at work. You stand:

a) Several feet away. You're fully aware that people need their personal space.

b) As close as you can. Snuggling up is the way to show people you really like them!

c) Between one and two feet away, which is close enough to be friendly, but not close enough to crowd other people.

Answer: c. Personal space is important in relationships, and different relationships call for different measurements of personal space. Close friends usually stand or sit one to two feet from each other; women tend to get closer than men.

2. You've just completed a project that is currently being criticised by the powers-that-be. You know your information is solid. You:

a) **Stand in front of the boss's desk with your hands on your hips, your feet planted far apart, your nostrils flared and your jaw locked while listening to his critique**. (We'll talk more about the possible implications of flared nostrils in Chapter 8.)

b) **Sit in front of the boss's desk, your back straight, your feet flat on the floor, your head level and your eyes focused on him**.

c) **Stand in the boss's doorway, legs crossed, arms crossed over your chest, head angled down**.

Answer: b. Option (a) expresses hostility; option (c) makes you look completely submissive, as though you know you're wrong and you're willing to accept the criticism. There's nothing wrong with using these gestures when the situation warrants it, but here, you only want to show that you're calm, cool and collected – which can best be accomplished with option (b).

3. You're new in town and haven't met any friends yet. You've decided to hit the local coffee shop in the hope of making a new acquaintance or two. Once you have your skinny latte in hand, you:

a) **Find a quiet table in the corner where you can watch as people enter and leave the place**.

b) **Sit at the window counter, where someone else is bound to come and sit near you**.

c) **Leave**. You don't really see anyone interesting here, after all.

Answer: b. When you want to meet new people, you have to be willing to be near them. (Again, this relates to personal space.) When you're close to people, conversation follows – as long as certain boundaries are respected. Options (a) and (c) send the message, 'Stay away from me.'

4. You sit with acquaintances in your company's canteen every day. You'd like to be better friends with them. Aside from using the appropriate amount of personal space, what are some other techniques to show your interest?

a) **As someone else is speaking, smile, tilt your head to the side and nod**. Hold eye contact for several seconds; look away, and then look back at the speaker. Laugh and touch her arm when she tells a funny story.

b) **As someone else is speaking, look to the others in the group and do whatever they're doing**.

c) **As someone else is speaking, make your eyes as wide as they can be, maintain constant eye contact, smile, nod profusely, and touch her as often as possible**.

Answer: a. While (b) seems like a safe option, you have to remember that these people are already friendly with each other, and their body-language cues between each other are likely to be more casual. Imitating their cues might show a lack of interest on your part, depending on how laid-back they are with each other. Option (c) is just too much – you'll scare the other person into thinking that you're a little too interested in her. Option (a) is middle ground – it's not too much, it's not too little, it's just right.

5. You're out on a first date with Mr Handsome, who is so perfect you just can't take your eyes off of him. It's all right to stare at him, because he must be used to it.

a) **True**

b) **False**

Answer: b. Unless you know someone well and/or are ready to face some unpredictable circumstances, staring isn't a great idea. Sure, this guy probably knows how good-looking he is, but don't forget he's also a human being. Maybe he wants you to fall in love with his mind. Staring can also make you look like a potential stalker. Use extended eye contact (something you'll read about in Chapter 7) to show your interest instead.

6. Every Friday at mid-afternoon, your colleagues start to show signs of relaxing: ties are loosened, people perch on each other's desks and there's laughter in the air along with the discussion of heading out to Happy Hour. How can you get yourself invited?

a) By joining in the relaxed atmosphere. Lose the blazer and work your way into the conversation.

b) By keeping your nose in your own business. If they want you to come, they'll seek you out.

c) You'll catch up with them later.

Answer: a. If you want to get in on the fun with these people, then get into their conversation. Many times, all you have to do is be present when plans are made. Keeping to yourself – as in answers (b) and (c) – will ensure that you leave the office alone while everyone else heads out together.

7. You're being interviewed for a promotion in your company. When you greet the boss, how do you present your hand for the obligatory handshake?

a) With your palm facing up towards the ceiling.

b) With the palm facing down towards the floor.

c) With the palm vertical.

Answer: c. Presenting a hand with the palm facing down (b) is a sign of domination (and can be perceived as an arrogant gesture); a palm held upwards (a) is a sign of submission. Best to shake in the traditional manner, with your palm vertical to the boss's.

8. You have to give a report to your boss about some irregularities in the office accounts. What should you do with your hands?

a) Keep them on the table in front of you where she can see them.

b) Stick them in your pockets.

c) They'll be safely tucked into your armpits as you tightly cross your arms during this meeting.

Answer: a. Hiding the hands (b) indicates that you have a secret; crossing your arms (c) can be perceived as a protective and/or self-comforting measure. If you have nothing to fear – because you're telling the truth – then you shouldn't need to comfort yourself. Let your boss see that you're on the up-and-up by keeping those hands out in the open.

9. You're out with your male friends and you meet up with some young ladies at a bar. How do you project confidence with your posture?

a) By shrugging a lot.

b) By standing with your back straight and shoulders back.

c) Who cares about posture? Slouching is more comfortable.

Answer: b. Standing straight and tall shows the world that you're comfortable in your own skin. Shrugging (a) and slouching (c) are both signs of insecurity. If you want these girls to think you're a man of the world, it's best to start with a good stance.

10. You're travelling abroad and notice that not one person has made eye contact with you since you got off the plane. What could be the cause?

a) Your outfit is horrendous.

b) Your haircut is horrific.

c) Minimal eye contact is appropriate in some cultures.

Answer: c. It's probably not your appearance; in some cultures, minimal eye contact is the rule of the day. Don't question it and don't try to change it, just adapt to it.

How did you do? Being in tune with body language can mean the difference between successful social interactions and complete isolation. But the ultimate outcome of these situations depends on how well you're able to combine your spoken messages with your body language. Again, you want to make sure your body language is sending the message you intend.

Correcting Errant Body Language

You've taken a good look at your body language and you see some areas for improvement. That's a step in the right direction. (Most people could use a little body-language overhaul, so you're in good company.) How hard is this going to be, and how long will it take? In other words, is it worth your time and effort?

How Important Is Non-Verbal Communication, Anyway?

As you've read in this chapter, your body sends two messages in any interaction – one spoken, the other non-verbal. If your non-verbal cues are contradicting your spoken word, there's a very good chance that whoever you're speaking to is going to:

- Be very confused.
- Make a mental note of the discrepancy.
- View you as a potentially dishonest person.

Body language can be misused and/or misinterpreted depending on the person displaying the cues and the environment in which he's displaying them. As you don't want to be the simpleton sending confusing or incorrect messages, it's worth your time to take a look at your behaviour and determine what you're telling the world.

These judgments are difficult to overcome in your personal relationships. But when it comes to wooing clients and closing deals, if you can't sell yourself along with your spoken message, the clients will move on to someone else – someone who took the time to perfect her non-verbal communication.

Back to Basics

Correcting your body language may be very easy or it may be more difficult – it all depends on how established your habits are. If you're a handwringer (a gesture that indicates insecurity), for example, and you have been for as long as you can remember, you're going to have to find something else to do with your hands. You'll need to be vigilant and remember to acknowledge what your hands are doing from time to time. Breaking your dependence on this comfort measure is the hardest part; once you're past that point, learning to use your hands in a more effective way (to project confidence, for example) depends on how much you practise and use your new moves. Soon enough, they'll become second nature. (Tips for expressing yourself effectively with your hands are found in Chapter 3.)

This chapter has focused on the ways that errant body language masks your true intentions and emotions, and how those mistakes may affect your relationships. Learning to use appropriate body language – cues that emphasise your verbal message instead of contradicting it – will not only help you in your personal relationships, but also in your professional dealings. When you have this relatively simply information guiding you, you put yourself at an advantage that many others are simply lacking. Throughout the rest of the book, you'll read about specific regions of the body, how to control the messages you're sending with your various appendages, and – just as importantly – how to decipher what other people are saying with their bodies, even when their mouths are saying something completely different.

Chapter 3

The Language of Hands

Some people can't complete a sentence (or even a simple phrase) without punctuating it by flailing their hands. Others like to keep their hands tucked away, taking them out for the really important occasions, like hailing a taxi or blowing kisses. Fortunately, the language of the hands is not only universal in many cases, it's also instinctual – surprisingly easy to learn and understand.

Hand Motions

You probably know someone who's a 'hand-talker', a person who can't make a point without doing so emphatically. He uses sweeping hand gestures, karate chops and questionably timed claps and snaps, and occasionally positions his fingers as if to strangle an invisible victim.

Your first introduction to a hand-talker can be startling, especially if you've never known anyone who communicates with his hands, or if the person in front of you is using gestures you've never seen and don't know how to interpret. Rest assured, hand-talking is an international occurrence. Some common hand gestures around the world include:

- The 'V' for victory sign: the back of your hand is facing you in this gesture. Turn your hand around and you will seriously insult someone, in Britain at least. (Hand insults are covered in Chapter 12).
- The 'OK' sign: form a circle with the thumb and forefinger, and hold the other fingers straight up. (Beware: in some cultures, this, too, is an insult).
- Thumb(s) up: this means 'good work' in many cultures.
- Waving: says 'hello' or 'goodbye'.
- 'Templing' the hands or intertwining the fingers: in many cultures, this conveys deep thought.
- Hand(s) to the heart: this commonly indicates love or heartache.
- Chopping motions, a fist, or a finger pointed at someone's face or chest: all of these betray hostility in the speaker.

There are many, many more hand motions, of course. You use your hands to indicate size (the fish you caught was how big?) and spatial relationships (to indicate how close you were standing to your favourite actress in Leicester Square) or to mimic activities (like holding your little finger to your mouth and your thumb to your ear to tell someone to call you later). In fact, some researchers believe that the hands actually convey more meaning and emotion than the face or the mouth.

In the next section, you'll learn how the positioning of the hands relates to the emotion behind the message.

Talk to the Hand

Let's say you're pleading with your parents for some extra spending money. Your mother holds her hands out to you, palms up, and says you have to be more responsible with your money. Is she willing to negotiate a loan or not? In the same situation, your father holds his hands up, his palms facing you, and says, 'Sorry, kid. I'm not lending you any more money.' Is there a chance that you'll change his mind?

There are several basic positions of the hands: palms up, palms down, palms facing the speaker and palms facing away from the speaker. Then there are fists, hand twirls and seemingly random finger-points. As you're reading this paragraph, you may be thinking, 'I do these things all the time. I don't mean anything by them!' Well, of course you do. (To find out what you mean when you use these hand motions, keep reading).

Bridge Builder

Holding your hands out with the palms turned upwards is a way of saying, 'I'm a peacemaker. Let's be friends.' It's also a way of asking for help, which is why you see religious clerics using this gesture, and why beggars reach out to people with their palms facing skywards. This is a non-threatening move.

How can you use this knowledge to evaluate real-life situations? Let's say your flatmate wants to have a chat with you because you haven't been doing your fair share of the housework and the place is starting to stink of old shoes and mildew. If the majority of his hand gestures are made with his palms facing upwards, what he's really looking for is a fair solution. He's open to new ideas and willing to discuss several options. If you can suggest a decent resolution to the issue, he's not going to fight you on it.

Here's another example: you're faced with a difficult situation at work. You have to get several people to blend their ideas into one project, and you suspect that everyone is going to hold firm to his or her own position. Sit them down at a table and extend your arms a bit while holding your hands in a palms-up gesture. This draws them to you. Not only is this a non-threatening move (one that lets your colleagues know that you aren't cracking a whip – yet), it also usually puts people at ease without their realizing it, making them more receptive to your ideas.

Palms-up is commonly seen in prayer as a beseeching move. Obviously, in this instance, the person is asking for something and is open to a response of some sort. When used in normal day-to-day conversation, this gesture is interpreted as being accepting of other people and ideas.

Come to Me

The palms-in gesture is similar to the palms-up move, except it's more of a 'drawing-in' motion. If you're speaking to someone and using a lot of palms-in movements, he is going to know that you like him, that you want to speak to him, that you want to bring him into your world. Now, this doesn't necessarily mean that you want him to move in with you (at least not right away), but it's definitely a friendly gesture. You're almost literally pulling him towards you.

Picture this: you're saying goodnight to your date outside your front door. You really want him to come in, but you don't want to pressure him. Suggest that he come in for a drink while using the palms-in gesture, which is friendly without crossing over into aggressive territory.

The palms-in gesture isn't always as obvious as it sounds. (You don't have to be making actual pulling-in motions to get your point across, in other words.) You can be waving your hands around in a seemingly random fashion; as long as your palms are facing you, this is an inviting motion.

Back It Up

On the flip side, the palms-down gesture is a dominating move that sometimes also indicates hostility. Think back to the angry flatmate example from earlier in this chapter. What if he sat you down and ran through his complaints, along with his solution for the situation, with his palms facing downwards? What's his underlying message?

• 'This is exactly what I mean to say. Don't question it or argue with it.'
And/or

• 'Keep your distance and listen to what I'm saying.'

Palms-down is not an inviting gesture. It's meant to hold others at bay while you speak. It indicates that you've already made up your mind and you're not open to any sort of input. Palms-down is often combined or replaced with palms-out (palms facing away from you), which basically tells the same story: back off and accept what I'm saying, because I'm not going to change my mind.

Remember the 1990s, when everyone was holding their palms in each other's faces and saying, 'Talk to the hand'? This was body language in full force! Holding your palms towards another person tells him to stop his talking, because you aren't listening.

The gist of the palms-down message is that you're firm in your message. But the strength of the palms-down message depends on the position of the fingers, something that will be discussed a little later in this chapter.

Fisticuffs

The position of the fist can indicate power or hostility. A fist is generally not an indication that all is well. Even if it's used as a display of power (as opposed to overt hostility), it's a means of letting others know that they have been (or will be) conquered and crushed. Dictators love this gesture. The wild, wielded fist looks like a judge's gavel and instills fear into their subjects. (Nikita Khrushchev and Benito Mussolini were particularly good at this move.)

When used to convey power or intimidation, there's no mistaking the message behind the fist. The problem is that the fist has become a caricature of its former self; that is, people often use it in jest. It's not uncommon to see the fake fist make an appearance in all sorts of situations, especially among men. When your friend pretends he's going to punch you after you've made a crack about his shirt, his hostility probably isn't genuine. But if he aims a fist in your direction after you make a crack about his girlfriend … duck.

The next time you see a newborn baby crying, look at his hands. They'll be curled into tight little fists. Even deaf-and-blind babies make fists when they're feeling out of sorts, indicating that the fist is not a learned gesture – it's an inborn response to anger or frustration.

Follow the Fingers

You've learned about the basic hand positions. But what about those random finger movements – those you see when someone is speaking to you with his hands flailing left and right accompanied by pointing and twirling fingers? He is probably just a bit more expressive than the average hand-talker. His message is best interpreted through the basic position of the hand (palms up, in, down or out). However, any time someone waves a finger in your face, go ahead and interpret that as a gesture of disapproval. And if that finger ends up poking you, that's a gesture of hostility and intimidation. (Interestingly, pointing is another move that's a favourite among dictators. Fidel Castro, for example, loves to emphasise his spoken word with his index finger.)

A hand with open fingers generally displays an open-minded attitude. Tightly closed fingers indicate that the person is uptight and rigid. Finding a happy medium is best; this shows that you're open to new ideas yet confident with your own knowledge. This idea can be combined with the palms-up/palms-down positions. Picture a person in a palms-down position with his fingers lined up like little soldiers, right next to each other. There's no way you're going to persuade him to change his mind on the issue. However, if his palms-down hands have fingers that are somewhat spread apart, you have two messages coming your way: he feels very strongly about his position, but he may also be willing to at least hear your take on things.

Hyped-Up Hands

In addition to the entire gamut of emotions, the hands send some of the most obvious and immediate signs of nervousness, most of which are fairly easy to pick up on. People who wring their hands, pull on or bend their fingers, dig their nails into their fists, or drum their fingertips on the tabletop are often brimming with anxiety. But don't be too quick to judge a hand by its motion. As you'll read in this section, some of these gestures may also indicate that the person is in the beginning stages of rigor mortis – that's right, she's been bored to death.

Comforting Measures

Self-touches are another sign that all is not well with someone, and may include gestures like:

- Rubbing the face (e.g. the nose or the chin).
- Rubbing the forearms.
- Crossing the arms in a tight hug.
- Cracking the knuckles.
- Clasping the hands together tightly.
- Clenching the hands in a fist.

These motions are comforting measures, even though some of them (like serious, dedicated hand wringing or digging the nails into any body part) appear to be painful. It's the person's way of assuring herself that everything is going to be all right. You'll most often see these gestures when someone is distressed – which can mean that she's nervous about being caught in a lie or that she's crippled by an anxiety disorder.

The more severe a person's anxiety, the more noticeable and drastic her hand gestures may be. For example, someone who's a little nervous about a job interview might release some pent-up stress by clenching her hands in a fist and releasing them several times while she waits for her name to be called. You probably wouldn't even notice what she was doing with her hands if you weren't so tuned in to body language.

A person who's telling a major lie – say, a spouse denying the affair he's been carrying on for several months – might tightly cross his arms while he swears he's been faithful. He's almost literally protecting himself from the accusation and the ramifications of telling the truth. This is such a common gesture that it's easy to underestimate or miss its significance in this scenario.

Morse Code for Boring

One more note on hands that can't sit still: they can also convey extreme boredom. You're unlikely to see ennui displayed in hand wringing or clenched fists; these moves are usually reserved for genuine nervousness. Boredom usually manifests itself through finger tapping, facial rubbing (including the head propped up on the hand) and knuckle cracking – motions that serve to rouse the person (of course, the head propped in the hand only serves to keep that head off the desk in front of it). As some of these gestures overlap with expressions of anxiety, you may have to use your skills of observation (including your knowledge of body language, naturally) to determine whether the knuckle-cracking kid sitting next to you on the bus is frightened about something or merely uninterested in his surroundings. (Chapter 9 contains more detailed information on nervous hands).

Shake It Like You Mean It

The handshake is such a critical first-impression–making gesture, and yet it is one that goes unperfected in so many people. Until you're confronted with a truly awkward handshake – you find yourself holding someone else's limp hand, for example – you may not even realise the power of a good shake. While a great handshake can make you seem wise and powerful, a weak shake can give you an aura of fearfulness or insecurity.

The Grip

The core of the handshake is the grip. How hard should you shake someone else's hand? Well, there's a middle ground you need to find and it lies somewhere between a limp grasp and a bone-crushing one. If you've shaken enough hands, you've no doubt experienced both ends of the spectrum, and you know that neither is especially pleasant.

If you are concerned about exposing yourself to germs, that's understandable to a point. However, as a limp shake gives the other person the idea that you're weak (physically or emotionally), you should try to get over your germ fear and develop a good grip. Just keep your hands – and the germs – away from your face until you've had a chance to wash them.

The limp shake is decidedly feminine, which, of course, is not in and of itself a bad thing. If you're a woman heading out on a blind date and you want to make sure that your suitor knows you're a softhearted female, by all means, use the limp shake. However, most handshakes are offered and accepted in the business world – which is often defined by an air of masculinity, even in this day and age. Therefore, once you put on a suit, the limp handshake should be left out of your repertoire, no matter what your gender.

How can you tell if your grip is adequate? First, make sure you're inserting your hand far enough into the shake. A limp shake often generates from one person attempting to limit her exposure to the other person's palm; the weak shaker does her best to touch only the other person's fingers or to touch the inside of the other person's palm just lightly.

Those Pesky Palms Again

You'll remember that this chapter talked about the palms as they relate to body language: palms-up is a friendly gesture; palms-down indicates a closed-off speaker who isn't open to new ideas.

The general idea applies to the handshake, with one small difference: Someone who offers his hand to you with his palm facing down is telling you that he's the top dog in the office. This is the kind of move that the president of the company might use when meeting with underlings. When someone offers you his hand in this fashion, it actually forces you to shake in a palm-up position, which is a submissive move. You're acquiescing to his power.

General Douglas MacArthur was the commander of the Allied forces in the Pacific and later head of the United Nations forces. Suffice to say he caused plenty of men to tremble in their boots. When President Harry S Truman fired MacArthur in the 1950s, he shook the general's hand using a palm-down motion.

So what are the lessons to be learned here? First, unless you're the boss, don't offer your hand for shaking with the palm facing downwards. Although some people may not know the literal meaning of this motion, most acknowledge that it's an out-of-the-ordinary move, a way of setting yourself apart from everyone else, a way of saying, 'I'm a little better than you are.' It might not be in your best interest to communicate this so blatantly to your colleagues, who may not necessarily feel that you are better than they are. They'll start looking for other subtle signs of arrogance in you.

Second, if someone offers you his hand in a palm-down position, it's all right to offer yours vertically and wait for him to shake your hand. The funny thing is that some particularly aggressive people will take your hand and try to turn it palm-up as they shake it. Go ahead and fight the twist and don't feel a bit strange about the wrist wrestling that you're engaging in. You're simply protecting your own standing.

Is it wrong to offer your hand in a palm-up manner? No, not if you're supremely confident and/or in a position of power to begin with. This is actually seen as something of a humbling move and will most likely make others feel more comfortable in your presence.

If you're the boss, you don't necessarily need to offer your hand in the dominating position. Shaking hands in the traditional manner – with both parties' palms vertical to each other – shows that you respect the other person, no matter what their standing in the company.

The Shake

Now that you've got the strength and positioning correct, how long should you hang on to that other hand? What's the appropriate length of time to shake?

The up-and-down motions are called pumps. Three to five pumps are usually adequate. Anything shorter feels too brief in most situations; anything longer feels as though you're holding the other person's hand for personal reasons.

Everyone has been in situations where the handshake is either abbreviated or extended, and many times this is because neither person knows how long to shake. Go ahead and take the lead here – give the other person five good shakes and pull back.

Other Touches

You've seen brothers and male friends shake each other's hands and simultaneously clap each other on the shoulder – obviously a way of saying, 'I'm so glad to see you!' Is this motion reserved for personal meetings? If your boss smacks you on the shoulder, is that a way of saying he really likes you, or is it a way of saying something else entirely?

The shoulder-smack, along with the elbow-grab, is almost always simply an extension of goodwill. It's a way of expressing genuine happiness at seeing the other person without moving into hug territory (though sometimes the shoulder-clap is a prelude to the hug, especially among male family members or friends).

The one situation where you should give in to the other person's whims is when you're shaking with your boss. He's the leader; if he wants to hold your hand all day long, let him (unless, of course, he's crossing into inappropriate territory with other body language gestures).

Here's a subtle move that often follows the handshake and is easy to miss: let's say you're finishing up a meeting with a colleague. You shake hands and as you turn to walk out the door, he walks with you, putting his hand on your shoulder. This is a condescending move, one that suggests that you're the underling in this situation.

If you work with someone who is prone to the condescending shoulder touch, move out of his range after shaking his hand. When he does this to you, it feeds his own perception that he's higher up on the ladder than you are, so to speak, which may not mean anything in the real world, but there's no sense feeding his ego.

You may not be bothered by the shoulder touch, but you don't want the other person to start believing that he has some sort of control over you. You want him to know that you're a force to be reckoned with. Steering clear of his attempts at intimidation is a great way to get this message through loudly and clearly.

Politicians and the Perfect Hand Positioning

The hands are so important in emphasizing a person's point (or betraying a lie), professional speakers are trained to use very limited hand gestures. The next time you see a politician in action, for example, watch his or her hands. You'll note that the more powerful the politician, the more controlled his hand movements are.

Politicians love their rehearsed hand gestures. JFK and Bill Clinton, for example, were famous for using a loosely closed fist with a thumb sticking out of the top to get their points across without appearing aggressive. Tony Blair perfected the 'come with me' gesture, starting with palms outwards then bringing them in towards the body. And George W Bush, often placed both hands on the podium when he spoke – a way of saying, 'I have nothing to hide.'

The Hand Complication

You might be wondering why politicians bother learning hand gestures. If they're so afraid that their hands are going to give away their deep, dark secrets, why don't they just put them in their pockets? This seems like an easy solution to a complicated matter, but don't go into the field of political consulting just yet. Hiding the hands is as good as saying, 'You won't believe the secret I have!' Obviously, this isn't a wise move in a field already polluted with closeted skeletons. A politician always wants to appear as though he's telling the truth, the whole truth, or something a lot like the truth.

As politicians generally want to give the impression that they're being as open and honest as possible, they usually don't cross their arms or legs while they speak. Although these postures may be unaffected and comfortable, they may also be interpreted as an attempt by the politician to hide information and/or protect himself.

The Truth at Hand

Politicians keep their hands on display to look honest and trustworthy, so they are very careful about the gestures they use. As discussed earlier in this chapter, the hands can say an awful lot – they can actually contradict the words coming out of the speaker's mouth. Picture a leader pleading for peace while emphasizing his words with a closed fist. (Unspoken message: 'I'll achieve peace – one war at a time.')

One reason speakers train themselves to use several neutral hand movements is so they appear honest and forthright even if they're fudging the truth. Using the correct hand gestures can allow a speaker to lull the public into a state of trust and comfort. What types of gestures do politicians favour?

- Palms-down motions: as you read earlier in this chapter, palms-down is a move of domination. In this case, the speaker is telling you that he's in control of the situation.
- 'Patting' gestures: this is a palms-down move where the speaker gently pats the air in front of him. It's generally interpreted as kind of a soothing move, as though the speaker is reaching out to touch you personally and tell you that everything is going to be all right.
- Palm raising: simply raising the hand with the fingers extended and close together is a neutral gesture that once again conveys the message that the speaker is calm, cool, collected and ready to handle the situation.

What kinds of gestures do politicians try to avoid? For starters, fists – in democratic countries, no one wants to follow someone who's out for blood. People want to see their leader has gathered his thoughts, is in control of his emotions and has come up with a solid plan of action. Pounding a fist on a podium generally means this person is ready to act, but may not have considered all possible outcomes.

Although politicians do use palms-up gestures, they do so sparingly. In every other sector this is considered to be a bridge-building move (and you'd think that politicians would love to be known as peacemakers), but it's also perceived as a gesture of relative weakness, as though the speaker is begging you to believe him. You might see a politician use this type of motion when he's trying to explain a difficult concept – or when he's apologizing for his latest scandal.

Signing

Sign language, as you know, is a way for hearing-impaired people to communicate with others through a series of hand gestures. You might wonder if these gestures have anything to do with body language. Can a person communicate anger or happiness through his hands, for example? When hearing people have a conversation, they focus on each other's facial cues, body position and eye contact. As a deaf person has to concentrate on the other person's hands in order to understand what the other person is saying, you might think that he might miss these body-language cues. But you'd be wrong.

Hearing-impaired people rely on body language (facial cues are especially important) to get the full meaning of any given interaction. Non-verbal gestures are to sign language what voice inflection is to spoken communication: a simple way to assess another person's emotional state of mind. And just as spoken dialects vary, signers from different regions of the country or from different ethnic groups or even from different families have their own 'accent', or way of imparting their intended messages.

As the hands have so much to say – in sign language as well as in verbal interactions – it's important to be aware of the messages that you're sending and receiving. Take the time to learn the basic meaning of hand gestures, and you'll always be in the know.

Chapter 4

Straight Talk: What Your Posture Tells the World

How many times have you been told to straighten up and fly right? Did you ever consider that maybe people aren't talking about your attitude, but your posture? If you're a sloucher, your stance is sending a definite message to other people. Believe it or not, a simple thing like adjusting the way you sit, stand and walk can have a profound effect on the way others view you.

Perilous Posture

Your mother wasn't joking: poor posture can cause plenty of problems in your day-to-day life. Not only does slouching lead to physical aches and pains, it can also project specific images of you and your personality, including:

- Insecurity
- Illness
- Shyness
- Boredom
- Indifference

Poor posture is one of those subtle characteristics that people often can't put their finger on. Your colleague knows there's something about you that rubs her the wrong way, but she's not sure what it is. She thinks perhaps you're stand-offish, but she can't really say why. She's a little afraid to approach you, in fact, and who can blame her? You sit hunched over at your desk, your head hung low. And when you do get up, the only difference in your appearance is that your legs are moving underneath you – you're still slouched over with your head tilted downwards. Is it any wonder that other people are reluctant to strike up a conversation with you? You're hardly the picture of friendliness – or confidence.

Not only does slouching make you appear insecure, it can also cause an entire range of ailments, like backache and headaches. Learning to walk tall not only makes you look confident, it might also have a positive effect on your physical health.

Sure Signs of Insecurity

So what is it about poor posture that makes a sloucher appear to be insecure? Why can't someone sit hunched over and simply be regarded as someone who's more comfortable that way? Why must people read any more into it?

Well, as you just read, slouching is one of those things that most people don't really think about – in terms of themselves or others – unless the deviation from the norm is very pronounced. If a friend of yours actually has a hunchback, for example, you can't help but see it – but interestingly, because you know she can't walk straight, you're more likely to acknowledge that this imperfection has nothing to do with her personality. The same doesn't hold true for those who can stand up straight but choose not to.

Slouching – and all of the gestures that go along with it – makes you appear smaller. Try it yourself by doing a simple home experiment: stand in front of your bathroom mirror. Pull your shoulders back and hold your head level. You look pretty good. You're as tall as you're capable of being, you're taking up a fair amount of room (this can be exaggerated by standing with your feet planted far apart, but that will be discussed later), and even if you don't feel it, you look prepared to take on anything that comes your way.

Straightening your spine is one of the easiest ways to transform your entire appearance. You'll appear to be taller, more interested in the world around you and ready to tackle anything.

Now, let it all go. Give into the slouch. And give it a good effort – really slouch. How are you looking now, with your shoulders hanging down and your waist creeping up in a disturbing manner? Smaller. Weaker. Less confident. Bored. Sick of the world. Depressed. The list could go on and on, but again, there isn't anything in this posture that says, 'Wow, I look great! I hope everyone else notices me.'

Your Posture is Worth a Thousand Words

Perhaps you're thinking, 'Well, so what if my posture makes people look away from me? I hate it when people are always concerned with how other people see them!'

That's fair enough, as long as you can truly live that attitude. (Dismissing the opinions of those around you takes an enormous amount of confidence, so you're way ahead of the game.) However, most people are at least a little concerned with the image they're projecting to others, especially when it comes to matters of love and business. They want to know what they're doing wrong, how it's impeding their progress and how they can correct it.

So it comes down to this: poor posture can say a lot about you – things that aren't true, and things that you don't believe about yourself. You may be the funniest, cleverest, coolest person you know (not to mention the most modest) but for some reason, you're single and your career is going nowhere. Meanwhile, your friends have absolutely no trouble meeting people wherever they happen to be and they're skipping rungs on their way up the corporate ladder. What's going on? Well, it could be that your stance is uninviting.

If you find you're having trouble meeting new and interesting people, take a look at your posture and remember it's one of the first things other people notice about you. Hunched-over people don't appear to be looking for fun – it's that simple.

Work-Weary Posture

While posture may throw you off track in the dating world, it can knock you for an absolute six at work. When you're competing for promotions and pay rises, you have to play the part of the confident employee – that means in addition to doing your job well, you have to look the part. Someone who walks around the workplace slouched over with his head pointed down towards the carpet and his shoulders pulled in close to his sides isn't likely to instil a whole lot of confidence in the boss. In other words, he doesn't look like he's ready to handle any situation; he looks like he's ready to run and hide. Although this probably isn't fair, it is certainly the reality.

Perfecting Your Posture

With posture and confidence, the taller and wider you make yourself appear, the more people will stand back and say (if to no one but themselves), 'Wow, that woman's capable of protecting herself and looking out for those around her – I'll bet she'd make a great [insert position of authority here]!'

If you see an animal standing trying to make itself look as large as possible – as when a bear or a horse stands on its hind legs – get out of the way! This posture means the animal is feeling threatened and is ready to attack.

Some people are very doubtful that posture has much effect on their everyday lives; they believe that looks and intelligence come into play far more often, and that may be true in some environments. However, most people aren't supermodel-beautiful, and most people aren't Einstein-level brilliant. In fact, most people are fairly average, and yet plenty of average people find themselves in amazing circumstances. So what propels some average people ahead of others? Attitude and confidence – both of which can be displayed in your posture.

Linking Posture to Animals

Posturing is linked to the animal kingdom. I know, you're thinking, 'I don't ever recall seeing a squirrel holding his head up high and forcing his shoulders back so that he could be promoted to Head Nut Counter.' Well, you may be right, but remember: animals have more serious concerns than earning titles – their main day-to-day worry is survival. And yes, nut gathering may fall into that category, but a more pressing issue is the age-old competition of predator versus prey.

Take a situation as simple as a dog terrorizing a cat. Because the dog is probably the larger animal, the cat is the animal in danger. As such, it can do one of two things – it can fight or try to escape. If you've ever seen a fearless cat in this situation, you'll notice that it does everything it can to make itself look bigger: it'll raise its haunches, and it might even stand up on its back legs as it prepares for battle. If the dog is on the timid side, it might decide that this cat isn't worth the trouble and retreat.

On the other hand, something very interesting happens in the moments when an animal realises it's being hunted. If the animal instinctually knows that it can't win and it can't escape the situation, it will try to avoid being seen by the predator. A cat, for example, might curl itself up and sit very still until the dog passes by. However, if the dog comes too close for comfort, it's going to become well acquainted with a set of sharp cat claws.

Animals try to maintain a 'critical distance', or safety zone, between themselves and predators. (Think of it as an animal's personal space.) If a perceived threat, animal or human, enters into this zone, the animal will attack. This is why it's important to keep a healthy distance between yourself and animals that you don't know.

Humans generally do the same things with their posture, and while much of it is based on instinct, there's no rule that says you can't work on changing the way you carry yourself so that you don't look like prey.

Posture in the Real World

Cats and dogs are interesting, but let's take this posturing business and put it in a human context. Let's say that you have a couple of colleagues who you're observing: There's Joe, who has a very high opinion of himself, and Kevin, who tries to stay out of everyone's way. Joe isn't the biggest bloke in the world – he's well under 6ft – but the only word you can think of to describe his walk is that he swaggers. This guy exudes confidence. No one messes with him. Whatever he says, goes.

Kevin, on the other hand, is taller than Joe, but you'd only notice this if you really looked. This is because Kevin's posture is all pulled in – he slouches when he walks and stands and his arms are always close to his sides or actually in front of his body. You're not sure if he's a very skinny person or if the way he carries himself just makes him look tiny.

One day Joe and Kevin go head-to-head over some project they're working on. You can see them engaged in a heated discussion: Joe is standing with his feet planted far apart, his hands on his hips, his head level to the ground. (In fact, he's looking a little like John Wayne, minus the cowboy gear.) For good measure, he throws his hands out to the side once in a while. Kevin, on the other hand, is standing with his arms tightly crossed over his chest, his legs crossed and his head angled towards the ground. You can clearly see now that Kevin is a good six inches taller than Joe, but if this were a fistfight, you'd put every penny you have on Joe.

Note that Joe is using fairly common gestures and postures. He's staking out his territory, making himself appear as large as possible so that everyone around him understands that he is not to be messed with. Meanwhile, Kevin is responding by trying to make himself as small as possible, either to hide or protect himself from Joe, who will inevitably win this argument and get exactly what he wants.

When you see a situation like this, it's obvious – to the viewer – that if the timid person would just learn to posture himself correctly, he would be at least on equal footing with his nemesis. So if you have a Kevin in your life, give him a few pointers on literally standing up for himself. Both of you may be surprised by the results.

Leg Language

Here's one more secret to a successful stance: don't cross your legs. You might find it difficult to envision someone standing with his legs crossed (unless he's also hopping to the toilet). But women, in particular, sometimes stand with their legs crossed at the ankles. Men may lean on the wall to cross their legs as they're speaking with someone.

Crossing the legs when you stand is a definite non-threatening move. It's coy and casual, and that's fine – as long as the conversation you're having is coy and casual. But if you're gearing up for an argument that's going to go down in history as the battle of the year, you'd be wise to position yourself with your feet about hip-width apart.

The wide-legged stance is another move that makes you look as large as possible. You may not win the disagreement (that has much more to do with your ability to piece together a logical argument than with body language), but you won't look (or feel) as though you're standing there with your tail between your legs.

Head and Shoulders Above the Crowds

So posturing works during an argument – but you don't really argue with other people, so what good is this information to you?

In society, people are groomed to believe that men should be able to protect themselves and their loved ones. Women, meanwhile, are supposed to sit back and be protected. Even in this day and age where these old stereotypes don't necessarily hold true, most couples are still comprised of the larger man/smaller woman combination. And sure, this may well be because men are naturally larger than women, but still, you think you'd see at least a few of the reverse (smaller man/larger woman) combinations. How many of these types of couples do you know? (One? Maybe two?)

Is this getting way off the point? No. The point is to make yourself aware of the way that you react to posture and size in your day-to-day life.

Stand Tall

If you're a smallish man, you can make yourself appear larger simply by standing tall and adopting an air of confidence. Remember Joe and Kevin from earlier in this chapter? Joe is smaller in stature and yet Kevin is afraid of him!

It's hard to be a small man in a world where most of your friends and colleagues seem to tower over you. Taller men sometimes love to lord their size over shorter guys, which forces the shorter men to either laugh along with their friends or to become defensive. Either way, the smaller men are left feeling as though their lack of height is a definite deficiency and that their taller peers have all the luck.

This is not true. There are as many tall insecure men as there are short insecure men. Confidence is what makes you attractive to other people; confidence is what wins the boss over at promotion time; confidence is what prevents fistfights; confidence is what wins verbal arguments. Good posture screams, 'I am confident!' so your mouth doesn't have to.

Tom Cruise, Joaquin Phoenix, Dermot O'Leary, Phil Collins – what do these men have in common? They are five-foot eight or shorter. Never noticed their size? Perhaps it's because they also know how to project confidence.

This isn't to say that you should stand up tall and act belligerent and argumentative just because you realise the power of good posture. (After all, fools come in all sizes.) But, just as poor posture can make people have their doubts about you, good posture might chase those doubts away.

Back Off!

While you don't frequently hear women complaining about being too small, sometimes size comes down to an issue of safety: a small woman doesn't want to appear vulnerable when she's walking through the park or down a city street, for example. What should a woman do if and when she finds herself alone in a questionable area? Stand tall; thrust those shoulders back; hold your head level or slightly angled upwards; put your hands on your hips and use a wide stance if you're confronted.

How is this going to help you if some weirdo has you in his sights? Think back to our animal friends who were preparing for battle: once the cat made itself look bigger, the dog left it alone. The cat simply wasn't worth the trouble – but you can bet that if a timid little cat skulks past the dog, the chase will be on!

Safety experts advise women to learn how to carry themselves with a definite attitude. If you can make yourself look formidable – simply unwilling to be the prey, just like a cat standing up on its hind legs – there's a better chance of scaring off a potential attacker. The truth is that it depends on the person and the situation.

Arm Awareness

When you're talking about posture, the issue of your arms always comes up – or down, or across the chest. Many people have a specific issue with their arms, as if they have a life of their own. These men and women don't know what to do with their upper limbs when they walk or stand or sit. Most give up and let them hang there, poor disconnected appendages. But what you do with your arms can make or break what you're attempting to do with your posture!

Cross My Heart

There is a world of theories associated with crossing your arms over your chest. Some people say that this is an attempt to defend yourself against the person you're arguing with; others say it's an attempt to make yourself smaller (and invisible); some say that this position shuts the other person out of the communication; and still others suggest that this is simply a comfortable position.

If you're witnessing an argument where one person is clearly the aggressor and the other is obviously frightened and the frightened person appears to be hugging herself in this manner, then yes, the arm-cross is probably a subconscious attempt to protect herself. But if you're watching a casual exchange between two friends and one has her arms crossed, it's likely that she just likes to position herself this way.

So what's the lesson to learn about the arm-cross? Be aware of it; be aware that it can send a message that says, 'I'm a little scared' or, 'I don't really want to talk to you.' If you're in a situation where you absolutely must come across as brave and/or interested, uncross those arms!

Hands on hips says, 'I'm confident and strong'

Hands on Hips

As mentioned earlier, posture can make you look bigger than you are. Placing your hands on your hips helps to exaggerate this effect, which is why you mostly see this in people who are angry or fairly aggressive. Just like in the animal kingdom, these people want to make themselves look bigger, powerful, fearless and ready to spring into action. Keep in mind that the angle of the elbows and the position of the thumbs are very important When your thumbs face forwards, you force the elbows backwards – a pose that appears to be feminine and weak. When your thumbs face backwards, your elbows are directed outwards, which makes you appear large and strong.

Find the happy medium. Pointing your elbows forwards makes you look like a contortionist; dropping them way back makes you look like Mick Jagger, a vision that, quite frankly, isn't likely to strike fear into the heart of your opponent. Holding your elbows straight out to the sides is the most effective position, as it makes you appear as wide as possible. That isn't a look most people are going for on a day-to-day basis, but it might just help you out of a sticky situation!

What's Your Angle?

Now that this chapter has covered every angle of posture; this section will talk about angles themselves. This section will teach you to position parts of your body to show interest (or lack thereof) in what another person is saying.

Baiting the Hook

Anglers are, as you know, fishermen. They're trying to lure and capture their prey. Whether or not they make a big catch depends on their skill. The same can be said for luring and trapping others with your body language.

What is this angling, you're wondering? The best way to understand it is to do it. Take a seat. Pretend someone is seated to your left and you're going to have a nice chat with this person. If you're a woman, cross your legs and point them towards your imaginary friend. If you're a man, you can stretch your legs out any way you want – just make sure they're pointing in the direction of the invisible person.

You don't have to be sitting to work the angle correctly. If you happen to be standing, use your shoulders to lure your new friend. Here's where your posture comes into play: stand straight and 'square' your shoulders towards the other person. You're creating a personal space that exists only between the two of you, a space that is both intimate and yet non-threatening (unless you start crowding that personal space – something discussed more in Chapter 17).

What does 'squaring' the shoulders mean?
It simply means to straighten them so they're at right angles to the body. Sit or stand straight; your shoulders will naturally fall into alignment. Now, when you speak to someone else, turn your shoulders in their direction.

Think this sounds too easy? Look for this type of angling in real-life settings. The next time you're at a club or you witness interoffice flirting, note the angle of both parties. Of course, angling isn't always sexual. It can (and should) be used in any conversation where you want to appear interested. Learning to angle your body correctly is simply polite; as you'll read in the following section, angling your body away from someone sends a completely different message.

Throwing It Back

To show your lack of interest in pursuing a conversation, all you have to do is angle your body away from the other person. You may look his way, your tone of voice may be pleasant enough – but if you don't turn your body towards him, you're sending a subtle yet unmistakable signal that you're not interested.

Here is a classic example of this type of angling. A woman sits perched on a barstool. She appears to be a friendly sort; she's laughing and talking with her friends. A man approaches her from the side and attempts to strike up a conversation. If she turns to point her legs towards him, he has a shot; if she doesn't, he's dead in the water. While there may be nothing he can do to bring her around (both literally and figuratively), if he knows how to read this signal, he can at least move on before he spends too much time on what's most likely a futile attempt.

The Position of Authority

There's one more body position that's worth discussing, and although part of it concerns angling, it has more to do with actual position. It's best to be at eye level with the other person when you're having a conversation; otherwise, the person who is in the physically higher position is perceived to have more power.

Imagine your boss calls you into her office and tells you to take a seat. She then proceeds to tear you limb from limb over a careless accounting error you've made. She's standing above you, listing your many flaws. You have no other choice but to look up at her. Maybe you have a perfectly logical explanation concerning this error, but she's making you feel like a child. So instead of speaking up, you take her browbeating and head back to your desk.

Some people are particularly adept at employing this tactic, and if you happen to be on the small side, it might be wise to learn a few subtle moves to put yourself on top. Let's say you're a short woman and you want to have a discussion with your husband about his seeming inability to help with the housework. Wait until he has parked himself on the sofa and then take your seat – on the arm of the couch. You've put yourself in the position of authority, whether he consciously realises it or not.

The way you position yourself either says, 'I'm in complete control!' or, 'Wow, I need some serious help.' If you can learn the simple tricks of powerful positioning, you can look like you're in control even when you feel as though you desperately need help. Stand tall and the world stands with you; slouch and you slump alone.

Chapter 5

The Remarkable Head

The head is one of the first areas you notice about someone else; it houses the eyes, the nose and the mouth, each of which offers a wealth of non-verbal cues. But there's even more to the story: your head itself is used to relay certain unspoken messages to the people around you. So you might say that the head is the powerhouse of the entire body language unit.

Is Beauty All in Your Head?

Any time you are discussing the head, you have to deal with the face. While there are several chapters in this book that deal with specific components of the face, this one will talk about the face in more general terms in an attempt to answer the question 'What makes someone attractive?'

First impressions are a powerful thing. Body language can help you put your best foot forward, but then there's also a little thing called physical attractiveness that factors into first meetings. You have little control over this factor because, speaking in general terms, there are some people who are empirically attractive and some people who aren't. As a society, people accept the terms of what makes a person beautiful – but what are those terms, exactly? Attractive people usually have a few things going for them:

- Their faces are symmetrical.
- Their faces are without obvious flaws.
- Their faces are relatively youthful looking.

In addition, the size and shape of certain areas of the face determine how other people perceive each other. Small or short chins, for example, lead to general interpretations of shyness. But is this a chicken-or-the-egg-type situation? For example, if people with weak chins can be viewed to be less attractive than their strong-chinned peers and are treated as such, then it's natural that they might also start to view themselves that way. Their body language will reflect their lack of confidence and may actually feed the belief that weak-chinned people have weak constitutions.

Just as unattractive people might express their lack of confidence through their body language, people who have always known they're gorgeous may feel superior to the common man. That attitude will be reflected in the way they carry themselves, and may in turn lead you to look for signs of arrogance in all beautiful people.

So beauty – or the lack of it – is another example of the filter through which people view each other's non-verbal cues. When you're evaluating the body language involved with the head's gestures, be aware that a person's appearance can make you see things that aren't there (you want to believe that that great-looking man is really nice, so you look for signs of it in the way he angles his head, for example) or can make you miss things that are there (you don't pay much attention to your not-particularly-handsome neighbour, but if you did, you'd find that he's always tilting his head to the side, really listening to what other people say). Proceed with caution!

Heads Up

You've probably heard the saying, 'Keep your chin up!', which is about being optimistic. What does your point of view have to do with the position of your chin? Well, it's not just where your chin is situated, but the way your head is angled. If your chin is looking upwards, then you will be, too – or so the theory goes.

Studying Your Shoes?

The idea behind the old 'chin up' adage is that if your chin is pointed down towards the ground, you can't help but have a grim outlook on life. A head that's angled downwards doesn't appear to be a happy little head; it looks like its owner wants nothing to do with the world surrounding her. If your head is pointing towards the ground, you don't look like a confident person, no matter what you do with the rest of your body language. In fact, if you combine a confident walk and friendly mannerisms with a downward-tilted head, people will be completely confused. 'She seems like she's got her act together,' they might say, 'but she also appears to be depressed about something.'

When you angle your head downwards, your eyes usually follow suit, which means you're not making eye contact with the people around you. This leads to other assumptions about your personality. Colleagues might think you're aloof; acquaintances might believe you're painfully shy; friends and family members might think you're trying to hide something from them.

The one situation where a head angled downwards works to your benefit is when you're trying to be coy with a member of the opposite sex. Picture this: you've just met a man who's sweet, conversational and good-looking to boot. You don't want him to think you're too worldly; you'd rather come across as innocent or naive at this point. Angle your head down and look up at him while he's speaking. If you really want to play the innocent-girl card, keep the head angled down when you speak, but make sure you're smiling and looking right at him; otherwise, you'll be in danger of seeming uninterested.

On the Side

If you want to appear to be really, truly listening to someone else, angling the head to the side is a move you'll want to add to your bag of body-language tricks. When you employ this gesture, you appear to be lifting an ear, as though to say, 'I'm doing everything I can to take in each and every word that comes out of your mouth.' It doesn't matter which way you angle your head – left or right works equally well. And keep in mind, this is just a slight angling of your head; you're not trying to touch one ear to your shoulder in an effort to prove that you can hear just fine out of the other one.

Although this gesture is used to emphasise listening skills, it's also employed when people are expressing sympathy. You might see someone say, 'I'm so sorry' as her head tilts to the side. What's this all about? Are these people offering – non-verbally – to listen to the other person's troubles? Sort of, but in this case, the head-tilt is more a way of showing that you feel for the other person's pain without making it your own. Later in this chapter, you'll read about other ways to express sympathy with your head.

Angling your head to the side is another way to play the cutesy, coy card with a member of the opposite sex. Not only does this gesture make you appear innocent and harmless, it's also a good way to show that you're a good listener.

The head-tilt can also come in handy if you want to appear innocent. Let's say your husband has accused you of scratching his beloved motorcycle. You honestly had nothing to do with the damage to his bike. You're upset and feeling more than a little defensive – two emotions that could easily lead to you throwing your head back in an effort to appear rather dominant (a gesture you'll read about a little later in this chapter). While you're well within your rights to express your indignation, your real goal is to end the fight before it goes too far. (After all, the more the two of you argue, the more likely it is that the initial issue will be buried in other accusations – like 'You've always hated my bike!' and 'You love that bike more than you love me!') To defuse the situation quickly, try angling your head to the side while you stick to your story. You'll appear much more innocent (which you are, after all), and this might be all it takes to convince your man that he's got it all wrong.

Levelling the Head

Do you want to appear confident? It all starts with your head. When you walk through your workplace or down the street, make sure your head is at an even parallel with the ground. Your eyes are straight ahead, your chin isn't dropping down or raising up towards the sky. Now broaden those shoulders and watch as people take notice of you.

Where else will a level head come in handy?

Well, in any situation, really. A head that's held straight and steady appears to be alert, so even if you're having a drawn-out chat with your sister or listening to a rather dull speech or presentation, a level head will say, 'I'm paying attention and I'm completely present in the moment.'

Head Up

Kids often refer to their arrogant classmates as being 'stuck-up'. This is shorthand for saying that the person in question has her nose stuck up in the air. The reason she has her nose stuck up in the air – metaphorically speaking, of course – is because her head is angled back. And her head is angled back because she's arrogant. It's a classic case of cause and effect.

Picture the most arrogant person you know. Now imagine you're having an argument with her (or him); how does she hold her head once she has let you know that you're wrong? Chances are, it's angled slightly back, with her chin pointing towards the ceiling. In fact, if you tune in to dramatic television shows where haughty women are the main characters, watch how they hold their heads during intense scenes. The head invariably lifts and you have a perfect shot of the character's nostrils. Angling the head back is a way of saying, 'You know, I really am better than you are.' It's a domineering move.

If you want to show someone that you're higher up the food chain than he is, make use of the backwards head-tilt. If it's done subtly, it's hardly noticeable, and yet this move makes you appear regal, somehow above the common man. Just be aware of its power and its implications – you're not going to win many friends with this move, but you might be able to stop an argument in its tracks, and you might be able to convince people to see your point of view simply because you look like a person who isn't to be trifled with.

If you want to come across as a normal, down-to-earth, friendly sort of person, don't tilt your head backwards! Learn to level out your head to project confidence while occasionally tilting it to the side to show you're not too confident.

Hair Basics

Is a hairstyle powerful enough to send a non-verbal message? The answer is yes. Your hair speaks volumes about you, even if it's less-than-voluminous, because it's one of those intangibles – it tells people whether you're trendy, you're unconventional, you're traditional, you're laid-back or you just don't care about trends. In addition, the way you treat your hair – at your desk or while walking down the street – can send another set of messages.

Hair is a lot like clothing when it comes to body language. Although it doesn't technically have a set of non-verbal behaviours, it's one of the first things people will notice and judge about you. In addition, the way you touch your hair expresses a whole set of non-verbal messages.

Hair-Raising Situations

A hairstyle is an amazing thing: it can define you to scores of people you don't even know. Imagine your very conservative grandmother on the train, holding on to her purse for dear life. A young man with a purple Mohican comes along and sits down right next to her. As she tells the tale later, she says, 'Well, naturally, I was terrified.' But what was she so scared of? Granted, she may have been uncomfortable being seated next to any young male, but there's little doubt that his unconventional hairstyle may have exacerbated her fear. The Mohican makes him appear to be someone who has little use for the rules and regulations of society. She was expecting him to be a criminal, of course, and kept her eyes peeled for any signs of suspicious behaviour (shifty eyes, for example, or bouncy, twitchy hands and feet).

You're surprised, then, when your grandmother tells you that when she dropped her knitting needle and he was kind enough to retrieve it for her, she ended up having a lovely conversation with this young man. She reports that he had the kindest smile she can recall seeing in ages, a body language cue that has obviously won her over and taught her a lesson about not judging a man by his hairdo.

What Your Style Tells the World

There's no single 'best' hairstyle, but there are styles that work better for specific ages, occupations and lifestyles. For example, a Chief Executive is very unlikely to enter the office with a spiky pink hairdo for the simple reason that she would be perceived as being unprofessional (and possibly a tad crazy for trying to pull off this look in the corporate world). In other words, the hair would make a questionable impression, and her body language would be read through this filter.

Donald Trump's hairdo is widely mocked by comedians, and if he were just the average man on the street, he'd probably get plenty of flack from friends and colleagues for his questionable sense of style. However, his body language lets everyone around him know that he is King Trump: he won't tolerate any criticism surrounding any decision he makes – including the way he combs his hair.

Art school students might expect their tutor to display some creative choices with a coif – in fact, they might have a difficult time taking artistic direction from someone who appears to be too conservative. Even if the tutor has an artistic pain – or, conversely, a joie de vivre – that comes through in his body language, his appearance is his first impression, and the thing that's likely to make or break his non-verbal communication, at least initially.

Generally speaking, modern hairstyles carry these messages:

- Short hair on women: you're sporty, confident, fun, but not necessarily a highly sexual person.
- Medium hair on women: you're intelligent, confident, outgoing, but again, not perceived as a sex object.
- Long hair on women: you're confident and completely comfortable with your sexuality.

What's the connection between long hair and sex, you wonder? Long hair is really an adornment for the body, a way of saying, 'Look at me', which is why most actresses and models wear their hair below their shoulders (and why hair extensions are all the rage). Long hair is especially popular among younger women, who are genetically programmed to find a mate, procreate and carry on the human race. Once they've made this contribution to society, the long hair is often the first thing to go. It's no longer needed to attract a mate, and it's not easy to simultaneously care for a baby and super-long tresses, anyway.

Fringes send the message, 'I'm young and fun!' (And you thought they were only good for hiding foreheads!) And no matter what the style, keep your head clean. Poor grooming and hygiene skills make you appear sickly, down on your luck and even depressed.

As for men, baldness is not the scourge it once was. (Think Bruce Willis, Jason Statham, Andre Agassi and Michael Jordan – very confident men with very bare heads.) Although males have spent plenty of money and time searching for a cure for the receding hairline, nowadays, it's not unusual to see a man embrace his thinning hair by shaving it all off. This is a definite move of confidence, a way of saying, 'Who cares about hair? My personality is what matters!'

Men who wear their hair in a neat, conservative fashion are widely viewed as competent, mature people; men who opt for wild, long locks, meanwhile, send the message, 'I'm slightly wild and don't have much use for society's boundaries.'

Hair Twirls and Flicks

Obviously, there are countless options for hairstyles out there. But no matter who you are, no matter what your hair looks like, once you start touching it, everyone sends the same basic messages. Hard to believe, you say? It's just not possible that your mother and your best friend could be expressing themselves in the same exact ways! Well, take a closer look at how they touch their heads and you might discover that they have more in common than you thought.

Flicking the Hair

You know the move – a woman with longish hair reaches up along her shoulder and throws that hair backwards. What does it mean?

Tossing the hair is one way of making yourself noticeable – but not necessarily in the way you might think. Although you can see plenty of long-tressed women swishing their hair in an attempt to make themselves more visible to the opposite sex, this can also be done in a rather aggressive manner, such as during an argument. By flicking the hair around, you make yourself look a little larger to your opponent, which, you might recall, is an animalistic response to conflict.

Self-Grooming

As mentioned earlier, good grooming is an essential part of appearing healthy and vibrant, but over-grooming sends another set of messages. Patting or straightening the hair over and over again is a form of self-touch and is often a sign that the groomer is nervous. You might see this when a girl is chatting with an attractive boy and she tucks her hair behind her ear continuously – even though the phantom lock hasn't moved once during the entire conversation. Men in this situation might actually reach up and draw their hands across their hair from front to back – smoothing the follicles, if you will – but are also more likely to reach one hand behind the head and kind of settle the hair down that way. This is a actually a form of self-touch that indicates anxiety, but it's disguised here as a different message: 'I'm just making sure all the hairs are in place back there.'

Running your fingers through your hair is usually a way to attract the attention of the opposite sex – unless your fingers take hold of the hair and pull it to the sides. This gesture usually means you're frustrated beyond belief and on the verge of tearing your own hair out.

Twirling the Hair

Wrapping the hair around a finger is a gesture that mimics the innocence of childhood and is often used as a flirtation device. If you're talking to a woman and she's twirling away, she's trying to tell you that she's interested in you.

Twirling the hair can also be a soothing habit, something that a person does when she's bored or trying to settle herself down – which is where this move ties into childhood. It's not unusual to see small children twirl their hair when they're put to bed, for example, or when they're crying. It's also not unusual to see a colleague twirling her hair madly while she's doing some very dull research on her computer. This is her way of releasing tension.

If you're a hair twirler, take heed: because this is a gesture that reminds people of young children, make sure you're not the employee who's twisting her hair during a meeting. It sends an unmistakable non-verbal communication: 'I'm kind of immature and I have a very short attention span. Pinch me when you've finished talking.'

Yes, No and Everything in Between

When you think about body language and the head, the two gestures that probably come to mind are head nods and head shakes. While nodding is the classic way of agreeing with a friend and shaking your head is usually the way to say 'No', there are other messages contained in these movements.

Shake It Up

Shaking your head from side to side is usually a way to tell someone that you're in disagreement with his point of view, whether you're telling a child that he can't eat chocolate buttons for dinner or you're telling your boss that you won't take on more work for the same pay. The headshake sends a clear message: 'No'.

However, the headshake has another layer to it. Let's say you're on your way into a funeral home. Mourners are gathered, speaking in hushed tones. What else do you notice? That's right, heads are shaking. In this instance, some people might be shaking their heads in disbelief, while others use the gesture to express their sorrow, but this is still usually a way of saying, 'I can't believe this has happened.' (This is an extreme example. You might also see a neighbour shaking his head as he surveys the holes his dog has dug in the yard. This is simply his way of saying, 'I can't believe that animal is so destructive.')

You might see people shake their heads during an argument as well. This is a way of expressing displeasure and disagreement with the other person's point of view.

It's really interesting when someone shakes his head no while he's saying yes – or when he says no while nodding his head yes. That's a sure sign that he is at the very least conflicted in his point of view and very likely being untruthful with his spoken message.

Nodding

Nodding is an easy way to say that you agree with something. However, nods can also indicate that someone is listening to what you're saying – a way of telling you, 'Yes, yes, I see your point, please go on.'

Someone who's very excited may also nod a lot. Picture your best friend seated at a concert for her favourite band. As she's singing along, she's also nodding that head up and down. She looks like she's simply bopping along (which she is), but she's also expressing her delight. Of course, very quick nodding is an even clearer indication of excitement. If you offered your housemate a free dinner at his favourite curry house, he might respond with a set of eager nods.

Nodding can also be a gesture of dominance, a way of saying, 'I'm in charge here.' Imagine that you've been pulled over for speeding, and as you try to argue your way out of the ticket (you're very sure you were actually driving too slowly), the officer interrupts you and lists all of the offenses he's booking you for. As he ticks off each point, he nods. He's emphasizing his point and telling you that there's no use trying to change his mind. Take the ticket and take your chances with the magistrate instead.

In the extreme, nodding can express anger. The police officer in the previous example wasn't truly enraged; he was simply asserting his power. When you're embroiled in a nasty argument with someone, it's not unusual for both heads to start moving up and down in time with the shouting. This is just a way of using your head to emphasise your point and make yourself heard (albeit very loudly).

As you've read here, the head can send some powerful messages – both positive and negative. Knowing how to decode above-the-shoulders communication can lead you to some interesting conclusions. Keep your eyes trained on your friends' noggins and you'll be way ahead of the body language game.

Chapter 6

The Mighty Mouth

You've already read that body language works to either emphasise your spoken word or contradict it. Your mouth, of course, is home to your words, which might lead you to believe that your spoken message would override anything your mouth is doing while you're talking. Wrong! In this chapter, you'll learn how the shape and position of the lips adds or detracts from your colourful verbal language.

Let Your Mouth Do the Non-Verbal Talkin'

You can understand how the mouth plays an important role in general communication, but why is it so important in the study of body language? Like the eyes, people tend to focus on the mouth during face-to-face conversation. The lips also play into romantic fantasies and have been the focus of attention for many years. Back in the silent film era, for example, when body language was almost a separate character in each movie, Clara Bow was one of the most famous actresses in the world due in large part to her physical qualities, most notably her lips.

Bow lips have a small dip in the top lip, almost forming a 'V' in the middle of the lip. Despite the likeness of the names, 'bow lips' weren't named for Clara Bow's famous mouth. Rather, the name refers to Cupid's bow.

Because the mouth is the focal point for chitchat and romantic interludes, men and women alike strive to achieve near-perfection in their oral cavities. Westerners, in particular, spend millions each year on whitening their teeth, freshening their breath and plumping their lips with artificial fillers.

Do any of these things really work in terms of non-verbal communication, or are the natural gestures of the mouth what really count? It's probably safe to say that anything that makes your mouth look clean and fresh is worthwhile. There's a fine line, however, between making your mouth look its best and making it look like a plastic factory. In fact, when you start putting too much work into your mouth – when you drastically change your teeth and/or your lips, for example – your mouth will move differently, thus affecting the way the non-verbal messages of your mouth are perceived – for better or for worse.

A completely different mouth isn't necessarily a negative thing – maybe you want to change the way your mouth behaves – but it's something to keep in mind when you're thinking about having cosmetic work done on this area.

Lip Behaviours

Think back to when you were a child. How did you know whether your mother or teacher or babysitter was really angry at you or whether she was merely irritated? You could probably tell by looking at her mouth. Happy mouths have one set of behaviours, annoyed mouths have another, and mouths belonging to furious people have a collection of characteristics all their own.

Compressing the Lips

The classic sign of the angry mouth is lips that appear to be smashed down and glued together, a gesture that's technically called compressing the lips. The lips are pushed together in a thin, tight line. Compressing the lips can also be a sign of extreme frustration – an emotion that's approaching anger, perhaps, but hasn't escalated to that point yet.

Before you dramatically change the look of your mouth, consider the final outcome. Will your mouth still look natural? Think of someone who has a set of too-big or too-small dentures; his mouth never looks natural or normal, and unfortunately, the odd look of his mouth is what you tend to focus on.

Imagine that you're trying to balance your ledger and you keep coming up short. You know there's a reason for this, and you can't rest until you find the missing money. If anyone happened to see your mouth at this very moment, he'd instantly know that you're tense, confused and fed up with the whole project.

The Purse

The lip-purse is often confused with compressing the lips, but there's a subtle difference between the two. As you just read, when you compress your lips, they appear to be joined together tightly. The lip-purse falls somewhere between compressing the lips and puckering them – it's almost a combination of the two. The lips are smashed together, but instead of being somewhat extended in a straight line, they come together in what appears to be a slight angry pucker.

Pursing the lips can indicate anger, but is more often used to convey confusion or disagreement on some level. Let's say a couple is discussing their dinner plans. The man wants to go to the new Thai place; the woman has her heart set on Italian food. Lo and behold, the boyfriend pulls out a voucher for a free meal at the Thai restaurant, which makes this an offer that's hard to refuse. His girlfriend mulls this over: she's not a fan of spicy food, but she is a thrifty person. Her pursed lips betray the indecision swirling around in her head.

Puckers and Pouts

What's the best way to extend a message of extreme affection from across the room? Just pucker up, baby! The lip pucker is the precursor to the kiss, of course, and is an unmistakable sign of love and affection.

Well-designed and very practised puckers can be seen on models in all sorts of advertisements, from cosmetics to alcohol. In order to read the message behind these lips, you have to take the rest of the face into consideration. A wide-eyed pucker is far less romantic than one accompanied by hazy, sultry eyes, for example.

Pouting – extending the lower lip just slightly further than the top lip – can indicate sadness, anger or frustration. Most people tend to think that pouting is something that small children do, but that's not always so. Children's pouts tend to be more obvious than adults', for the simple reason that kids don't bother to temper their emotional expressions. So while a child may jut his lower lip way out and over the top lip in a most effective manner, an adult pout is usually more subtle, with just a slight protrusion of the lower lip.

Interestingly, as the pout is one of those body-language traits that instantly reminds you of childhood, it's also a move that's used in flirting.

Sticking your lower lip out makes you appear young and innocent. Take heed, though: if you choose to employ the pout, do so sparingly. Although it's coy and cute, it also happens to be a gesture that can go from endearing to annoying in about one minute.

A Kiss Is Still a Kiss

As you'll read in Chapter 12, some non-verbal cues vary from culture to culture. Holding your hand in a certain pose might be completely acceptable in Europe, but it is insulting in regions of South America. Fortunately, what you've heard about the language of love is true – it's international. In every culture, kissing is a sign of affection – but did you ever stop to wonder why people are compelled to join themselves together at the oral cavities, which are potentially fraught with peril (in the way of germs and bad breath)?

The area around the nose and mouth is one of the most sensitive regions in the body – it's packed with nerve endings. Kissing excites those nerve endings and gives you a sense of exhilaration, peace and/or well-being. So there really is a reason you feel exhilarated after that first kiss with a new love interest – your nerves have been fired up!

Because of those nerve endings, just touching the lips can affect your mood. This is why you'll see people rub their mouths when they're upset or confused – by touching the mouth, they're literally soothing their nerves. It's also why the simple act of brushing your lips across a special someone's cheek can be almost as exciting as giving him a smack on the kisser.

Tongue Twisters

Throughout this book, you'll read about body-language cues that are supposed to remind others of the innocence of childhood. Most of these are gestures that make you appear youthful in a good way. Sticking your tongue out at someone as a means of saying, 'I don't like you' isn't one of them, so if you've left primary school, it's probably best to consign that little communication device to the past.

That isn't to say that the tongue doesn't have other uses in the realm of body language, of course. You can put it on display in other ways in order to get a more positive message across to the one you love.

Licking the Lips

Licking the lips can send a variety of messages, depending on who's doing the licking and in what setting. Consider these scenarios:

- You've just ordered dinner. Your date is excitedly licking his lips. Is he looking to get intimate with you right now?
- You're hanging out with your friends in a nightclub. You notice a girl staring at you, licking her lips. Does she need some lip balm?
- You've just finished running in the park. As you're stretching, you see another runner licking his lips. Is he flirting with you?

The answer to each of these questions is no. Licking the lips as you're preparing or waiting for a meal indicates that you can hardly wait to devour your food. Licking the lips as you're checking out a member of the opposite sex in a nightclub indicates that you can hardly wait to get your hands on him or her. Licking the lips at any time can simply mean that they feel dry. So, again, it's important to take the environment into play (it's kind of unlikely that a bloke who's focused on his marathon training is actively looking to score with ladies in the park) as well as the rest of the person's body language (if that runner is winking and licking his lips, then maybe you've found yourself a new fitness partner).

Licking the lips is a cue that's very easy to misunderstand – and it's usually men who are misreading women's lips. Be sure to factor in other body language when trying to interpret this particular gesture. Men are more likely than women to misinterpret lip-licking as a sign of flirtation, so it's especially important for them to understand that in the real world, lip-licking can be a completely innocent gesture. In other words, it's best to observe a woman's body language in its entirety before making a romantic move based on the way she's moistening her mouth.

Playing Peekaboo with Your Tongue

Imagine you're watching your favourite reality chat show and the host is interviewing a guest who's recently become embroiled in a particularly juicy scandal involving his missing spouse. The host asks her guest if he has any idea where his wife might be. You're on the edge of your seat, waiting to compare his spoken word against his body language.

Fortunately, you have the latest digital technology and are able to play the interview in extreme slow motion. You notice that his eye contact never wavers, that he holds his hands folded in his lap – so far, he appears to be rather forthcoming. But then he does something that catches your eye: he allows his tongue to push through his lips – just a tiny bit – before he answers, 'No, I don't know where she is.'

What does that tongue tell you? He isn't sure of his own answer. He may not know her exact location at the moment, but he may have some idea of what's become of her. Obviously, this is a classic case of splitting hairs, but that's the exact reason that his tongue popped out when it did – he was giving an answer that isn't exactly a lie, but it's not the entire truth, either.

The tongue-show indicates some kind of turmoil – uncertainty, disagreement, even contempt for a person or her message. If you don't happen to agree with something your friend is telling you, for example, your tongue might pop out in this manner. Whether you choose to pursue an argument is another story, but your tongue has done a lot of the talking already.

The Law of the Jaw

You have all sorts of information on the non-verbal cues of the mouth, but don't forget to look in the area surrounding the mouth – specifically, below it. Like bread and butter, the mouth and jaw go together. The lips might affect the appearance of the jaw, but it's more likely that the jaw pulls the lips into formation based on its own mood.

The Locked Jaw

What's an easy way to tell whether someone's at ease or if he has some weighty matters on his mind? Take a look at his lower jaw. A jaw set in stone is sure sign of tension. You can actually see the muscles contract in an angry jaw, which is one way to know for certain when a person's emotions are taking a turn for the worse. The jaw might carry the burden of the emotion on its own, or it might be accompanied by pursed or compressed lips, which serve to emphasise the appearance of anger, tension, sadness or whatever negative feeling the person is having.

The size and shape of the jaw also play an important role in body language. A square jaw makes the face appear strong; a serious underbite makes the face look weak; a protruding jaw can make a person look somewhat unintelligent. Each of these characteristics can affect how the rest of a person's non-verbal cues are received.

Keep in mind that although some people clench their jaws because they're tense, others do it out of habit (although many times this habit starts out of a desire to relieve tension of some kind and develops into a long-term soothing routine). In these cases, the lips are usually not pursed. The compressed lip/locked jaw combination is almost exclusively reserved for expressions of anger or frustration.

A clenched jaw can also be a sign of hostility. The next time you witness two people having a serious disagreement, take note of their jaws, especially the jaw of the person who isn't talking at the moment. The muscles will be drawn so tightly, they'll look like violin strings.

The Jaw-Drop

You're watching a horror film. The heroine is characteristically heading towards the one area of the entire world that she should be running away from (a basement, a funhouse or a cabin in the woods). Unlike her careless peers who've already met with their disastrous fates, she's approaching this dangerous situation very slowly. Now, her jaw may be clenched at first – naturally, she's tense – but as she gets closer and closer to the actual danger of the situation, you'll note that her mouth is opening wider and wider.

The jaw-drop tells you that a person is shocked or perhaps even confused – however, the mouth doesn't necessarily have to be wide open, as it might be in the case above. Let's say you recently split up with your partner. As you're driving home from work, you spot his car in the lane next to you. As the two of you have vowed to remain friends, you pull up alongside him to wave – and then you spot your best friend in his passenger seat. You're understandably confused (did her car break down? Are they car sharing?) and surprised. Anyone looking in on this situation would immediately be able to read your thoughts by way of your open mouth.

The jaw-drop is a reaction to surprise, confusion or fear. Of course, surprises can be good or bad. If you watch the news, you might see one person win the lottery and another watching his own house burn to the ground. Both of them might express their shock with an open mouth.

Chewing

Babies and toddlers stick everything in their mouths. They slobber, they drool and they drive their parents crazy with worry that this child will eventually choke. This is what experts call the 'oral phase' of life, and it's meant to be a means of discovery (how does the coffee table taste?) and a way to relieve tension. Most kids outgrow this by the time they go to preschool, but some don't. There are plenty of adults who give in to the urge to stick things in their mouth.

The Adult Chewer

Does your workmate chomp on his pencils from 9 to 5? Some experts might say that he became 'stuck' in this oral phase of life, that he never found a more mature way to soothe himself and that he continues to chew on his shirt collar, toothpicks and bits of paper because he needs this kind of soothing to get through his day. If you happen to be very close to someone who chews on everything in sight, you might try explaining this concept to him and suggesting other ways for him to deal with stress. The problem is that an adult chewer is very set in his ways – and he can't really avoid the very thing that he relies on. (His mouth is always right there, after all.) If you can get a pencil chewer to switch to chewing gum, that's an acceptable compromise.

All infants are born with a sucking reflex, which they need to eat and to settle their nerves. This is why crying babies respond well to dummies and learn to suck their thumbs – the sucking calms them down.

Mouth Chewing and Biting

Lots of people chew on their own lips, tongues and the insides of their cheeks. If you're not one of these people, you might be wondering why anyone would do such a thing – doesn't it hurt? Probably not. Chewing on the mouth is usually a way to relieve stress or boredom. Most people don't bite themselves hard enough to cause any harm, though in times of extreme upset, a person might accidentally bite down harder than he intended and draw blood.

So what about people who bite other people? What if your neighbour's child regularly tries to chomp on your son? This is a sign of aggression, obviously, but it's also not all that uncommon in kids. Again, they explore the world with their mouths; also, once they bite someone to express their frustration or anger, they learn that it gets a reaction. Some kids really enjoy having that kind of power in their tiny little teeth.

Adult biters are a different story, of course. Hopefully, the only biting you've experienced in your adult life has been passionate in nature. There's really nothing to read into it beyond this. Some lovers are biters; others aren't. If your mate's biting bothers you, don't assume that it's a character flaw of some sort. Just tell him to stop. If he can't or won't, then you should look for other non-verbal cues of aggression, like dominant eye contact, a set jaw and an aggressive stance.

Happy at Last

Last but not least, you'll learn what the happy mouth looks like. It's no great mystery, actually: happy mouths smile. They laugh. They don't stick their tongues out at other people. But are there varying degrees of how pleased a mouth can appear?

Smiling

There's nothing more pleasing than a genuine smile – it warms your heart to see someone you care about grinning broadly. And when the real smile belongs to you, you physically feel at ease, if only for a moment.

Everyone knows that there are real smiles and fake smiles. Julia Roberts is known for showing her pearly whites in a genuine manner. Beauty pageant contestants generally wear plastic grins. What's the difference – and should it make a difference to you if someone else is flashing you a fake sign of happiness? A real smile has the following characteristics:

- The lips move upwards.
- The nose may crinkle slightly; nostrils may flare.
- The muscles around the eyes are fully engaged.

This is what experts call the zygomatic smile (so named for the zygomatic major muscle, which pulls your cheeks and lips into a genuine smile), and when you see it, it means the other person is truly happy. If your interviewer or date gives you a fully engaged zygomatic smile, you can sit back and relax a bit – things are going your way!

By contrast, the fake smile has these characteristics:

- The lips move laterally.
- The muscles and features of the rest of the face remain somewhat stagnant.

The key to the genuine smile is in how the eyes behave. Although you can surely learn to fake a real smile by consciously contracting your facial muscles, you can be certain that someone whose lips are moving sideways and whose eyes remain rather blank is faking that grin for your benefit – perhaps out of politeness (as may be the case on a first date that isn't going all that well), perhaps in an effort to deceive you (as may be the case when you're talking to a used-car salesman). Assess the situation carefully and proceed with caution.

Laughing

What place does laughter have in body language? People either find something amusing and laugh, or they don't. How can you read into that, other than say that some people have a more developed (or more immature) sense of humour than others?

A person with a great laugh is generally perceived to be a friendly sort. He's often the hit of any gathering, simply because people love to hear his chuckle – it makes them feel good because it makes them laugh, too. Now, there's the crux of laughter – the way it spreads. And it doesn't spread the way a fad does – people don't simply copy one another's laugh attacks, they actually experience real amusement at watching someone else guffaw. Everyone's experienced this sort of thing, and usually at the absolute worst time.

Perhaps in your school classroom, your teacher sat down in her chair and it made a most unflattering squeaking sound. You did your best to ignore it, but then you saw your best friend trying to stifle his own laughter. Pretty soon, the two of you were watching each other trying not to laugh and finding it more difficult to keep a straight face. At this point, the laughter was as much about the laughter itself as it was about the teacher's indignity. (If only you'd been able to articulate this to the headmistress.)

A laugh doesn't need to be loud in order to draw other people in. It's the act itself that makes other people view the laugher as a lighthearted, good-natured person.

A person who doesn't laugh often is thought of as being uptight, even if she merely happens to have a very reserved sense of humour. Just as boisterous laughter makes a person appear sociable, a complete absence of laughter can make people think you're a humourless hermit-type. If you don't laugh much, at least learn to smile at the appropriate times – and make sure that smile appears genuine!

The moral of the story: when people want to know what's on your mind, they'll look to your mouth, so give your public what they're looking for. It's hard to mistake authentic movements of the mouth so don't be surprised if people are suddenly reading your communications a lot more clearly. It's not that you've become a great orator – you've just learned to put your message where your mouth is.

Chapter 7

The Eyes Have It

Have you ever had a dream where you're speaking to someone who is looking away from you, just having a normal conversation – until the person turns towards you and you see his eyes are glowing red? Pretty scary stuff, even if he appears to be completely normal otherwise. In real life, the eyes are usually a little less frightening, but they do often hold the answers you're looking for in a person, including whether he's truthful and/or interested in what you're saying.

Looking Awful?

There's just no getting around it: if your eyes don't look healthy and bright, neither do you. Unfortunately, many common conditions and ailments can cause your eyes to appear red, puffy or otherwise sickly, including:

- Allergies
- Colds
- Lack of sleep
- Poor diet
- Hormonal changes
- Normal aging/cosmetic issues (bags, crow's feet, etc.)

Of course, there are also anatomical issues at play here, namely the size, shape and symmetry of the eyes, along with conditions like serious dark circles, which can be caused by capillaries surrounding the eye.

Since you see people every day of your life and you know everybody's physically different, you might wonder why the eyes play such a huge role in how you perceive somebody at first glance. A person's eyes can tell you many, many things about him: his age, his mood, his level of health, whether he's paying attention to you when you speak. Throughout this chapter, you'll learn how to interpret and use specific eye movements.

Eye Awareness

The cosmetic industry sells billions of pounds' worth of make-up to women each year; a large chunk of that profit is made from the sale of eye shadow, eye liner, mascara, eyebrow gel and concealer (used to cover up unsightly dark shadows surrounding the eyes). In addition, Botox – a toxin that paralyzes the muscles, in this case those surrounding the eyes, thus eliminating crow's feet and making the eyes appear younger – is the aging woman's new best friend.

Girly Glances

Why do women, in particular, place so much stock (almost literally) in the appearance of their eyes? The answer comes from your school biology book: females are genetically programmed to make themselves appear fertile to the male gender so that the human race may go on. Young women are fertile women; and as these women are destined to carry on the human race, they're held in high regard by males. The first signs of aging – fine lines, dark circles and wrinkles – often appear around the eyes, so women do everything in their power to camouflage those little flaws, lest they be regarded as somehow less valuable to society than their younger sisters.

Another reason women spend long hours applying eye make-up is to mimic the big-eyed innocence of youth … and we're talking about real youth, as in childhood. When a woman makes up her eyes to look wide and innocent, she looks as harmless and as inexperienced as a young child, which may help to attract men who are looking for a date who's filled with virtue or who's simply gullible.

Rugged Eyes

All in all, though, even with the emphasis on youth in this country, age still isn't the issue for men that it is for women. Men can theoretically remain virile right through their old age. Many women are attracted to older mates for practical reasons – he's wiser, more mature and financially stable. In other words, a little age can look very good on a man's face. So although many men will knock themselves out to keep physically fit, it's not likely that you'll regularly see men at the cosmetics counter any time soon. They're finding dates without spending hours in front of the mirror and/or huge amounts of money on cosmetic surgery, correcting or hiding the fine lines around their eyes.

Those Mysterious Brows

What kinds of messages do you send and receive through the windows of the soul and their frames? Let's start by discussing the eyebrows, an area of the face that's once again usually the exclusive concern of women, who spend time and money waxing, threading, plucking and shaping them in the quest for the perfect arch. Why are the eyebrows so important? Well, it helps to think of them as two horizontal exclamation points – they can emphasise (or completely contradict) the words coming out of your mouth.

Raising Eyebrows

Picture this: you're speaking to your colleague, asking what time you can expect him to have his part of your joint report completed. As he tells you it'll be ready for you when you get back from lunch, he raises both of his eyebrows. Is he being true or false? Well, you'll have to base your answer on more than his eyebrows, but here's what those strips of hair can tell you: he wants you to believe him. When both eyebrows are raised, it's like someone is underlining his verbal message. If your colleague happens to be a generally trustworthy person, then he's most likely telling you the truth about the report. If he's a compulsive liar, the eyebrows shouldn't convince you of the veracity of his message.

Typically, the double eyebrow-raise indicates that someone wants you to see her as a sincere person. Raising both eyebrows is a way of saying, 'I'm telling you the truth.' However, liars are just as likely to employ this move as truthful people are, so don't base your judgment of the message solely on the positioning of the eyebrows.

Raised eyebrows can also indicate confusion, though furrowed eyebrows are more common in these instances. If someone raises his eyebrows while questioning your take on a particular issue, you'll typically note other body-language signs, like an open mouth and flared nostrils. Taken together, these gestures indicate that the other person doesn't exactly think you're a championship-level fibber, but he has some serious concerns about what you're saying.

Raising One Eyebrow

While the double brow-raise can sometimes indicate confusion, there's no mistaking the single brow-raise. Let's say that you're the one who's being asked to produce a report by the end of the business day. You give your colleague an enthusiastic, 'Can do!' and notice that he's looking at you with one eyebrow raised. Should you interpret this as a sign that he has complete faith in you and your abilities?

Hardly. The single eyebrow-raise is a non-verbal way of saying, 'I don't believe you.' Note that this is a step beyond being confused by what you're saying; at best, this person believes that you're being deliberately deceitful. At worst, he thinks you're a simpleton who has no idea what you're talking about. So how can you convince him that you're competent? Redo that 'can-do' … and this time shoot him a double brow-raise!

Frown's in Town

Perhaps the easiest brow signal to read is the frown, which is usually interpreted as a sign of anger, but there are other times when people wear a knitted brow, namely during times of sadness or confusion. Imagine a child trying to put a wheel back into his rollerblade after it's flown out of its socket. He's having a difficult time of it – that wheel just wants to stay out. What do you notice about the child's face? His eyebrows are pointing downwards, probably in a fairly severe manner. Is he angry that he's having so much trouble or confused about how to get the wheel back into place? Maybe a little of both. It's hard to tell by the eyebrows alone, so you'll have to take a look at the rest of his face. (Pursed lips, for example, are a sign of frustration and/or anger, while an open mouth is usually a sign of confusion.)

Interestingly, many patients request Botox in the area between the eyebrows in order to eliminate a 'permanent' frown. The lines that appear in this region can make people look angry all the time. Ridding yourself of this facial gesture allows others to view you in a completely different light.

Sadness can also be seen in a frown, especially the types of sadness that lead people to deep and serious thought – events such as a break-up, an illness, recovering from being fired – anything that might trigger a sense of regret and a feeling that different actions might have prevented the situation. In these cases, the frowner may actually be contemplating some big issues in her life. The downward eyebrows are an indication of frustration and confusion.

If someone you know frowns almost constantly and walks into the wall on a regular basis, there's a good chance that he's suffering from poor vision. No need to read into his eye movements – get him to the optometrist!

Eyelashes

Eyelashes, individually taken, are tiny hairs that are supposed to catch debris before it enters the eye, but those little hairs hold a lot of power in their collective strands. Women think about their eyelashes a lot – they curl them, apply mascara to them to make them appear longer and thicker, and know how to bat them to win a man over. When you look at an artist's drawing of a baby, you'll note that the child will inevitably have gorgeous eyes and long, beautiful eyelashes. That's right – the allure of the lashes is another one of those non-verbal things that ties in to the innocence of childhood. The longer and more beautiful the lashes are, the more harmless you appear to be. (You can read more about the technique involved in the successful lash-bat in Chapter 17).

Long eyelashes are considered beautiful, but only if they appear to be somewhat natural. When lashes are so caked with mascara that they look like spikes coming out of the eyes, you've crossed the line from innocent to quite frightening. Wipe off some of that mascara and go for a cleaner look.

The average person blinks about 20 times a minute. When any sort of anxiety or excitement comes on to the scene, that number shoots up noticeably. This surge in emotion is why women may bat their eyes on a date, but also why you might blink more than usual when speaking with your boss or when telling a lie.

Open Wide

Eye communication is sometimes so subtle that you can sense the message coming from the ocular area without knowing why you're responding the way you are. Squinty eyes, half-closed eyes and wide-open eyes all have their own means of communicating with the outside world. What if you're sending the wrong message? Have no fear; the fixes for these situations are actually quite simple, as you'll read in this section.

Get Your Eyes Checked

Squinting at people when they're speaking to you tells them that you're very doubtful of their integrity and/or competence. You might be having trouble seeing – a very common cause of the squint – but other people won't necessarily know that. All they see is you, squinting and staring as though you're attempting to find the truth in this person's face – and failing.

While squinting is sometimes caused by poor eyesight, it can also be the result of your personal anatomy or it might simply be an unfortunate habit. People might also respond to a threatening situation by narrowing their eyes (picture Clint Eastwood as Dirty Harry). Whatever the case, lose the squint if you want to appear friendly and open-minded. Force those lids open, either by reminding yourself to do so or by getting some contact lenses or glasses, and you'll see that others will view you differently – namely, they won't think of you as someone who's always looking for the flaw or potential danger in a situation.

Sorry I'm Boring You

Let's say you're visiting your doctor, relaying your most troubling symptoms, sharing the most personal sort of information with him … and he looks at you with his eyes half-closed. Are you boring him, or is this his way of telling you that your prognosis isn't good? Before you start writing your will on the paper covering the examination table, consider that this might be the way your doctor looks at everyone, in every situation, good or bad.

An open eye indicates that you're fully present in the moment: you're engaged in the conversation, the wheels are turning in your head, and you actually care about what the other person is saying.

The half-closed eye is interpreted as a sign of boredom and/or fatigue. If you tend to walk around with your eyelids at half-mast, then you're probably used to people being a little stand-offish or offended by you – but perhaps you've never realised why. Because of their anatomical structure, some people physically can't hold their eyelids open all the way. Plastic surgery can correct this condition, but for people who'd rather not go under the knife, there are plenty of other ways to show interest in what someone else is saying. Eye contact (which will be discussed shortly), smiling and angling the body towards the other person will help compensate for eyes that don't look 100 percent alert.

Double-Wide Eyes?

If half-closed eyes indicate boredom, then you can go ahead and assume that a wide-open eye shows interest in another person. Just don't go wild – there's no need for you to look googly eyed if you can help it. Eyes that are too open (as wide as possible, so that the entire white of the eye is showing) can appear fearful or intimidated.

If your eyes are naturally wider than most other people's, there are ways to overcome misinterpretations of your ocular language. Keep your eye contact a bit briefer than what's considered polite (you'll read about this in the following section), and use friendly body-language cues (smiling, proper angling, friendly touches when appropriate) to assure others that you are neither anxious nor domineering.

Look at Me!

Eye contact is one of the most asked-about topics in the study of body language. When you are learning to communicate non-verbally (and to read the non-verbal cues of friends and colleagues), you will want to know:

- How long should I hold eye contact with someone else?
- Does appropriate eye contact change according to the situation?
- What might happen if my eye-contact skills are poor?
- What kinds of messages can I send with eye contact?
- How do I interpret someone else's eye movements?

Hold ... and Release!

There is perhaps no question about eye contact as pressing as, 'How long should I look at someone while I'm speaking to him? How about when I'm listening – do the rules change depending on who's leading the conversation?'

Imagine you're walking home from work and you bump into your best friend. You stop to say hello and make plans to meet for dinner later. Assuming the two of you have seen each other recently, you'll probably make eye contact for a few seconds while you're talking before looking down or off to the side for a few seconds – then you'll make eye contact again, look away and back again. This pattern will be repeated throughout the conversation.

If you happen to run into a long-lost friend instead, your eye contact might linger a little longer. Longer stretches of eye contact indicate an extreme interest in what the other person is saying.

It's natural to be more interested in someone new than in someone that you see every day. In cases like these – where you meet up with someone who is intrinsically fascinating for whatever reason – it's fine to use more eye contact than you normally would. You probably already do this without even thinking about it.

Make a Lasting Impression

People tend to worry about eye contact most in situations where they're concerned about making a good impression on someone else, like first dates and job interviews. Even someone who has a natural aptitude for using an appropriate amount of eye contact can over-think these situations and end up sending a false message by staring or avoiding the other person's gaze altogether.

Communicating at eye level establishes an equal relationship. Standing above someone while you're literally talking down at him puts you in a position of being superior; looking up while someone browbeats you puts you in an inferior position.

Eye contact is tricky in the early stages of dating, because even though you may be incredibly interested in everything your date is saying, you don't want to come across as being over-the-edge-of-sanity-interested (having a tendency towards developing obsessions, in other words). Use normal eye contact in the beginning stages (hold the gaze for a few seconds, look away, repeat) until your date's body language (he's moving closer and closer to you, he reaches to take your hand, he's smiling non-stop) indicate that he's really into you.

And what about that eye contact in a job interview? The same rules apply: steady, consistent eye contact combined with well-timed breaks can work wonders for your overall image, especially as so many other interviewees don't know what to do with their eyeballs in this situation. The general recommendation is that you hold eye contact for no longer than five seconds before glancing away.

Breaking Contact

You might be wondering where your eyes should be looking when you briefly break eye contact. Your best option is either to look downwards briefly – what's called the 'gaze down' – or off to the side of the person who's speaking. Looking downwards is a submissive move that shows that you're still listening. Glancing off to the side sends a similar message: I'm still here, even though my eyes are taking a little break from you right now.

Note that any time you look away from the person you're speaking to, it's just a brief glance before regaining eye contact. If you're speaking to someone while actively keeping an eye on everyone walking past you, you're sending the message that you're not engaged in the conversation. You're coming across as distracted and rude, as though you're looking for something or someone more interesting to save you from this interaction. And if you happen to be on the receiving end of this type of behaviour, feel free to follow the other person's glance to determine what or who she finds so fascinating. You can get a good feel for someone's interests, intentions and level of attentiveness in this type of situation.

It's considered impolite to look at everything around you when you're involved in a conversation. However, when you're being reamed out by your boss or spouse, this kind of lack of eye contact is a way of indicating that you're not in agreement with the other person; the gaze down, on the other hand, is a way of expressing shame.

Up, Up and Away

Breaking eye contact and looking upwards isn't a good option – at least not if you want to keep the conversation friendly. Even a brief glance upwards indicates boredom or frustration on your part. There are situations where this type of glance is appropriate – during an argument or whenever you're hearing something that's completely out of sync with your thinking, look upwards if you want the other person to know how you feel. But be aware that most people will take immediate offense to this gesture and your conversation will almost certainly become heated or come to a screeching halt.

The upward glance is similar to the eye roll, with a small exception: the upward glance is a bit subtler. The eye roll is an overt move – the eyeball starts at one corner of the eye and moves up and around the orbit. Now, if you asked your friends what this motion means, you might get several different answers, including anger and frustration. What differentiates the eye roll from the upward glance is that the rolling of the eyeball is usually motivated by condescension – it's a way of saying, 'That is absolutely, positively the stupidest thing I have ever heard in my life.'

While the upward glance and the eye roll are related, they're interpreted very differently by other people – so be careful when your eyes start migrating to the tops of their sockets. Your spouse might forgive an upward glance during an argument, for example, but an eye roll is going to count as a different and more serious type of offense.

Shifting Suspicions

If you ever watch old crime movies, you'll no doubt hear some villain described as having 'shifty eyes'. What does this mean, exactly, and why are bad guys more prone to having these strange eye movements?

Eye shifting really refers to the eyeballs darting all over the place. When you read about breaking eye contact earlier in the chapter, you were advised to look away briefly, to the side or downwards, and then make eye contact with the other person again. When someone breaks eye contact (or refuses to meet your gaze) and instead appears to be looking to the left, right and back of you, you can't help but wonder what's going on with him. He appears to be on the lookout for something, but what?

Shifting or darting the eyes can mean several different things:

- The person really is watching out for someone else, so he can either meet up with her or avoid her.
- The person is completely uninterested in what you're saying.
- Whatever you're saying is making this person nervous, and he's looking for any opportunity or excuse to escape.

The bottom line on shifty eyes is that if someone is really into the situation and conversation he's currently involved in, he won't be looking all over the place. Take note of where your eyes are focused during your day-to-day interactions. If you find that you're looking everywhere but into the eyes of the person you're talking to, you're sending a message that says, 'Let's wrap this. I can't help but notice that everything around you is far more interesting than you are.'

Emotional Eyes

Now that you know all about the eyes, you'll have no problem decoding someone's emotions by looking at her orbital sockets, right? Not exactly. Just like any other subtopic of body language, the eyes have to be read in conjunction with what the rest of the body is saying. Earlier this chapter mentioned how anatomical differences in the eye can make someone appeared bored when in reality her eyes are always half-closed. So while the eyes are a fairly good indicator of someone's feelings, you can't rely on them 100 percent to interpret emotion.

Let's take a situation where the eyes could confuse you. You're dating a new girl and even though she expresses a lot of interest in you through her body language – she smiles, laughs, angles herself towards you, gives you lots of friendly little touches – her eyes are always on the move. She's looking all over the place, and rarely into your eyes. What's going on here? Is she interested in this relationship or just biding her time?

Based on her other body-language signals, she's definitely somewhat interested. The overactive eyes are cause for concern, though. Give her the benefit of the doubt and assume that she's just easily distracted. Find a place that's quiet and distraction-free and gaze into her eyes. If she makes eye contact in a shy manner – for a second before looking away and looking back – then she's probably just a little timid (and unschooled in eye-contact technique). But if she still seems as though she's looking around for an escape route, there's probably a deeper issue (fear of commitment, or she's simply just not into you) at play here.

The eyes are a powerful set of tools in the body-language workshop. When you learn to use those peepers effectively (say, to woo an attractive neighbour or to intimidate an annoying colleague), you're putting yourself at a definite advantage – and exerting very little effort, by the way. So start perfecting your looks. Make sure your eyes aren't giving you away when you'd rather hide the truth; make certain that you appear to be sincere when honesty is what you're offering. And when you've perfected your orbital moves, don't be surprised to find that all eyes are suddenly on you.

Chapter 8

Nosing Around

People say that the nose knows. Obviously, your nose plays a big part in the way you interact with the world and the people in it. (Your nose is what tells you that a great-looking man is way less attractive when he's suffering from body odour.) Aside from its practical uses, the nose has a language all its own, and you'll learn all about it in this chapter.

A Flare for Emotion

When it comes to understanding the language of the nose, the nostrils are a good place to start. Have you ever noticed that when someone is sad, her nostrils flare? When that same person is shocked, her nostrils flare. And when she's angry beyond belief … well, what do you know? Her nostrils flare. Why does this happen, you wonder, and how should you react to widening nasal openings?

Animalistic Instincts

As often as you see it happen, you may never stop and ask yourself why nostrils flare and why it's usually in response to some unexpected or adverse event. This is something else that goes back to your primitive ancestors who were fighting to survive with the daily threat of animal predators knocking on their cave door. The fight-or-flight response had to kick in in order for your relatives to assess the situation and prepare themselves for battle (or to run away). The nostril flare is a physical adaptation that helped them to literally sniff out the enemy.

Modern Flare

The flare can signal an unpleasant state of mind. Now, this could well be in response to a perceived attack, but it doesn't necessarily indicate that it's physical in nature. Let's say you're driving to work with your friend Mary. She's telling you all about her boyfriend (a bloke you can't stand). Seems he's found himself in trouble with the law and Mary's had to cough up the money for a solicitor. You're concerned for your friend and tell her that she's being taken advantage of, that her boyfriend will never amount to anything, and that you can't believe that she'd blow her holiday money to help him stay out of prison.

Mary sits quietly listening to your outburst, so you assume that she's agreeing with your point of view. At the next red light, you look her way and notice that her eyes are squinted, her jaw is set in stone and her nostrils are flared widely. Because of her body language you know you've just crossed a line and sent her into an internal rage.

The nostrils are a great indicator of someone's emotions; as a result, you might see flared nostrils in all sorts of situations, depending on the nose in question. For example, the nostrils might open widely in response to:

- Fear: non-verbal cues are similar to surprise.
- Anger: you read about Mary's strong reaction, how her eyes and jaw changed.
- Disgust: an emotion somewhere between anger and disdain, where you might see crinkled eyes, curled lips and flared nostrils.

Is it always easy to read the nose? In other words, do flared nostrils always indicate one of the above reactions? Unfortunately, this isn't always the case, as you'll read in the following section.

Naturally Nostrilly

Some people have naturally large nostrils that appear to be flared even when they aren't. In other cases, rhinoplasty can alter the size or shape of the nostrils, so that, again, they appear to be permanently enlarged.

Before you go pinning an emotion on someone, take care to note the normal state of her nostrils. Someone who has big nostrils will become angry if she hears 20 people ask her why she looks so angry.

If you happen to have nostrils that are on the larger side, just be aware that flared nostrils are often perceived as an expression of emotion. You might want to think about adjusting the rest of your non-verbal cues so that your face is sending the messages you intend. For example, if you tend to frown out of habit, this gesture, combined with your flared nostrils, is probably making you look angry a good part of the day. Maybe people are afraid to approach you – and if they do, they are automatically on the defense, because they think they're entering into your bad mood zone.

The Nose on Cloud Nine

You've just read how the nose flares in reaction to adverse situations. Let's not forget that the nose can react in the same way to good news. For example, when athletes win the much-coveted season-ending prize in their sport, you see their emotions displayed in all their raw glory – the smiles are broad, the eyes are wide open and the nostrils are often flared.

Now picture waiting for a friend to walk into her own surprise party. When she's caught in the glare of the lights and a crowd that was heretofore hidden from view, her emotion will be somewhere between fear and happiness. You'll see that displayed in her wide eyes, her open mouth and her flared nostrils. And don't be surprised if you see that your date's nostrils are flared. This can also be an indication of arousal or excitement.

It's important to keep in mind that just because someone touches his nose doesn't mean he's up to something dastardly. He might have a legitimate itch, after all. Take care to note how long the rubbing and itching goes on, especially if he appears to be healthy.

Read My Nose

People often centre certain non-verbal cues around the nose. For example, if you're in an interview and the person behind the desk keeps tapping the bridge of her nose, is that a good sign or a signal that you're not at all the type of person she's looking for? If you ask your spouse about a suspicious charge on his credit card bill and he keeps scratching his nose while explaining himself, should you believe him or throw him out?

The key to deciphering nose-touches is keeping tabs on the frequency and/or length of the touch. After all, unless your hubby is suffering from some sort of cold or an allergic reaction, his itch shouldn't require ten minutes of rubbing the tip of his nose.

Nose-Touching

Harry is a graphic designer in an advertising agency who's known for being slow to respond to any question asked of him. He's no dimwit, he simply likes to choose his words very carefully. When a new boss came on to the scene, she asked Harry for his input on his budget. Harry raised one finger and placed it right on the tip of his nose. First, he pressed up on it, making it appear as though he was creating a pig nose. Then he went the other way – pressing the tip of his nose flat against his face. Anyone could clearly see that the new boss was confused not only by his silence, but by his finger–nose connection.

Excessive nose-touching – touching that goes beyond a quick rub – can be highly distracting to the people around you, especially if you're twisting or pushing your nose into strange shapes. Making a conscious effort to keep your hands off your nose could change the way others see you.

Harry's a deep thinker, and like many of his kind, he employs self-touch as a way of comforting himself while he runs through the options in his mind. Other deep thinkers might raise a finger to the forehead or the temple. His colleagues are accustomed to this behaviour and don't find it distracting or disturbing; however, since it was clear that the new boss didn't know what to make of Harry and his fondness for his nose, a friend suggested that he keep his hands off his face in the office – and then Harry was confused! His nose-pressing habit was so ingrained, he didn't even realise he'd been doing it.

Once Harry took a good look at his body language, he realised that thinking with his nose, so to speak, was probably a strange thing to be doing. He made a concerted effort to desist with this behaviour, and lo and behold, things between him and the boss improved.

If you employ the nose-tap in the UK, you wouldn't be surprised to receive some questioning looks, as here the gesture means 'We're sharing a secret.' However, across the pond in the United States, and in other cultures, people use the nose-tap to communicate a different message. The tap is similar to the nose-press: it's a way of indicating that you're thinking something over.

Nose-Rubbing

You're on holiday and you've just checked into your hotel, only to find that your 'super-luxury' accommodation is nothing more than a shoebox filled with plastic furniture. You traipse down to the lobby and demand the room that you booked – the one you saw on the hotel's website. While the receptionist tells you the hotel is sold out and there isn't a thing she can do for you, she rubs the front of her nose. You're not giving up; you've paid far too much for such a dump of a room. You ask to see a manager, and the receptionist tells you there isn't a manager on duty; you'll have to wait till tomorrow morning. And now she gives the side of her nose a good up-and-down rub. What's going on here? Does working for such a shady operation make her nose itch?

That nose-rub is a self-touch, a means of calming the nerves of a person who isn't being entirely truthful. In this example, there's a good chance that the employee is discouraged from handing out room upgrades but that doesn't mean that she can't do it.

Does the nose-rub have any other purpose? Of course it does. As you already read, rubbing the nose can be a response to an actual itch or sense of discomfort. But it can also be a sign that someone's not being honest with you. If your date keeps rubbing his nose, what does that mean? First, make sure he isn't allergic to your perfume. If he insists he's feeling fine, then the excessive touching or rubbing of the nose might indicate he's feeling uncomfortable. Now, this could be a good thing or a bad thing for you, depending on what's making him feel uneasy. If he's worried because he likes you a lot and he's sure he's making a fool of himself, then that's not so bad. But if he's squirming in his seat because he can't wait for this date to end, that's obviously another story. How can you tell the difference? By reading the rest of his non-verbal cues. Is he angling himself towards you or away from you? How's his eye contact? Have the two of you touched at all during the course of the evening?

Crinkle, Crinkle, Little Nose

The nose's first priority is to let you know when something stinks, literally. In fact, the smells entering into your nasal passageways en route to the brain's olfactory centre can alert you to danger (as in the case of noxious fumes or smoke) or they can help you to relax (aromatherapy is based on this principle). Pleasant smells are, of course, always welcome, but when an unpleasant stench comes on the scene, the nose often reacts by crinkling. This response is also suitable for expressing your displeasure with someone who may actually smell quite pleasant.

For example, you've just finished your workout at the gym. You're supposed to pick up your friend for lunch, and since you're running late, you don't bother to hit the showers; you just grab your coat and run. When you pick up your friend minutes later, she climbs into the car and the two of you start chatting away. Soon, you notice that she's looking around uncomfortably and pressing a tissue to her nose. You ask her if she's ill; she says no, but still, that tissue remains blocking her nostrils. Without actually plugging her nostrils, she's telling you that something stinks.

After lunch, you head to the office. You have a big report due tomorrow. You're hard at work, when one of your colleagues pops into your office to discuss your thoughts. As you summarize what you've come up with so far, you notice that he's crinkling his nose. Instantly, you start to panic. Do you smell? It's possible – the nose does initially crinkle when a hint of offensive waft hits it – but it's more likely that this nose crinkle is an expression of the way your colleague feels about your report, and it isn't good. The nose crinkle is used to convey displeasure or disagreement on some issue. You might see a woman crinkle her nose when an undesirable man asks her for a date, and you'll also see nose crinkles when children argue with each other.

This isn't a gesture that's used to express a positive message, so when you see someone's nose crinkle in response to something you're saying, you might want to stop right there and get to the bottom of the issue.

Sneezing and Snorting

Every nose makes strange noises from time to time (some more than others), but do these sounds really mean something in terms of reading someone's personality, or are they just side effects of nature, the result of too much pollen in the air or fluid in the sinuses? The answers might just surprise you. In fact, you might just find yourself taking 'nose notes' on the people surrounding you.

Ahh-Choo!

Everyone sneezes, of course, some people more than others. It's not really the number of sneezes, but the way you sneeze that tells other people something about you (aside from the fact that you have some sort of nasal irritation going on). Don't believe this theory? Pay attention to the people in your life and how they let loose with their sneezes and whether this physical release of the itchy nose fits their personality.

People are highly conscious of the way they sneeze, even though they can't control when they sneeze. It's uncommon to hear an earth-shattering sneeze from a person who's very timid, for example.

Someone who's loud and boisterous is more likely to sneeze with full force, making such a ruckus that he scares the daylights out of everyone around him. (He's also less likely to turn his head away from whoever has the misfortune of standing in front of him.) Someone who's fairly conservative and considerate in his day-to-day dealings will try to sneeze away from everyone else and keep the volume as low as possible. Very delicate women often have a little meow of a sneeze, while high achievers of both genders give a short, loud sneeze.

Is this the best way to determine someone's personality? Probably not, but it is interesting to take note of the sneezes of the people you already know.

Oink!

In our culture, snorts are generally considered to be rude – unless you have a good reason for sounding like a pig. (There aren't many.) If you're suffering from a head cold, your spouse will probably forgive a snort-snort here and a snort-snort there.

Snorting in public is likely to disgust the people around you, making them think you know nothing about common courtesy. If you must do it, try to carry out your sinus exercises when you are in private.

People who snort when they laugh are generally thought of as being good-natured and uninhibited. You might expect this from your little brother, but when a snort-laugh comes from a grown adult, it's sometimes disconcerting – and embarrassing. If you accidentally snort-laugh in a meeting or during a dinner party, you can use some other body language to make amends: laugh at yourself first; if you show that you are good-natured and uninhibited, then maybe that snort will have done you a favour.

So now you know that your nose is more than an ornamental decoration in the middle of your face. It's all right to get nosy with other people's noses; just remember that the size and shape of the nose are often given certain non-verbal attributes, even though these factors don't change with emotion flare-ups. You'll do well to read your colleague's entire set of non-verbal cues before deciding that her flared nostrils are a sign of extreme anger. (If she's smiling, you're safe; if she's frowning and pursing her lips, run!)

Can't Stop Moving

Twitching, shaking or constant movements are signals of boredom, nervousness or extreme excitement. As these emotions are obviously very different in nature, you don't want to be sending the wrong signals at the wrong time (otherwise your dentist will think you're excited to see him and your significant other will think you have an extreme case of nerves). This chapter gives you an overview of why people bounce and twist their body parts at the strangest times, and also gives you advice for interpreting these unusual moves.

Movers and Shakers

Children are naturally prone to constant movement, and if you think about it, that makes sense: they have an entire world to explore and conquer, and they don't want to be confined to one spot any longer than is absolutely necessary (and sometimes not even that long). As kids mature, their attention span increases and their pinball existence (bouncing from activity to activity and place to place) gradually slows down.

If you watch someone who's prone to panic attacks, you can actually see the progression of an episode: what starts out as mild anxiety (wringing the hands) may progress to a state of terror (rocking back and forth, hugging himself tightly) before settling back down into a state of relative comfort (hands clasped tightly).

By the time kids mature into adults, they're supposed to be able to sit through boring lectures, long meetings, endless films and dull dates without exhibiting obvious signs of physical or emotional discomfort. Still, at some point in your life, you've probably known an adult who just couldn't sit still for more than a few minutes. Some people are truly bored if they're not working at something, so they keep moving as a way to ward off the negative emotions of boredom and frustration. Constant movement is an alternative to focused action for these people, even though they do it without thinking about it. For other people, continuous motion is a way to soothe away the anxiety and worry they already have. There's a subtle difference between the two, but one thing is the same – both sets of people derive a certain amount of comfort (if not pleasure) from being constantly on the move.

Nervous Hands

In Chapter 3, you learned that some behavioural experts believe the hands display more emotion than any other part of the body. This is perhaps most true when you're talking about nervousness projected through hand movements. Someone who's anxious may pull out all the stops, using those hands to express every emotion she's experiencing at the exact moment those feelings strike her.

The Power of Touch

Anxious hands often engage in self-touch. Self-touches include things like wringing the hands, rubbing the face, clenching the fists, hugging oneself, cracking the knuckles and so on.

But why do anxious people feel the need to massage various parts of their body? The sense of touch is incredibly powerful – so powerful, in fact, that studies have shown that premature infants who receive massage fare better than those who don't. Parents use touch to soothe fussy babies and children. As adults, people learn that a simple touch from a boyfriend or girlfriend can cause more of an adrenaline rush than bungee jumping. In addition, the benefits of regular massage for adults – such as improved sleep patterns and a boosted immune system – have been documented in medical studies. In fact, today many hospitals employ massage therapists.

So from the first moments of life, you learn that touch has a magic, soothing quality. It's really no wonder, then, that during anxious moments you might use self-touches to calm your nerves.

There are all sorts of self-touches that are used to soothe the nerves. Running your hands through your hair, pulling on an earlobe, or touching the back of the neck are indications that you're feeling out of sorts and attempting to calm your nerves.

Finding Comfort

Self-touches centring on parts of the body with high nerve concentrations (such as the area around the lips) may be more comforting than other sites on the body, but this probably depends on the person and the cause of his anxiety. As you might imagine, mental health plays a role in the kinds of touches one might find most soothing. A person who has a slight case of nerves due to an upcoming job interview might find the around-the-chin-and-mouth rub very comforting, but it's probably safe to say that someone who has an irrational worry (for example, someone who's concerned that a meteor is going to hit his house at any moment) is experiencing an entirely different, more severe type of anxiety. His self-touches will probably be more pronounced (he might, for example, hug himself or wring his hands) because he needs more comforting.

One form of self-touch, called dermatillomania, also referred to as compulsive skin picking (CSP), afflicts men and women suffering from obsessive-compulsive disorder. These people are compelled to pick at the skin until it bleeds. Obviously, most people wouldn't find comfort in this sort of self-touch, but the relief that these people experience is real.

Self-touches can also indicate lying, uncertainty, or even a certain amount of hostility. All of these emotions are based in anxiety; the difference is that anxiety itself is classified as a mental illness, so someone can be suffering from anxiety without an external cause. In other words, where one person might be exhibiting signs of nervousness because he's been leading a secret life, another person can exhibit the exact same behaviour for no apparent (external) reason.

Other Self-Touches

Of course, there are many, many kinds of self-touches. Someone who puts a finger up to her chin or to her head appears to be in deep thought; touching the nose is thought to be a sign of deception, as is rubbing the forehead; pulling at the hair indicates a high level of frustration.

Again, most of these emotions are rooted in anxiety, but some self-touches actually serve a specific purpose. For example, if you see your friend rubbing his stomach, he might have eaten too much. When your mother rubs her temples, she might be soothing away a headache. Someone who clasps his hands in a meeting is probably just using polite body language.

One touch to the back of the head indicates anxiety; in fact, this is a telltale sign of lying. Someone who puts both hands behind his head, however, is simply getting comfortable.

So what does this mean to you? It's a reminder that all body language is best interpreted through patterns of behaviour and along with other non-verbal cues. One lone gesture, like wringing the hands, may mean little in itself, but combine that with darting eyes and tapping feet (which you'll read about later in this chapter), and you're looking at someone displaying a lot of nervous energy.

Tap, Tap, Tap

Every time you talk to your boss, he drums his fingers on his desk. It drives you up the wall, and rightly so. Drumming the fingertips is widely considered to be a rude gesture, something that indicates profound boredom. But as you're learning more and more about body language, you're starting to wonder if perhaps you have been too hard on your boss. Maybe the man is suffering from chronic anxiety. Could this be the reason his fingers are tapping out a mysterious rhythm?

If you're in the habit of drumming out a song every time you have to sit for more than 30 seconds, stop. This gesture is considered impolite, a way of saying, 'I don't have all day to sit here and listen to you drone on and on.'

Let's say you're the tabletop drummer and you know that you don't mean to be offensive by expressing yourself with your mad rhythms. In fact, you sing along with your finger-drumming, hence letting everyone know that you're simply into the music playing in your head. This doesn't lessen the annoyance factor. You have to realise that drumming is highly irritating to those around you. In this instance, your body language is saying, 'I don't care if you're annoyed. I must drum!'

The one place you can continue on with your hand-band is in the privacy of your own car or at home, but even then, your drumming should be suspended if someone else is occupying the seat next to you.

Shifting Seats

Is it possible to tell from a person's midsection that she is feeling anxious? What do you look for – a tightening of the stomach, or the rhythm of a heart pounding so hard you can see the person's chest pulsating? While these are genuine ways to read high levels of anxiety, you'd have to be very close to a person to assess these types of changes. There's an easier way to tell from the torso if someone's feeling uncomfortable: watch how she moves in her seat.

At some point, you've no doubt seen a woman receiving unwanted attention from a man in a social setting. If the woman is seated, she might appear to sink back into her seat (if the chap is in front of her), or slide her torso off to the side. What she's really doing is curving her spine away from the man in an attempt to increase the space between her and him.

Shifting the spine away from a person you'd rather not deal with is akin to angling (turning) yourself in the opposite direction. Both carry the same message: 'Go away.' Even if the shifter remains polite, her spine is telling you all you need to know – she hasn't been won over, and it's not likely that she's going to change her mind.

The Bigger, The Better

Another shifty response to anxiety is something called the broadside display, something animals do when they're threatened by a predator. This is exactly what it sounds like – the animal will turn to the side and make itself seem as large as possible, sending a clear message to its opponent: 'Are you sure you want to mess with me?' People don't usually turn to the side when they mimic this stance; instead, they stand with their legs wide apart, their chests puffed out and their shoulders thrown back. They're sending the same message as their animal counterparts: 'Think twice before you come at me, because I'll be coming right back at you.'

When faced with fighting a predator, most animals prepare to fight, but some may choose the opposite route. Animals – and people – can make themselves appear as small as possible to hide from a predator. You might see a person literally trying to curl his spine inwards in this situation.

Happy Feet?

While some people employ the soothing relief of the self-touch to calm their nerves, others put their feet in motion – literally – by wiggling and jiggling their lower extremities. These movements often occur at the most inopportune moments, which is usually why they're very noticeable. It's not uncommon to see someone cross her legs and jiggle the top foot around, maybe during a job interview or perhaps during a heated argument at home. That bouncing foot will betray your true emotions every time, even if you've taken great care to project confidence with your other non-verbal gestures.

Rockin' and Rollin'

Rocking back and forth on the feet – from the balls of the feet to the heel and back and forth again, or from side to side, like a rocking ship – is usually interpreted as a comforting measure. This movement mimics the rocking of a baby, and may continue to be a self-comforting motion throughout childhood. When adults become parents and learn to soothe their children by rocking them back and forth, they're reminded of this comforting motion and might start using it when their kids aren't around. You might see adult men and women standing in a queue at the bank, for example, keeping their blood pressure down by rocking from side to side.

Remember, don't be too quick to judge behaviour. Obviously, people are different, and some may balance themselves on their toes simply to while away the time. For people who are normally calm, however, bouncing around in their seat and/or shaking every body part they own is a sure indication that something's up.

Bouncing on the balls of the feet is an action that's difficult to miss, particularly when you're involved in a one-on-one conversation with a spring-soled person. The bounce is a sign of excitement or nervousness, in which case it's another self-comforting measure. Fortunately, the other non-verbal gestures associated with these emotions are different enough that you can almost immediately determine which issue you're dealing with when you come face-to-face with a bouncer. For example:

- The nervous toe-bouncer will make little eye contact, possibly hide his hands in his pockets, and use other means of self-comfort, like occasionally rocking back and forth on his feet or crossing his arms tightly in front of himself.
- The excited bouncer will make good use of eye contact, smile and use hand gestures to express his happiness.

There's also a third possibility for foot-bouncing: for some people, it's a habit that just feels good. (That's another reason why it's important to view body language as a pattern of behaviour instead of a series of random events.)

Are You Cross?

Although there's some debate about whether leg-crossing is a non-verbal attempt to hide some sort of message, it's generally believed that most people simply find that crossing their legs while sitting is a comfortable position.

When you cross your legs while you're standing, however, other people might think that you're nervous. You've already read that when confronted with danger, animals and people will either make themselves as large as possible in order to scare off an attacker, or they may pull themselves in, in an attempt to 'hide' from an enemy. Crossing the legs while standing is a move that falls into this latter category, even if your main goal is to remain as comfortable as possible while standing for long periods of time. The bottom line is that to strike your most confident-looking pose, you should stand with your legs hip-width apart.

A Foot-Long Message

You know these people: they tap their feet when they sit down. When they cross their legs, the top foot jiggles. When they're lying on the sofa, both feet are wiggling. You want to grab those feet and restrain them – glue them to the floor, tape them to the sofa, whatever it takes! What's up with all the jiggling?

There are two possibilities: jiggling the feet is either a comforting measure (it simply feels good to the jiggler) or it's an indication of anxiety – or both. So if your friend taps his feet only when he's heading out on a date, it's probably just his way of soothing his nerves. But if he taps his feet all the time and doesn't appear to be a particularly nervous person, it's probably a habit, something that he doesn't really think about as he's doing it.

This information comes in handy when you need the truth from someone. Let's say your housemate, whose feet could be characterised as two cement blocks – they're usually unmoving, unless he happens to be walking – has sworn up and down that he doesn't know where your leather trousers are. He'd never wear cow skin, he claims, and besides, they'd never fit him, as he's several sizes larger than you. While he's telling you this, he has his legs crossed in the typical male figure-four position, and his top foot is shaking so much, he's holding on to his ankle to make sure that foot doesn't fly off his ankle and hit the TV screen.

Hmm … what kind of information can you glean from this scene? Your normally calm friend appears to be awfully nervous about something. Is it possible he tried those trousers on and split their seams? Did he use them to polish his car? Did he sell them on eBay? You may never know for sure, because you can't force him to tell you the truth. However, his foot has already told you that he knows more about the whereabouts of your trousers than he's letting on.

Jumping for Joy

At the beginning of this chapter, you read how children are normally very active little people, that their restless behaviour is often due to curiosity and a sense of having to get things done right now. Some people never lose that sense of wonder and/or urgency. For them, overabundance – of activity, of happiness, of everything – is the norm, and the way they express themselves best is with an overabundance of body language.

Handing Out Happiness

The hands are once again are at the centre of the emotional display here. Happy hands clap at the slightest mention of good news, and are often more expressive than the hands of a less enthusiastic person. Cheerful people are likely to share small, intimate touches with their friends and acquaintances, as well, perhaps in an attempt to draw others into their circle of contentment. (Hey, there are worse places you could be.)

Small touches bring you into another person's intimate circle. This is one way the hands remind you of the first, presumably safest intimacy in your life, the relationship between you and your mother.

When excitable people receive good news, they may punch their fists into the air as a way of saying, 'I did it!' You'll remember from Chapter 3 that clenched fists can be a sign of anxiety or hostility, but the body language that accompanies this sort of excitement isn't likely to be mistaken for any sort of nervousness. In place of the pumping fists, you might also see gleeful arms waving in the air or outstretched to the side.

Happiness can morph into elation, which may lead to self-touches, like hands raised to the chest or mouth, or clasped hands. Occasionally, you might see someone place his hands on the top of his head in reaction to good news, as though he's trying to keep his mind together while he processes this information.

Leapin' Legs!

When someone on TV is surprised with the news of having won a million-pound prize, the winner's behaviour is the most entertaining thing to watch – people jump, twirl, faint … It's enough to make you want to practise your own reaction to incredible news just in case someone shows up on your doorstep with an oversized cheque. (You don't want millions of people watching you drop like a stone, after all.)

Speaking of leaping limbs, you can see body language in action in traditional ballet. When the storyline is happy and lighthearted, the dancers prance all over the stage; when the action takes a turn towards tragedy, you'll see more grounded, down-to-earth moves. You don't need to know the story behind the dance; you'll know instinctually what's happening just by watching the movements of the men and women on stage.

Redirecting Nervous Energy

Mike is a thirty-something corporate player who is plagued by anxiety: 'I have so much on my plate on any given day, I need to continuously evaluate and reprioritise what's been done, what's being done, and what needs to be done by the close of business. Some people are naturally suited for that kind of stress. I'm not. I can literally feel when my blood pressure starts rising, and that makes me tense in my shoulders and my neck. I have to get up and pace until I feel like I can breathe a little more easily.'

Stress comes knocking on everyone's door at some point, whether you're a big wig in the workplace or a stay-at-home mum. As Mike mentioned, some people find that stress can be a positive, driving force; it helps them to focus and get things done. Other people don't react as well to life's pressures. And as you've read throughout this chapter, anxiety can exhibit itself in a variety of body movements.

There are many ways to manage stress and to reduce its physical manifestations (such as fidgeting, pacing and wringing the hands). The key is to take that nervous energy and find some way to use it. Exercise, for example, has several benefits for the highly strung man or woman:

- Pent-up energy is put to good use, either by competing with teammates (in a game of football, for example) or with yourself (trying to beat your best time for running a mile).
- Exercise should theoretically tire your body, taking the edge off anxiety and helping you to sleep more soundly, which also helps to reduce stress.
- Endorphins released during sustained physical activity give you a feeling of euphoria, which helps to dull nervousness.

Experts also recommend yoga, meditation and martial arts for refocusing negative emotions into positive visions of how your life can be. If these options sound a little too New Age for you, don't despair. Find an activity that you enjoy (it could be knitting, sailing, writing, gardening, woodworking or swimming) and throw yourself into it. If you don't know much about your chosen hobby, learn everything you can about it.

No matter how busy and harried you feel at work or at home, redirecting some of your focus to an outside interest will help to 'split' that nervous energy and soothe your anxiety. Your body language will reflect your new state of mind. You'll relax those clenched fists, stop the incessant tapping of your feet and generally appear to be more at ease in the world. In turn, people will view you as an approachable human being instead of a walking bundle of nerves, and you'll reap the benefits of more meaningful relationships with colleagues, friends and family members.

Keep in mind that nervous energy isn't necessarily a bad thing; many people do their best work when they're under the pressure of a deadline or when they're inundated with tasks. However, when your body language is saying to others, 'Stay away from me or I'll cry/scream/run away,' then it's time to find a different way to deal with pressure so that your non-verbal communication sends a more positive message.

Your body language is usually a major part of the first impression that you make on other people. Take a good look at your nervous habits and ask yourself whether others see you as someone on the verge of a nervous breakdown or someone who has everything under control. Learn to relax and keep your anxious movements to a minimum, but also remember that other nervous fidgeters and twitchers may never change their behaviour. No matter what emotions you're dealing with from other people, try your best to react to them with calm body language. Putting an anxious person at ease with your own non-verbal communication could have a direct positive influence on your life, if that other person (such as your boss or your spouse) happens to have some measure of control over your happiness (which, honestly, is one of the most practical uses of learning about body language).

Chapter 10

Children and Body Language

Young kids are blissfully ignorant of most non-verbal communication, which makes them all the more interesting to observe. Meanwhile, older kids who do know a bit about body language are also fun to watch, because they're often very obvious in their attempts, which is good news for parents who want to know if their child is lying to them. In this chapter, you'll learn when children begin using and reading body language, and how non-verbal communication changes as they get older.

Nature or Nurture?

Some non-verbal cues, like crying, laughing, frowning, blushing and smiling, are innate, and for the most part, universal. The human reactions to these cues are also innate. Studies have shown, for example, that a baby will react by cooing and smiling at a caregiver's happy face, while responding to an angry, frowning face with a pout and a furrowed brow.

There are other newborn reflexes that should disappear altogether. For example, if you run your finger down the sole of a baby's foot, her toes will open up like a little fan. But if the same thing happens when you run your finger down an adult's sole, it could be an indication of neurological damage.

Other non-verbal cues are learned from watching other people. Even the tiniest babies are dependent on their parents for learning about appropriate social interaction. Once kids move into the toddler and preschool years, before language is fully developed, they depend on non-verbal cues to help them express their emotions. And when the non-verbal cues aren't enough, you see the ultimate display of body language: the tantrum.

Going on Instinct

Babies are born with certain innate behaviours and responses. Some of these behaviours begin as normal newborn reflexes, most of which disappear within the first year. However, the behaviours aren't gone for good; they merely morph into childhood and adult behaviours. For example:

- Sucking: in infancy, the sucking reflex is essential for feeding, but it's also a way for a baby to comfort himself. Ever wonder why older kids suck their thumbs and why some adults chew pens or smoke? They're just soothing their nerves.
- Startling: every now and then, an infant will 'startle' – he'll tense up, thrust his arms out to the side and make a fearful face, as though he's falling. Adults have a similar type of reaction when they're faced with true danger.

• Gaze aversion: how can you tell when a baby has had enough of your goo-goo-gaa-gaa-ing? He'll avoid making eye contact with you, a behaviour that's referred to as gaze aversion. Adults do the same thing to indicate boredom or displeasure.

Baby See, Baby Do

Have you ever played peekaboo with a baby, or sat and smiled at an infant in the hope that he'd smile back at you? You were actively teaching this child about the world of non-verbal communication. Although babies are born with certain instincts concerning non-verbal cues (no one teaches a baby to cry, for example), infants also learn to communicate by copying caretakers' facial cues.

Babies are fascinated by the human face and strive to imitate the expressions they see. In fact, even a newborn infant is capable of mimicking certain facial gestures, like sticking out his tongue in response to seeing his father sticking out his own tongue.

Facial cues have a big impact on a child's social development. Studies have shown that babies with depressed mums (children who presumably see fewer smiles and expressions of happiness than children of happier mothers) display classic signs of depression (a 'flat affect' or frowning, a tense mouth, lack of eye contact), even when a chipper caretaker steps in and attempts to amuse the baby.

Researchers theorise that children of severely depressed mums often go on to have serious problems with their social development because of the way their mothers interact with them. These infants are exposed to non-verbal cues that are less affectionate and more negative in nature than the babies of mothers who aren't depressed. You'll remember that some non-verbal cues – and the reactions to them – are innate. Babies who are exposed to negative facial cues (frowning, crying, pursed lips, lack of eye contact) react to them in a negative way – either by fussing and/or crying or by making negative faces of their own. They don't receive positive feedback (a parent's smile, wide eyes or laughing) for accomplishments (rolling over, crawling, feeding themselves – all the usual milestones), and that lack of nurturing can affect a child's willingness to try new activities. Unfortunately, these reactions turn into negative attitudes, and by the time the child is ready to go to school he lacks self-confidence.

Depression is very common, especially in women, and especially during the postpartum period. If you're a depressed mum, talk to your doctor about different treatment options. You and your child(ren) will be better off for it.

Tantrums

How do adults express their displeasure with someone or something? Most use their language combined with a few pointed gestures, like pursed lips, a lack of eye contact, hands on the hips and either a dominant stance or angling away from the objectionable person or situation. It's rare to see a grown-up who ends up kicking and screaming and throwing her beloved possessions around the room. In fact, when you see someone behaving in such a childish way, it's fair to ask, 'How old are you? Two?'

Of course, when toddlers are angry, tired or not feeling well, you know straight away. There's the aforementioned kicking, screaming and throwing of things, but there's also the banging of the head against the wall or floor, the tears and the attempts at biting others.

Most experts will tell you that as long as your child isn't hurting herself or others, tantrums are harmless in the long run. Remember – she's still baby-like in that she doesn't have many other options for expressing herself. When you're upset, you can use your extensive vocabulary to explain your thoughts (and even then, slamming a door can still feel pretty good). Imagine not being able to verbalise your feelings in times of extreme stress. You'd kick and scream, too.

Preschoolers

Here's the age where body language starts to get interesting. If your preschooler is eager to please, you'll be treated to smiles, hugs and cuddling. If he's a rebellious little thing, you'll see frowning, pouting, and the need for him to do everything on his own (stay out of his personal space when he orders you out!). Of course, the same child can change personalities from week to week.

While tantrums are usually harmless to a toddler's overall development, don't allow your child to hurt himself. Hitting his head on a concrete floor, for example, could cause permanent damage to his little skull. Find a safe (soft) place for him to express his outrage at the world.

The thing to remember with this age group is that they're still far from being manipulative with their body language. Yes, preschoolers know that certain behaviour will get them rewards and others will get them put on the naughty step, but most are not truly in control of their emotions at any given moment. An angry child will exhibit signs of sadness and hostility (a pouted lip, arms crossed tightly over the chest, eyebrows furrowed, nostrils flared), and a happy child will exhibit signs of contentment (a smile, relaxed posture, friendly touches to her friends or caregivers).

School Days

As children enter primary school, their body language is still pretty much in the 'what you see is what you get' category. A shy child will maintain plenty of space between herself and other kids, she won't look them in the eye, and she might also exhibit some comforting measures, like rubbing her hands together or playing with her hair. All you have to do is look at her to know that she's feeling uncomfortable; you don't have to wonder if she's arrogant or angry (as you might with an adult displaying similar body language). If she were either, she'd be displaying different, very obvious non-verbal cues, like prolonged eye contact or a smirk (both signs of overconfidence), or a frown and a pout (obvious signs of discontentment).

Because they're so obvious with their behaviour, kids are also fairly good at reading each other's body language, even though they don't realise what they're doing. Four-year old Susie doesn't need to be a psychologist to know that there's something amiss when a friend sticks her tongue out at her and runs away, or a kinesiologist to know that a smiley friend is going to be kind to her. And Susie doesn't need to read a book about body language to know that a fight is breaking out between her brother, who's standing with his hands on his hips, and his classmate, who's towering over her brother in a menacing way.

Live and Learn

Somewhere along the line, children realise that they can fake certain behaviour to get what they want. Your 10-year-old daughter might have a friend who knows how to smile so sweetly that most adults think she's the most enchanting child who ever walked the earth. From the behaviour you've observed at your own house – particularly how this child turns her perfect behaviour on in the presence of adults and off in the presence of her friends – you know that she's learned how to charm and disarm authority figures.

Because sophisticated, manipulative non-verbal communication is learned – from peers, parents, siblings or the media – these behaviours develop earlier for some children than for others, and not at all for some kids. Your child might never acquire these kinds of gestures, even if her friends do.

You can't prevent your children from learning about manipulative body language, but if you see them using their non-verbal powers for less-than-honourable purposes (lying, cheating, taking advantage of other kids), call them out on their behaviour and try to put a stop to it. While there's something to be said for an adult who knows when and where to use effective body language, a child who's well versed in using manipulative gestures is heading down the wrong path. These kids simply can't handle the feeling of power that usually results from using dishonesty to get what they want.

Children with autism are often described as 'being in their own world', as a result of their inability to recognise, respond to or use non-verbal cues. Since autistic children often aren't capable of reading and responding to non-verbal cues, they may appear to be lacking in empathy. This, in turn, can lead to social isolation. With early intervention, many autistic children are able to find meaningful ways to interact with their family and peers.

Exclusion Zone

Children's body language is so extreme and powerful at times, they can make one another miserable even if they've never had any one-on-one interaction. 'Relational bullying' is the term experts use to describe one child being excluded from a larger group. No one picks on the outsider; no one touches her; no one expressly says, 'You can't play with us,' but the non-verbal messages of the larger group send a crystal-clear message. These behaviours may include:

- Lack of eye contact.
- Angling away from the child.
- Keeping lots of physical space between the group and the child.

What does this look like in a real-life setting? In a classroom of eight- and nine-year-olds, Annie is the outsider and Emma is a standout student. When Emma is called on in class to give an answer, everyone turns in her general direction. All eyes are on her. If she makes a mistake and laughs it off, everyone else laughs with her. When Annie is called on, the rest of the class stares down at their papers or at each other as though she isn't speaking. No matter what she says – whether it's brilliant or hysterically funny – it goes unacknowledged by the rest of the class. No one has done anything outwardly cruel to Annie (no one has made a face, called her a name or hit her), but the way the class is shutting her out is every bit as hurtful. Even the nicest kids in the class may go along with this kind of exclusion-by-ignoring behaviour because they're mimicking their peers.

> Relational bullying is something that parents and teachers really struggle with, precisely because it's so hard to pinpoint. You can't make kids like and accept each other, after all, and unless a child is being threatened with physical harm, authority figures are often reluctant to step in.

As a parent, what can you do about this? If your child is the one who's being singled out, encourage her to stand up for herself. Teach her how to project friendliness and confidence, and by all means, talk to her teacher. She may have some ideas for working your child into a group project or another setting that will help her break down the invisible walls that are keeping her out of peer activities. If your child is excluding another student, explain to her how hurtful this behaviour can be, even though it doesn't meet the definition of physical bullying. Teach her the difference between friendly body language and unfriendly gestures and encourage her to be a leader in showing the outcast child some kindness.

Little Liars

It isn't hard to learn to recognise the signs of lying in a young child. The key is to look for signs of nervousness, which are usually easy enough to see – as long as you know what you're looking for. The important thing here is to know what's normal and what's not for your own child. If he has a habit of blinking excessively all the time, for example, then you can't take his fluttering eyelashes into consideration when you're trying to determine whether his words are true or false.

Eye Spy

As you just read, excessive blinking is often a sign of lying; disrupted eye contact is another. When a child can't look you in the eye while he's telling you his version of the truth, it's because he's afraid of being caught or he's ashamed of what he's done, or both. When he stares into your eyes (and makes his own eyes as large as possible), it's an attempt to say, 'I'm looking right at you so you can see that I have nothing to hide.'

Most kids don't perfect the art of lying until they're around middle-school age, and even then, unless they're completely devoid of emotion, they're likely to give away one or two non-verbal cues when they're trying to pull the wool over their parents' eyes.

Another classic sign of anxiety is a flushed face. Some kids turn red faster and more easily than others, so if your child is prone to blushing when someone looks at him the wrong way, then just your accusation could be enough to make his cheeks and neck burn bright red. However, if he's red in the face as he's telling you he's off to play next door, you might want to check on him in about five minutes. There's a good chance he's really heading down to the stream where he's been forbidden to play.

Watch Those Hands

Little fibbers use self-touches to calm their nerves, but since some kids tend to do this kind of thing even when they're sitting around watching TV, it's not always the best way to determine your child's state of mind. If your child does something truly unusual, like holding his head in his hands or putting a hand over his own mouth while he speaks, those are pretty good indications that he has something on his mind that he doesn't want to share with you.

Children often hide their hands when they're lying. Let's say you've just come home to find that someone has knocked a plant off the table. When you find your son, you ask him what he knows about this unfortunate occurrence. He won't look at you, and he jams his hands in his pockets as he tells you that the cat did it. Don't chuck that cat out of the front door just yet … it looks like someone else might have had something to do with this little mishap (and his name isn't 'Kitty').

In adults, self-touches are a good indication of anxiety. However, some children love to touch themselves: they play with their hair, they pull at their eyelids, they twist their noses into strange shapes. These aren't necessarily signs of nervousness; they're probably just the work of idle hands and curious minds.

Extreme Expression

Marie's nine-year-old daughter, Jemma, isn't prone to emotional outbursts; in fact, she's a fairly calm child. Imagine Marie's shock, then, when Jemma had a major meltdown after Marie had asked her a seemingly innocent question. 'I had just bought these new high-heeled boots,' Marie says, 'and I couldn't find them anywhere. I mean, I hadn't even taken them out of the box yet, so I knew I hadn't left them somewhere around the house. I asked Jemma if she knew where they were. She tried to pull the classic, 'I have no idea what you're talking about' routine, but her face was just frozen in fear and she was turning bright red, so I knew something was up.

'I calmly said, 'Jemma, tell me the truth,' and all hell broke loose. She yelled at me for accusing her of 'stealing' my boots, then she stomped off to her bedroom, she slammed the door, and she cried her little head off. When she finally calmed down, she told me that she had worn the boots sledging in the back garden. She had hidden them under her bed, and they were completely wrecked.'

A child will ratchet up her emotional response when she's about to be caught in a lie. When a kid who isn't normally given to lots of hand motions, arm gestures, hopping, tapping the feet or rocking back and forth starts displaying these behaviours in reaction to a seemingly harmless question, your antennae should be standing at full attention. There's trouble swirling in that little head. With some careful prodding, you might elicit a full confession.

Emotional Overdrive

Most people have their own set of non-verbal gestures, and many of these gestures fall into fairly 'average' terrain. If they didn't, you'd never be able to analyse and decode another person's unspoken messages. But there are some people – and many of them are kids – whose behaviour falls into a rather extreme realm. They're highly expressive souls and they use their bodies to emphasise their spoken message. Is this a good thing or a bad thing, and what can you do to help others understand and accept your child's conduct?

Free as a Bird

Parents of highly animated children often describe their offspring as 'dramatic', 'theatrical', or just plain crazy (but in a good way). Not only are these kids very verbal, but every word that comes out of their mouths is accompanied by wild hand gestures, flailing arms, twirling, jumping, rolling on the floor … whatever non-verbal cues are necessary to get the point across. If you recognise your own child in this description, you've also perhaps received reports from her teachers who believe she's disruptive and distracting to the other students in the classroom. What's a parent to do?

If problems between your well-intentioned expressive child and her teacher persist, take the matter up with the head teacher. Your child may be better off in another classroom, or even in a more progressive school.

Purely expressive gestures, like flapping her arms as she describes the wingspan of the bald eagle, or jumping for joy when she receives perfect marks on her spelling test, are not only harmless, they're also healthy. Your child isn't hurting anyone, after all, and her enthusiasm may inspire her peers to look at life in a new way. That's an issue that deserves a one-on-one conference with the child's teacher, so that you can give her a better understanding of your child's sweet (if over-the-top) personality.

On the Other Hand …

Kids who are past the preschool and nursery years are old enough to understand that some behaviours are acceptable at school and others aren't. If you receive a call from your child's school about her behaviour, take an honest look at how your child is acting. Hostile non-verbal cues (such as smacking and making faces at other students or attempting to dominate them by glaring at them or stepping into their personal space) need to be addressed. These types of behaviours aren't simply a means of innocent expression, they're indicative of a mean streak that's going to land her in hot water again and again. Just as importantly, these non-verbal cues are also likely to lead to social isolation at some point. (Who wants to play with someone who's going to haul you off and hit you?)

Kids Will Be Kids

You've heard it a hundred times: bullies tend to be insecure people who treat other people badly to bolster their own egos. A child who uses hostile or inappropriate non-verbal gestures can often be led to express herself in another way, whether that's verbally, artistically or athletically. Don't expect the child to take the lead here; she'll need guidance and nurturing to find her niche. Once she learns to channel that energy and/or anxiety into an activity that she enjoys, reassess her non-verbal cues. If you find that she's still displaying unfriendly body language (old habits die hard, after all), teach her to use non-verbal cues that send out a positive vibe (such as smiling, keeping her hands to herself and respecting others' personal space).

In the end, it's important for parents and caregivers to remember that kids are blank canvases. They're just beginning to learn life's lessons, and a lot of what they'll discover will come from the non-verbal communication they see in their parents, teachers, siblings, friends and even strangers. Although these sources of information are wide and varied, there's one thing every child needs: to feel safe and secure at every age and every stage of life (even when they're disagreeable toddlers or teenagers). You can help your child to develop a sense of confidence – which will show up in his body language – by making sure that your gestures send a message of love and nurturing.

Business Body Language

By this point, you're well aware of the uses and pitfalls of observing body language. What you may not know, however, is that some people are trained in the art of assessing what you're saying with your eyes, posture and handshake. Some of these people happen to be employed by MI5; others happen to be ordinary businessmen and women who are on the lookout for promising job candidates. Before you head into your next job interview, you should know all the ways in which you're being evaluated.

Chapter 11

Talk the Talk, Walk the Walk

Some people are seemingly born knowing how to win over potential employers. These men and women know how to flash the smile, shake the hand, nod at the right times and land any position they go after. And then there are those who suffer through every job interview (and suffer is not too strong a word). The first group has a handle on how to behave professionally, even if they actually have no clue as to what they're doing in any other part of their career. The latter group either doesn't know about playing the part or doesn't see the importance of it. In fact, these people often feel that their unwillingness to go with the flow is what sets them apart from the other candidates and is the very thing that's going to win them the position they're after! Unfortunately, they're often wrong.

When in Doubt, Conform

When you're vying for an entry-level position in the corporate world, conformity is often your best shot at landing the job. Don't worry – you'll have plenty of time to make your mark once you've set up camp inside the company, but first you need to show the powers that be that you're a team player. And every member of the team displays a few common characteristics through his or her body language.

In an extremely creative environment, where conformity is synonymous with poor job performance, it's often wise to take the I'm-a-complete-original stance. In fact, the 'interview' may be a look at your portfolio and an assessment of just how eccentric you're capable of being.

When you sit down with an employer, you want to send the following unspoken messages:

- I'm interested in this company.
- I'm confident I can do this job well.
- I'm eager to be part of the team.

While it's important to be articulate during your time in the hot seat, it's just as important to back up your words with the correct gestures. You can tell your interviewer how confident you are, but if you're gnawing at your fingernails while you're saying it, you're sending him a definite mixed message. Nail biting may be the thing you do to pass the time, but it's perceived as a nervous habit.

Part of the message you want to convey with your body language is that this is where you plan on hanging your hat for the next several years (even if you have absolutely no intention of staying longer than six months). Companies don't want to spend money training an employee who isn't going to stay with them.

Listen to Your Grandmother!

Remember when your grandma would say, 'Stand up straight!' as she smacked you between the shoulder blades? She wasn't trying to be abusive; she honestly had your best interests at heart. Grandma knew that good posture conveys a positive message to the outside world. When you stand or sit straight up – as opposed to slouching – you look bigger. You appear ready to take on the world. When you sit up straight in an interview, you show that you're alert, interested and eager. This may sound like a minor detail, but it might be the thing that sets you apart from other job seekers.

You're not experiencing déjà vu. You did already read about posture in Chapter 4; however, since posture is part of projecting confidence, and confidence is vital to landing a job, you'll read about it here in the context of the job interview.

Depending on the other types of body language that you combine with slouching, you could appear to be hiding from the world. Picture someone who's walking hunched over, his arms close at his side, staring at the floor as he walks. People might wonder what this person is so afraid of!

Count on Me, Boss!

How does this carry over into the world of work? Every workplace has its crises and stressful situations. Your interviewer might specifically be looking for someone who can handle situations with ease (in other words, someone who'll drive a hard bargain with business contacts) and not succumb to the pressures associated with doing business (in other words, you won't allow clients to take advantage of you or your company).

Good posture gives you an instant attitude and sends out an unmistakable message to other people. Slouchers tend to be viewed as less confident, more nervous, less outgoing people. In a work setting, good posture makes you look like you're capable; poor posture makes you look world-weary.

People who stand tall appear to be comfortable in their own skin. They're ready to meet challenges head-on and tackle any problems that come their way. When you sit tall in an interview, you project the image of confidence – something your potential employer wants to see – even if you're shaking in your high-heeled boots (or loafers). For more information on posture, read Chapter 4.

Be There and Be Square

Posturing yourself correctly in an interview begins with your spine and ends with your legs. Sitting up straight is a good start, in other words, but if you let your lower body go wild, no one's going to notice how confident your upper body appears to be. More likely, they'll be asking 'What's going on with that guy's legs? Why are they over there?'

When you seat yourself in an interview, you want to square your shoulders and angle your body towards your interviewer. This simply means that you want your body to be facing him. It's not such a difficult task, actually; you want to avoid sitting so that your head is turned towards the interviewer with your lower body turned away from him, a position that can make you appear uninterested or shy. Angling yourself away from another person is an attempt to distance yourself from him (the technical term for this is 'angular distance') and is seen in situations from which there's no immediate escape (like a job interview). You can't increase the physical distance between yourself and the other person by, say, pulling your chair to the other side of the room, so you angle yourself away from him instead.

In any event, angling your lower body away from a person while your upper body is angled towards him is an awkward position to be in while you're in the middle of a Q&A session, for one thing; for another, it can come across as looking far too casual. (Try it at home and see for yourself. You can't help but feel as though you're lounging.)

To angle your body towards your interviewer, sit facing him with your back straight and your shoulders back. This creates a natural straight line between you and him, and try as you might, you are not going to get your legs very far off to the side. This means that your legs will also be angled towards your interviewer, which is right where they should be. (More on angling in Chapters 4, 17 and 18.)

What about those legs? Should you cross them or leave both feet flat on the floor? You want to avoid looking too comfortable – or too on-edge. It's all right to cross your legs, but don't jiggle your foot around; that tells your interviewer that you're nervous (or worse, bored). You should not stretch your legs out in front of you at any time during a job interview. That shows you're way too comfortable.

Here's one more tip on angling and positioning yourself: watch your interviewer and mimic his movements without being obvious about it. For example, if he asks you a question and then leans back in his seat, go ahead and lean back in yours a little. When he leans forwards, slowly move yourself to a forward angle. This creates a kind of symmetry between the two of you. When it's done correctly, he'll know he likes you, but he won't know why. (When it's done too obviously, he'll spot it in an instant – so be careful!)

Some Handy Tips

Although your mouth should do most of the talking in the interview, your hands will play an important role, too. For example, you'll have to shake a few hands, and you'll have to deal with the age-old issue of what to do with your hands while you're being interviewed.

Shake It

Chapter 3 discussed handshaking but since this is such an essential part of making a good impression on your potential employer, you'll learn more particulars of the proper shake here. First things first: a good handshake is firm without crossing over into bone-crushing territory; it's brief – three to five pumps (up and down) is a good rule of thumb; and you should always offer your palm in a vertical position when you're an employee.

Never shake hands with your interviewer by offering your hand in a palm-down position. This is a domineering move that shows you think an awful lot of yourself (too much, in fact, considering you haven't been hired yet).

You may have seen plenty of men and women offer their hand in a palm-down manner when shaking hands with a colleague, and you like the way it looks. In fact, you've been practising and perfecting this move. Well, lose it! The palm-down handshake is a dominating gesture. It's a way of saying, 'I'm the alpha fe/male here.' Now, if you happen to be the 'big cheese', go ahead and shake hands any way you want. But since most interviewees are fairly low down the ladder (especially in comparison to the interviewer), be sure to offer your palm in a way that says, 'I'm no threat.'

Other important tips on the handshake:

- If you suffer from sweaty palms, try to discreetly dry them before shaking.
- If your skin is dry, moisturise before your interview.
- Keep your nails short and neat.

All of the above issues point to your personal hygiene. Someone who pays attention to small details makes a good employee. Chapter 3 covers the handshake in more detail.

Hand Placement

What are you supposed to do with your hands while you're answering questions? Try not to wave them around like semaphore flags, even if you're a natural hand-talker. Do your best to keep them corralled without looking like they've turned to blocks of concrete on your lap. In other words, you want your hands to emphasise what you're saying with your mouth; you don't want them to be the centre of attention in the conversation.

Overusing your hands when you speak simply distracts the interviewer. And as hand-talkers are usually perceived (correctly or not) to be emotional people, he may wonder what you'll do with those hands when you're faced with a serious crisis in the office.

You also want to avoid touching your face, rubbing your arms or hugging yourself. Self-touches like these convey nervousness or a lack of confidence. (They're thought to be self-comforting measures.) Your best bet is to fold your hands on your lap in a natural-looking way. And leave them there.

Face the Interview

Using your face to maximum effect can also help you impress a potential employer. You don't have to be the most beautiful person on the face of the earth to land a job, but you do have to show that you posses some basic skills – like listening. You won't have to take a hearing test, but you should know how to look interested, friendly and eager to discuss any topic the interviewer throws your way.

No Angry People Need Apply

There are certain head and facial gestures that won't win you many points with an interviewer. They include:

- Excessive frowning.
- Bad eye contact.
- A head angled towards the floor (or towards the window, for that matter).
- Pursed, tense lips.

Basically, you want to avoid appearing as though you're angry or bored, because angry, bored people generally don't make excellent employees. They tend to do things like complain about their work and/or fight with their colleagues. (You also don't want to go to the opposite extreme and act as though you've just had a shot of pure adrenaline prior to entering the interviewer's office. Employees who are all hyped up tend to make other people nervous.)

Wanted: Shiny, Happy People

You want your facial expressions to give the impression that you can slide straight into the work environment without causing any disruption. You want to appear to be someone who works well with others. To that end, you want to wear a somewhat 'neutral face', at least for part of your interview. What does this mean, exactly? The true neutral face is devoid of emotion. This isn't the exact look you're going for, so you can dress yours up a little – for example:

- Your eyes are wide (but not overly so).
- Your mouth is neutral, perhaps just on the verge of smiling.
- Your eyebrows may be slightly raised.
- Your head is slightly angled to the side, and/ or perhaps nodding from time to time.

This face lets the other person know that you're engaged in what she's saying. You're listening intently and formulating your answers even as the other person is speaking. You're making the interviewer feel as though she is important and interesting – and that's not a bad signal to send to the person who has the authority to offer you a job.

Win or Lose

Now that you know some of the uses and pitfalls of body language, how should you put them into action? Here is a look at one interview from two angles. The differences should be obvious to you as you read through both scenarios, but the important thing is to recognise yourself in either situation and strive to correct any body language that isn't helping you in the job market.

Kate Conquers

Kate has been pounding the pavement in search of her first post-university job. She's been granted an audience with the Human Resources director of the local hospital and she's a little nervous. But at least she knows to dress appropriately – nothing too tight or too ill fitting. Her shoes are polished. Her hair and nails are clean and neat, and she looks great.

The interviewer calls Kate into his office and offers his hand. Kate takes it, shakes it four times (within the recommended three-to-five-pumps range), and sits up straight in the seat – but only after she's invited to do so. So far, so good.

While she's asked questions regarding her schooling and experience, she sits with her head slightly cocked to the side, her eyes wide open, her legs crossed at the knee but angled towards the interviewer. From time to time, she nods as the interviewer is speaking and smiles when she likes what she hears. When the interviewer leans forwards in his chair, Kate leans slightly forwards in hers. Her hands are loose in her lap; she's not fidgeting with them. She holds the interviewer's gaze for no more than five seconds before looking slightly off to the side of his head or dropping her eyes for a moment before making eye contact again. (Chapter 7 contains more information on eye contact.)

All in all, she's done some good work here. She came across as cool, calm and collected with her body language. Hopefully, she had some intelligent things to say, as her body of knowledge will have quite a bit of bearing as to whether she gets this job or not.

Kiss This Job Goodbye, Kate

Let's say Kate was in a bad mood on the day of the interview. She decided she didn't want this job but she felt as though she should go for the experience, so off she went, still dressed nicely enough, but without the will to land the position.

She walks into the interviewer's office and lightly touches his hand, pumping it once before seating herself. She leans too far back in the chair, stretching her legs out in front of her. She concentrates on the pattern in the rug, looking up at the interviewer only when she's asked a question, and even then her eye contact is fleeting. She doesn't smile. She has her arms crossed over her chest. The interviewer knows she doesn't want this job and resents having to interview her. Kate has wasted her own time as well as the Human Resources director's.

You Can Do Better Than That!

The differences in the two situations are fairly easy to spot. In the first interview, Kate has shown that she is confident and is an engaged listener. In the second interview, she didn't make eye contact, she slouched in her chair and she gave a poor handshake. She ended up looking unprofessional, unengaged and not at all interested in working for this company.

Here's the really interesting thing: Kate could have said the exact same thing in both interviews, but by using appropriate body language, she's far more likely to make a good impression on the employer.

Good interview body language doesn't come easily to everyone, but learning it is well worth the effort. If you're completely opposed to using your smile to get ahead in life, try to think of this as a game that everyone else is playing. You can refuse to join in, but somewhere, sometime, you're going to get left behind. (And then someone else will be sitting at your desk, earning your salary.)

Turning the Tables

Actually, you can't turn the tables on your interviewer (he already has a job, after all), but you can take a look at his body language and evaluate how well the interview is going. Just be aware that the person who's conducting the interview might not care in the least whether you're hired or not. His job might be limited to conducting interviews and passing along your information to someone else who makes the hiring decisions. Why should you know this? Because if your interviewer's body language is saying to you, 'I hate you. Get out of my office,' you should still hang on to your professional image. It's not going to hurt you, and in the end, there's always the possibility that it'll help.

So what are some signs that the interview isn't going as well as you'd hoped? Generally, be alert to any body language that indicates boredom or hostility coming from your interviewer, such as:

- Non-existent eye contact.
- Constant frowning.
- Arms crossed tightly over the chest.
- Head angled away from you.

Keep in mind that body language is a study of patterns of behaviour, another reason for you not to lose hope. For all you know, this man always looks bored, or maybe he does this to test an interviewee's mettle. It's best for you to continue on with your plan (which, if you've forgotten, is to project an air of confidence) no matter what your interviewer's body language is saying.

Inside the Office

What if you're gainfully employed but you're just spinning your wheels in the company? You're not getting promoted; no one seems to take notice of you or your contributions, and you're starting to wonder if anyone would even notice if you didn't turn up for work. Meanwhile, your colleague – let's call him Dan – is rocketing his way up the corporate ladder. What does he have that you don't? Is he cleverer? Does he have some sort of important connection with the president of the company? Is he blackmailing someone? Before you start throwing accusations around (even in your own mind), take an inconspicuous look at Dan's body language. Perhaps you could learn something from him.

I'm a Pro

You might think you're a better person than Dan, and you may be right. But being nicer doesn't get you ahead in the business world – being the better worker does. And sometimes you don't even have to be the better worker; you just have to know how to project the image of being the better worker.

Again, this goes back to showing your confidence and a positive attitude. Walk tall. Sit straight. Know how to look like you're listening to others. Cultivate a professional handshake (something discussed in Chapter 3 and earlier in this chapter). Look other people in the eye. Smile. All of these body-language cues make you look interested and approachable – like someone who's willing to jump in and help at any opportunity. Chances are, Dan knows how to display these characteristics without looking like a fake. He looks like he knows what he's doing, so other people assume that he does.

I'm a Con

What kind of body language hurts you in the workplace? Any actions that make you look abrasive, unsure or uninterested, such as:

- Poor posture.
- Bad eye contact.
- Weak handshake.
- Any nervous gestures, like hand wringing or foot jiggling.

Now, take another look at Dan. He stands tall, he makes a point of making eye contact with people, he shakes hands like he's running for parliament.

Can you see the difference? Dan looks like a port in a storm, like the man you can run to if something goes wrong. The worker who never makes eye contact and shies away from other people with his body language is going to go unnoticed at all times, including times of crisis, which is when leaders are made (and later promoted).

Here's the important part: given two equal job performances, a boss is likely to promote the person he likes better. And it's probably easier to like someone like Dan, because he gives everyone ample opportunity to see him making his impressive way through the office. It's not fair, but it happens all the time. You have to know how to play Dan's game if you want to get ahead in your workplace.

Walking Disasters

There's body language that will get you promoted, body language that will get you ignored, and body language that will get you fired. Everyone knows that some motions – like obscene gestures of any sort – are totally inappropriate in the workplace. But there are some body-language cues that fall into grey areas. Technically, they aren't offensive, but there's something about them that makes other people uncomfortable. These may include things like:

- Prolonged eye contact.
- Excessive use of the hands to emphasise a point.
- Excessive sighing or throat clearing.
- Round-the-clock frowning.
- Lingering touches.

The last item on the list may actually fall into a legal area, depending on who's doing the touching and where. The other actions, however, might be perceived as just 'creepy'. You know these things when you see them – the colleague who never looks away (or even blinks) while he's talking to you; the colleague who flaps her arms like wings when she's excited about something; the person who always looks angry (and whom you're afraid to ask a question of).

Again, the successful employee gets along well with everyone and appears eager to jump into any project or problem. This isn't to say that someone who doesn't know about appropriate eye contact is a bad person, but he may make other people nervous, which in turn may result in colleagues avoiding him.

For better or for worse, body language has a marked effect on interactions in the business world. It's a dog-eat-dog world out there, but you don't have to join in the backstabbing and gossiping that go on in far too many workplaces in order to get promoted. By learning to carry yourself as a true professional (someone who isn't afraid of what the day may throw your way, someone who's ready for action at a moment's notice – in other words, an office superhero), you make a distinct impression on the people around you, including your bosses. Stand tall, shake firmly and make eye contact, no matter how foreign these actions seem to you at first. No one remembers a wallflower – use your body language to make yourself visible, memorable, employable, and promotable.

Gestures Around the World

When learning the nuances of body language, it's important to note that depending on the country or culture it's displayed in, the same gesture can be acceptable or offensive. You might be thinking 'I'm not a world traveller, so this isn't really relevant to me.' You're wrong. As the United Kingdom is a melting pot of cultures, you're very likely to come across people of different backgrounds many times during your life. Knowing why they do the things they do – and why they react to certain gestures – could save you from embarrassing yourself.

Chapter 12

Once More, From the Top

The non-verbal language of the head seems fairly simple: you've got headshakes, nods and maybe an angle or two to deal with. In certain parts of the world, though, everything you know about the head is backwards. In fact, you could say 'yes' when you mean 'no' or insult onlookers with just the touch of a hand. Use that noggin to learn how to avoid making a bad impression once you cross these borders.

A-Head of the Pack

You're in India, visiting with your old university chum and his family, catching up, sharing some good times. Just as you've done a hundred times in the past, you reach out to playfully smack him on the head. Suddenly, his family is looking aghast and your friend is looking uncomfortable. You assure everyone that you didn't hit him hard enough to hurt him, but your explanation does nothing to smooth their ruffled feathers. What's going on here?

In India, as well as in Thailand and Tibet, the top of the head is a sacred area – it's actually considered part of the soul – and you don't just go around touching it. If you're not a regular visitor to these parts of the world, you might wonder how and when this knowledge will ever come in handy in your life. Here's a practical application: don't pat children of Indian, Thai or Tibetan descent on the head. (And here's another: don't smack adults on the head, no matter what their nationality.)

Yes? No? What?

Picture this: you're holidaying in Greece. You're supposed to meet up with friends for dinner, but as usual, you're running late. When you arrive at the restaurant, a waiter asks if you're meeting someone. You shake your head up and down, and he seats you ... all by yourself. Did he misunderstand you? No. He did what any Greek would do in the same situation. By nodding your head, you actually said no.

In British culture, of course, you nod to indicate your approval of something and you shake your head to show that you disagree or that you feel strongly that some point of view is wrong. This concept seems so simple, you might wonder how and why this gesture gets mixed up in other countries. Well, maybe you're the one who is getting it backwards – maybe 'yes' is 'no' and 'no' is 'yes' and we Brits are moving our heads in the wrong direction! The important thing to know is that even the simplest non-verbal cues can change from country to country and it's best to learn about them before you embark on any trip.

Greece isn't the only country where shaking the head from side to side means 'yes' and a nod means 'no'. Several countries in the Middle East, including Pakistan and Iran, also adhere to these rules of the head. If you're travelling to this area of the world, check with a guidebook to make sure your gestures of affirmation and rejection are moving in the right direction.

Tossing the Head

Nodding isn't the only gesture that might throw you off kilter in a foreign land. In Thailand, Laos and the Philippines, for example, the non-verbal cue for 'yes' is tossing the head backwards. In India and Thailand, people rock their heads back and forth very slowly to show that they're listening. Because these gestures aren't common in the United Kingdom, it's not likely that you'd mistake them for other body-language cues, as you might mistake nodding to mean 'yes' in every country.

As important as it is to acknowledge that the same cue can have different meanings around the world, it's as important to know that some gestures are unique to the culture in which they're used – another reason to do your homework before crossing international borders.

Eyeing International Body Language

Eye contact is such a big issue in British culture, and something that's often so hard to master, that you might be disheartened to know that what you learned in Chapter 7 doesn't necessarily apply to other cultures. Don't worry. Different cultures have different levels of appropriate eye contact, but in some cases it boils down to all (in other words, extended eye contact) or nothing (no eye contact at all). Once you work out which cultures expect lots of eye contact and which expect none, the rest is easy.

Look Away!

In Chapter 7, you learned how to use eye contact to your benefit and how to read the eyes of those around you. In Western culture, eye contact is not only polite, it's used to decode almost every relationship and interaction you have. Too much eye contact means one thing; too little means something else entirely.

While British people cherish eye contact as the definitive marker of a friendly interaction, other cultures avoid the intimate gaze altogether. Let's say you've just arrived in Tokyo. You're lost and trying to catch some friendly eye so that you might ask for directions. No one will look your way, however. You're wondering if you've done something to offend – is it your shirt? Your shoes? Your hairdo?

Even if your hair is looking a bit scary after your long plane journey, it's not the reason that no one is meeting your gaze. The Japanese routinely avoid eye contact with other people. It's considered disrespectful to stare into someone else's eyes, so they keep their eyes to themselves. It's helpful to know this if you're visiting Japan, but it's especially important to put this into practice if you have business dealings with a Japanese company. Because respect is part of the identity of a Japanese person, you need to go out of your way to follow their cues and keep your eye contact to a minimum.

Western cultures love to use and analyse eye contact, but eye contact is kept to a minimum in Japan, Africa, the Caribbean and South American countries. Keeping the eyes to oneself is a sign of respect for the other person.

It's also helpful to know about this difference in cultures on a personal level. Your Japanese neighbour might appear unfriendly if you don't understand why she never looks your way. Knowing that this is the way she was raised and that a lack of eye contact is actually her way of being polite will help you to reserve judgment until you know her better.

Looky Here

Let's say you've arrived in Saudi Arabia for a business meeting. You arrive at the office where you shake hands with your hosts before you begin to talk shop. You notice that as you're speaking, all eyes are on you, and they don't take a break. Not once. There's no looking away, or off to the side or down at the ground, even for a second. You're starting to feel very uncomfortable, wondering if this is some sort of attempt at intimidation.

It isn't. Prolonged eye contact (coupled with close proximity) is the norm in Arab countries. Extended eye contact is a sign of respect here, just as the avoidance of eye contact is a sign of respect in Japan. In fact, people who don't comply with this expectation in the Arab world are viewed as rather suspicious. Your best bet is to get comfortable with all eyes being on you and to return the gaze when someone else is speaking.

Did I Lose You?

You've been asked to give a presentation in your office. You've worked hard to prepare, and you're feeling confident as you stand up to regale your colleagues and superiors with your knowledge of the intricate workings of your industry. After you've been talking non-stop for 15 minutes, you stop to take questions and you notice everyone's eyes are closed. Your first thought is, 'I've bored them into comas.'

This is undoubtedly a bad sign in the British workplace, but if you were presenting your work in Japan, Thailand or China, you'd actually come away from this meeting thinking that you'd given your audience something to mull over. Closing the eyes in these cultures is a way of saying, 'I hear you and I'm giving your idea some serious thought.'

Brow-nie Points

If you raise your eyebrows at someone else in this country, it's a way of indicating that you want him to believe what you're saying, whether or not you're telling the whole truth. Raised eyebrows might also accompany an expression of fear or shock. In parts of Asia, however, raised eyebrows take the place of the head-nod; that is, to say 'yes' in these countries, you simply raise your brows.

Meanwhile, in the Philippines, don't try to agree with someone's point of view by shimmying your eyebrows up and down. In that country, the brow-raise is a way of saying 'Hello'. Continually raising and lowering your eyebrows is the equivalent of saying, 'Hi. Hi. Hi. Hi. Hi.' (Don't be surprised if you make friends very quickly over there.)

Worldwide Noses

What do these situations have in common?

- A changing room full of sweaty kit.
- A car filled with old fast-food containers.
- A kitchen with an overflowing rubbish bin.

They all stink. And to show your displeasure with the stench, you might do what people all over the world would do in a similar situation – grab your nose and pinch it. (It's good to know that some non-verbal gestures are the same no matter where you go!)

If you're at a gathering in Asia, keep your hanky hidden, even if you have an itchy nose. While Westerners don't exactly embrace nose blowing in public, they tolerate it. However, blowing your nose at a social event in Asia is considered very rude.

There are some other gestures centred on the nose that vary from culture to culture. For example, if someone taps her nose in the United Kingdom it means that whatever information is being passed at the moment is to be kept private. However, that same gesture in the United States is usually a way of saying, 'I'm thinking.'

If you're travelling to Beijing, don't pack your tissues. The Chinese blow their noses by shooting their nasal mucus on to the ground!

Slip of the Lip

The mouth is, of course, the prime instrument for verbal communication, but as you read in Chapter 6, body language experts believe that along with the hands, the mouth expresses more emotion than any other body part. This makes perfect sense, since the mouth often agrees with the verbal message – that is, if someone is conveying an uplifting verbal message, his mouth is rather happy looking. If that same person is expressing sadness, outrage or grief, his mouth tells the tale, both verbally and non-verbally.

In some cultures, especially in South America, the lips are used to point to something. An unschooled tourist might think that everyone around him is puckering up, just waiting for a pair of lips to smooch with, but in reality, this gesture is as intimate as using your index finger to indicate which way you're heading down the street.

Love Those Lips

The mouth is capable of expressing such complex emotions that it should come as no surprise that its non-verbal messages can vary depending on where you happen to find yourself on the globe. Kissing, for example, is a universal gesture of love and affection and you're likely to see partners and friends smooching on city streets all over the world. In many European countries, friends kiss each other on both cheeks anywhere from two to four times when meeting and departing. However, in parts of Asia kissing is considered a highly intimate gesture, which isn't allowed in public – not even as a form of friendly greeting.

If you find yourself waiting on tables in Mexico and notice that people are trying to kiss up to you, don't be too flattered. The kissing sound is a way to get a server's attention in that country.

That's Italiano!

If you happen to be travelling through Italy, you might see someone gather his fingertips together and kiss them. This is a way of showing appreciation for beauty or some sort of positive occurrence. Let's say you've just tasted the best cannoli you've ever had. You might turn to the baker and kiss your fingertips. Don't worry – he won't mistake this as some sort of romantic overture. He'll appreciate the compliment.

The Messages of the Upper Appendages

In Western culture, the arms and hands are highly expressive. Some people love to use them during every conversation, to emphasise every point, to indicate every feeling they're having at any moment. Are these cues the same everywhere, or is one man's gesture another man's insult? In this section, you'll read when it's all right to use your own handy non-verbal gestures and when you need to keep those limbs under wraps.

Armed and Ready

In some cultures, the arms are used with grace and skill to express the full range of emotions – happiness, sadness, frustration, grief, anger – while other cultures are more reserved. In these cultures, the arms are used sparingly, and never in an over-the-top manner.

The Japanese, as you know by now, are a rather conservative culture, so it may not surprise you to learn that they don't get their points across by using a lot of arm gestures. It's more important to them to get their point across in a respectful, spoken message and to keep non-verbal gestures to a minimum. In general, Asian people keep their arms in front of them as a way to show respect to others.

In most countries, standing or walking with the arms behind the back indicates that the person is reserved and relaxed. Standing with the hands clasped in front of the body is a respectful gesture.

In places like Italy or South America, however, where expressing emotion is essential to the human experience, the arms are part of even the most casual conversation. To the untrained eye, the use of a lot of arm gestures can appear to be rather aggressive, but here's where it's especially important to read the rest of a person's non-verbal cues. Is her face angry or content? Is her stance aggressive or relaxed? Assessing these gestures will give you the answers you're looking for.

Hand Me a Body-Language Guide

Hand motions are one set of non-verbal gestures that might get you into trouble once you pack your bags and leave the country. There are just so many of them that we use in this culture, it's difficult to leave them behind and adapt to a whole new way of expressing yourself with your mitts. In fact, many travellers think of body language as a superficial thing. They've taken the time to learn the language of the foreign country they'll be visiting; the rest, they think, will just fall into place.

In Chapter 1, you read that some experts in the field of non-verbal communication believe that approximately two-thirds of all communication is unspoken. If you don't take this into consideration before travelling the world, you're going to feel lost – and not because you can't follow a map, but because your behaviour is bound to make you stand out as a stranger in a strange land.

If you see two women or two men holding hands on a London or New York street, your immediate inference is that they're a couple. But take another look – are they part of another culture? They may just be friends. In Russia, Asia and India, friends of the same gender routinely walk hand-in-hand.

Handy Ways to Get in Trouble

Because the hands are so highly visible and because they do so much 'talking', they get a lot of attention. They might help you make some foreign friends, or they might land you in international hot water. Consider the potential for trouble in these situations:

- You're meeting with a Japanese client. You hand him your business card. He looks taken aback. Why?
- You're holidaying in Greece, watching the women on the beach. You give one particularly beautiful lady the thumbs-up sign. She gasps, grabs her boyfriend and the two of them begin marching in your direction. Do they want to make your acquaintance, or should you start running?
- In Brazil, your pedicurist wants to know if she's done a pleasing job on your toes. You're on your phone, so you give her the symbol to indicate 'OK. She bursts into tears. Was she hoping for a thumbs-up sign?

You've just offended three lovely people without realizing it. Your errors were:

- With the Japanese businessman, perhaps you flippantly tossed the card his way. The Japanese usually pass business cards with both hands. When they accept them, it's also with both hands, and they treat them as though they're a gift.
- Your intended friendly gesture on the beach carried just the opposite message; thumbs-up means 'Up yours!' in Greece (and in Western Africa, South America, Iran, Russia and Sardinia).
- In Brazil (and in Greece, Turkey, Italy and Russia), the sign Brits use to mean 'OK' is actually a grave insult. Better start gushing about how your toes have never looked better, or this girl might never return to the salon.

Are all of your favourite hand signals off-limits overseas? Of course not! You can walk around Paris and Los Angeles all day long flashing people the thumbs-up sign. They may find you highly irritating, but no one's likely to take great offense at your gesture.

Shaking It Around the World

You learned the right way to shake a hand in Chapter 3. Does that translate in foreign countries or must you also rethink your business greetings once you land on foreign turf? You're wise to be so proactive, since the shake is a product of the Western world. Generally speaking, the handshake crosses boundaries of all sorts these days, with just a few modifications. In the United States, Canada, Australia and New Zealand, the appropriate handshake is the same as the shake that you'd use in Britain. But in the Middle East, it's customary to use a lighter grasp in place of the tight, firm clasp that's commonplace elsewhere in the world. This handshake also includes placing the free hand on the other person's forearm, a sign of friendliness and goodwill. Mexicans also grab hold of the other person's free arm, but they're likely to throw a hug into the greeting as well.

In China, handshakes are never shared between people from different social strata. So while it's perfectly acceptable to offer a handshake to a friend or a colleague, a labourer would never attempt to shake his boss's hand. The French shake with a quick, light grip. Germans offer a firm shake with a little bow. And speaking of bows, the Japanese do shake hands (as opposed to only bowing), but they do so with the arm extended all the way. A bow is also part of the shake.

How do you bow properly?
Bowing is a traditional greeting in parts of Asia. To execute a proper bow, keep your hands at your side; in Thailand, bow with hands in prayer formation. The deeper the bow, the more respect you show for the other person.

The Lower Appendages

You've worked your way down the body, and you might feel like you're standing on solid ground, ready to go forth and not offend other cultures with your non-verbal gestures. Not so fast. The legs and the feet – and where they're positioned – are every bit as important in the study of international body language as any other part of the body.

Hold It Right There!

In Chapter 17, you'll read all about proxemics, or what is commonly referred to as personal space. The more intimate the relationship, the less personal space you need between yourself and the other person. Strangers in this country tend to stay about three feet apart when walking down a street; close friends give each other about a foot and a half in the same situation. Because Brits tend to develop close relationships in all aspects of their life – personal and professional – it's not unusual to see two colleagues standing very close to each other as they discuss business. Americans, Australians, Mexicans and Middle Easterners also tend to stand quite close to one another, whether the conversation is business or pleasure. This isn't the case around the globe, however.

Asians and many Africans tend to give each other much more space than British people do – about three feet – no matter what the relationship. This is especially important to know in situations where creeping into someone's personal space might seem intimidating or aggressive. For example, let's say you're a professor trying to help one of your foreign students grasp the concept of what you're teaching. If the student happens to be Asian or African, it's wise to keep several feet between the two of you. Any closer, and the student may feel as uncomfortable and/or threatened as you would if a stranger were standing right next to you.

Filthy Feet

Let's go back to your visit to India. After you've apologised profusely for your head-smacking debacle, you settle back into your chair and resume the friendly discussion you were having with your friend. You're feeling tired and relaxed, and you do the old Western male figure-four leg-cross. And once again, you find that you're on the receiving end of some very dirty looks.

What have you done this time? In some cultures (particularly in the Middle East and in parts of Asia), the sole of the foot is considered to be filthy. Displaying the bottom of your foot to someone else implies that the other person is lower than the dirt on your shoe. You'll have to do some pretty fancy footwork to convince the family that this wasn't your intention, and then you might want to take those feet for a walk … all the way home.

Travel should be interesting and exciting, not anxiety-provoking. One sure way to make yourself feel unwelcome in another culture is to use inappropriate body language while visiting. There's a great big world out there and a lot to see and learn – start by learning how to charm the locals in the country you're heading to. Continue by learning how not to be offensive. When you take your show on the road, proceed with caution. Ease into the culture, take note of other non-verbal interactions, and do as the Romans (or Indians or Russians) do.

Dress Up your Body Language

It's one thing to know how to rein in (or let loose with) your body language; it's another to understand how the way you dress affects your non-verbal communication. Not only is clothing one of the first things that other people notice about you – one of those facets of appearance that's up for judgment – but what you're wearing (and how you wear it) can also affect the way you feel about yourself, which in turn affects the way you present yourself to others and the way they interpret your body language.

Chapter 13

Clothing and Common Sense

Right or wrong, the way you dress is seen as a reflection of who you are and what you're trying to prove. Imagine you're interviewing candidates for a position opening up in your workplace. Your first interviewee arrives dressed in jeans and a crinkled short-sleeve shirt. Your immediate thought is 'Where's his suit? I've never interviewed anyone dressed so casually.' Now, you might like this casualness about him or you might think he's a real cretin for not making more of an effort (crinkles are a sign of poor grooming, after all) – the point is, you've already made a huge assumption about his personality based on his outfit.

Until you know someone well, you're likely to assign certain personality traits based on appearance alone (e.g. how she's dressed) – and then see what you expect to see in terms of her body language.

Candidate number two enters dressed in a suit two sizes too large, which makes him look childlike and sloppy. Again, your mind jumps to conclusions as you think, 'This bloke doesn't even know how to buy a suit that fits!' You might pity him and give him a break or you might think that he couldn't possibly handle the details of your office if he can't dress himself decently. But again, his clothes have sent a message all their own.

Your third candidate turns up dressed in what appears to be a custom-made suit, leading you to believe that this man is either already very successful or that he knows what it takes to ascend the corporate ladder. You think, 'He has a real eye for detail,' which makes you believe that he could be an asset to the company (especially when it comes to impressing clients).

Of course, an employee cannot survive simply by wearing his clothing well. Each of these men will also display certain body-language characteristics – some of these gestures may suggest extreme confidence; others may betray serious self-doubts. You'll view these gestures through the lens of your own judgment – and that judgment begins the moment you lay eyes on the men.

The Fashion Police

If you're at all doubtful that clothing adds to or detracts from a person's body language, think about this: when criminals head to court, their solicitors usually advise them to dress as conservatively as possible in the hope that the mere appearance of innocence might hint at good character and consequently sway the jury in their favour. Unfortunately for these hardworking advocates, their clients often do themselves down with their non-verbal behaviour.

Fabrics have a language all their own. Cashmere and cotton, for example, are soft and inviting, suggesting that the wearer is a gentle soul. 'Hard' materials, like leather or boiled wool, keep others at a distance.

In one legal case, defense lawyers advised their clients to dress in pastel-coloured jumpers. The hope was that this look would help the jury envision these men as innocent young boys, incapable of cold-blooded murder. But why not just dress them in blazers? Why jumpers? Pullovers and cardigans simply look friendlier and less intimidating than a blazer or suit.

Dressing the Part

The old adage 'the clothes make the man' implies that the right outfit can help you pull off the image you're trying to project. However, the idea extends beyond the business world. Footballers' wives have their own dress code, which differs from the way politicians dress, which is far different from the way bikers dress.

Trick or Treat

The funny thing about dressing the part is that it affects your body language. You start acting the way you think you're supposed to. Put a bloke in a studded leather jacket and suddenly he's not so mild-mannered anymore; he has been transformed into a rough-and-tumble biker, complete with the commanding posture and tough-guy facial expressions. Now take a mum who's used to wearing jeans and T-shirts and put her in a flowing ball gown. She'll feel more feminine than she has in ages, and you'll see it reflected in her body language as she steps lightly around the room, her shoulders back, her neck extended, doing her best to behave in a ladylike manner.

Accessories – like jewellery, belts, handbags and scarves – also reveal a lot about your personality. People who cover themselves with fancy accoutrements are perceived as confident and outgoing.

Dressing for success is the first step towards achieving your goals, whatever they may be. Learning the appropriate non-verbal gestures – strutting like a biker, for example, or traipsing around like an elegant lady – is easier when you know you look like you can pull off the behaviour.

If these types of clothing can affect the way a person carries and projects him or herself, think what completely overhauling your wardrobe could do for your life!

Fight the Frump

Take a closer look at how your clothes affect the way you feel about yourself – and hence, the way you display your body-language cues. Perhaps you stand in front of your wardrobe every morning on the verge of tears, wishing you had something better to wear. You think you look frumpy in most of your outfits, and that makes you feel invisible compared to your colleagues.

Someone who feels invisible is, for all intents and purposes, not visible. You're not going to go out on a limb when it comes to taking risks and moving big projects along; you're not going to make yourself heard even when you have the most thought-provoking ideas in the room; you're not going to secure the pay rise and promotion you deserve. Instead, you'll use timid body-language cues (poor posture, drooped head, little eye contact), which will keep you out of the sight and minds of the people who count most.

Dressing like a shy, mousy person can make you feel that way and your behaviour will reflect your lack of confidence. New opportunities may pass you by (at work and in the rest of your life) because you don't look or feel worthy of them!

Power Up

If you have any hope of overcoming your insecurities, you have to start by dressing like you're in the game, not sitting on the sidelines. Look at your highly successful colleagues and take notes on what they're wearing. Then find a shop that specialises in businesswear and describe the look you're going for to the salesperson – and listen to her advice! A business-casual dress code varies from workplace to workplace and unfortunately leaves a lot of room for error. But remember it is all about looking the part. You want to blend in with the high rollers in your office.

In a more conservative office setting, you'll need traditional business attire (tailored, dark-coloured suits for men and women). The 'power suit' is so named because the mere act of wearing one can change your body language from meek to mighty. It also tends to influence the opinions of the people around you. So what is it about the power suit that makes others take notice of the wearer? Several things, including:

- Custom-made (or custom-tailored) suits accentuate the position of the shoulders, making them appear broad and strong.
- The jacket closes without dimpling or puckering between the buttons.
- The sleeves fall just below the wrist. (No childlike sloppiness here!)
- The trousers or skirt are neither too long nor too short, and there isn't any sagging or pulling in the rear quarters. (This showcases your attention to detail.)
- The power suit is never synthetic! (Plastic-based materials simply look cheap and diminish your potential dominance.)

Shoes also play a part in announcing your personality to others. Men and women who wear expensive, polished footwear are somewhat intimidating. Trainer wearers appear to be friendly. Trendy shoes make you look like a fun person. Your non-verbal cues will be compared to these perceptions.

Defying the Dress Code

Some people have an innate sense of who they are, a level of confidence most of us only dream of achieving. When an ultra-confident person is lacking any sense of dressing appropriately, however, confusion is the order of the day. How can someone who is so aware in every other area of her life be unaware of the negative impression her clothing is making?

If you are wondering how a bad outfit can trump even the most confident body language, consider the following example. Let's say you work in a fairly conservative setting. You want to send a message to your boss that says, 'I'm knowledgeable, responsible and confident enough to become a supervisor.' You've mastered the upright walk and shoulders-back posture expected of the employee-on-the-rise; your use of eye contact is legendary; your smile lights up the office. But your long, gauzy skirts and flowing tops are better suited to the artist's life than the business world. Your boss is concerned that your mystical outfits are sending clients the wrong message – and he's right. While your body language is sending a positive message, your clothes are giving customers very different ideas – not just about you, but about the entire company. Conservative clients want to see employees dressed in traditional office wear. It simply makes them feel safe doing business with you.

How serious is this body-language/poor-choice-of-clothing rift outside of the business world? Among people who know you well, your clothing probably doesn't make a bit of difference. They're tuned into your personality first and foremost and even if you regularly dress rather oddly, your friends aren't going to hold it against you. The problem is until someone gets to know you well, he makes a lot of assumptions about you based on your appearance. It can be tough to move those relationships past an acquaintance phase, especially if the assumptions are wrong. So your clothing can invite certain people into your life while keeping others at bay.

Errors in dress can make succeeding professionally, socially and even romantically difficult, to say the least. Business attire (whether traditional or casual) is like a team uniform: by dressing like them, you're telling your colleagues that you're all in this together. Defying the dress code, on the other hand, suggests that you're a rebel, and hence a threat to the status quo.

Common Errors in Judgment

Personalities change. Trends change. Life changes. And yet, people somehow forget to change their clothes. Not literally, of course – most people actually do remember to put on clean socks and underwear every day – but men and women get stuck in clothing ruts. They grab on to a style that works for them at aged 18 and try to pull off that same look well into their 30s and beyond. Your clothes need to change with the phases of your life, with the events surrounding you at any given moment, and with the persona you're trying to project at any point in time.

There's a Reason They're Called 'Gym Clothes'

Wearing your tracksuit bottoms to the office on Saturday morning might seem like a fine idea, until – surprise! – you find that your boss is also there making up lost time, and she's not dressed in scruffy trousers and an old, stained sweatshirt. She's wearing combat trousers and trainers, which are decidedly casual but not childlike or sloppy. Her clothes are saying, 'It's not a normal workday; I'm a little more laid-back this morning,' while your outfit is saying, 'I could barely drag myself out of bed,' regardless of whether you're actually working like a dog.

Some outfits – like tracksuit bottoms at work – send such a strong message that your body language has to work double-time to make up for the bad impression your clothing is putting forth (unless, of course, you work at a gym). For example, if your boss walks past your desk and sees you sitting there in your scruffs with your head in your hands, she's going to think you're slacking off (even if you're simply working out a problem in your mind). However, if you're dressed in more appropriate weekend working-wear (say, something more similar to what the head honcho is wearing), she might overlook the exact same behaviour. Why is this? In a more professional-looking outfit, your non-verbal cues say, 'I'm making an effort.' In your tracksuit bottoms, your body language says 'I resent having to be at my desk.' Any non-verbal cues that emphasise either notion will be duly noted.

Should people have wardrobes for each of their different personalities?
No. You just need to realise the clothing that's appropriate in one setting or at one point in your life isn't necessarily going to be the same clothing that's appropriate as your life progresses, your situation changes, and your horizons expand.

Act (and Dress) Your Age

Dressing your age can be a confusing matter in this century, as we've become more and more casual and youth oriented. When your grandmother was in her 40s, for example, she probably dressed very conservatively. These days, mothers and their teenage daughters often share clothes and no one thinks much of it, unless the mother is dressed inappropriately for the setting. Is it outrageous for a fit forty-something woman to wear a bikini at the swimming pool? No. But will she draw stares if she arrives at her child's school play dressed in a short skirt and a midriff-baring T-shirt? Well … yes. But why?

Baring a lot of skin says, 'Come and get me,' whether or not your non-verbal cues back up that message. Society tends to accept this from younger women, who are biologically programmed to attract a mate and procreate with him. Once she's done that, she's supposed to want to cover herself up and stop trying to draw the attention of males. An older woman is viewed – biologically speaking – as less fertile and possibly less healthy. For these reasons, she isn't the ideal candidate for propagating the human race and is therefore seen as less desirable. And lest you think that only average women come under fire for this sort of thing, a thirty-something celebrity was recently criticised in a fashion column for wearing a miniskirt and a tiny T-shirt. The writer claimed the woman is 'too old' to be showing so much skin, even though her physical appearance hasn't changed drastically in the last ten years. Is this prejudice or prudent advice?

A recent scientific study found that young women who are nearing ovulation will often dress to attract the attention of men. Not all women opt for low-cut blouses and thigh-high skirts, however. Some simply add accessories that sparkle (like big earrings or a rhinestone-studded belt) to make themselves more visible to the opposite sex.

From Outsider to Insider

No one's saying that it's fair for others to judge you and your non-verbal communication by the way you're dressed; it's just the way the world works. Don't take this information as advice to change everything about yourself, but do think about it whenever you feel like you're on the outside looking in, a situation that can easily occur when you're dressed differently from everyone around you. In these instances, you're viewed as an interloper of sorts. Some people might view you as a threat, others may think you're a loose cannon, and some may relegate you to the 'not worth getting to know' category.

It's not easy to defuse these types of judgments unless you understand them and work against them using friendly and confident body language. Show others that beneath your outfit lies a heart of gold, and they'll eventually come to know and accept you for who you are. And of course, there's always another, easier possibility: dress appropriately for the setting (in the office, for example, wear that power suit) or the occasion (an elegant wedding calls for a classy outfit – not jeans). Don't think of this as being untrue to yourself – think of it as making your life a little easier.

In order to make a good first (and lasting) impression, your attire needs to be sending the right signals. Think of your outfits as 'frozen gestures', that send the same message all day long. What do you want your clothes to say about you?

Looking for Love in All the Wrong Places

In the world of dating, you're often judged based on how you look, which is based in large part on how you're dressed. It's just human nature to be attracted to someone who looks (i.e. is dressed) like your fantasy of the perfect mate. However, if the people you're dating aren't meeting your expectations, think about what's drawing you to these men/women in the first place. Physical beauty and attraction can be enhanced (or minimised) by clothing. So maybe what you're really attracted to are the glittery tops or bum-hugging trousers.

Here's a story from the dating world that's far too common: a young man – Joe – was sick and tired of having meaningless one-night stands. He was ready to meet a fun girl, someone he could have a good time with. He headed down to the local nightclub with his friends and surveyed the female population gathered there. Then he spotted her: an attractive girl dressed to kill in her sequined top, tight jeans and high heels. Joe says, 'She just looked like someone I had to get to know. She looked fun – not like some uptight girl.' Joe made his move, bought her a drink and played the part of the nice guy … and shortly thereafter realised that she wasn't the person he expected her to be. Not only was she not fun, she was, indeed, very uptight. Joe recalls, 'She had her arms crossed the whole time I was trying to talk to her, never smiled, kept complaining about how many people were in the place and how someone had stepped on her new shoes. I'll tell you what – I couldn't wait to get away from her. Sure, she knew how to dress, but she was sucking the life out of me.'

Later that same evening, one of Joe's friends introduced him to an old friend named Laura, a plain-looking girl dressed in a T-shirt, jeans and trainers. Of that first night Joe says, 'We sat and told stories about our mutual friend and laughed our heads off. And it was then that I realised that not only is she fun, she's also really pretty.' They started dating and they're still together three years later.

Did you ever wonder why beautiful women can treat their partners badly and still not get dumped? Studies show that men are more likely to rate a highly attractive woman as 'compatible', regardless of her personality. Women, on the other hand, rank physical attractiveness below personality when they're evaluating a prospective mate.

But what if Joe hadn't been introduced to Laura by a mutual friend? Would he have looked right past her because she was dressed so simply? He says, 'I probably would have, yes. I guess that's a big lesson everyone needs to learn. There are a lot of quality women out there who just aren't into all that flash and glamour.' (And of course, the same holds true for quality men.)

For much more information on the body language of dating, read Chapters 16 (an overview), 17 (tips for women) and 18 (advice for men).

A Trip Around the Colour Wheel

Earlier in this chapter, you read a little bit about the role colour plays in clothing. This section will get more specific and discuss how colour affects the psyche and can turn you on – or off – someone in a split second. Don't consider colour as an aside, something you don't really need to think about. Because colour has such a powerful influence on human perception, many schools and businesses (not to mention homeowners) consult with colour experts to choose wall colours that stimulate productivity, tranquility, leadership, creativity, passion – you name it, there's a colour to enhance it. But there's no need to limit these hues to workstations and living rooms. You can literally wear your emotions (or at least the colours that represent certain emotions) on your sleeve.

Men and women are attracted to each other by physical beauty, which can be enhanced, exaggerated or negatively influenced by clothing. When a relationship doesn't work out, you may be left wondering how you could have missed all the signs that your ex is the most dishonest person on the face of the earth. Maybe it was because he looked so good.

Which colours are best for relaying your unspoken messages?

- Red: the colour of power, energy, danger, force, passion and love. Red increases the body's basic functions (metabolism, respiration, blood pressure) and also encourages quick thinking (which is why many road signs are red).

- Orange: indicates excitement, happiness, encouragement, determination and creativity. Orange enhances cognitive abilities, as it increases oxygen to the brain.
- Yellow: happiness, energy, intelligence. Yellow makes people feel at ease.
- Green: associated with nature, harmony and evolution. Green provides a sense of safety and protection.
- Blue: signifies intellect, trust and confidence. Blue promotes feelings of peace and tranquility.
- Purple: the symbol of luxury and extravagance. Purple is also associated with creativity and mystical living.
- White: indicates purity and light. Makes people feel clean and safe.
- Black: elegance, power, evil, death. Black is mysterious, unsafe, aggressive.

Take a look at your favourite outfits and consider which colours you've been working with. If people tend to think of you as overly aggressive, for example, retire your red tops and give blue or green shirts a whirl. It could be that the shades you're wearing are exaggerating your non-verbal cues, making you seem hostile when you're really just excitable. On the other hand, if your employees regularly ignore your orders, steer clear of orange and white clothing. Put your power on display by opting for black or red clothing instead.

If you learn one thing from this chapter, let it be that judging someone's character by their clothing alone doesn't always work. Learn to look beyond the wrapper and take the time to evaluate non-verbal gestures. You may not find the love of your life or a new best friend straight away, but by giving everyone a fair shot, regardless of how they're dressed, you'll become much more tolerant of people in general and greatly improve your chances for bringing new and interesting people into your life.

Physique and Body Language

It's no secret that non-verbal communication is usually attached to a body of some sort (the exception being online communications, discussed in Chapter 19). So does your body type affect how your non-verbal messages are interpreted? And if that's the case, if you change your body – slim it down, bulk it up – will people respond to you differently? In this chapter, you'll read how the ideal physique has evolved throughout the ages, and what you can do with your own body to obtain the results you're looking for in your day-to-day interactions.

Chapter 14

The Incredible Shrinking Woman

For centuries, women have struggled to meet the criteria of the 'ideal' female body, not only to win the affections of men but also to hold a certain status in society. The interesting thing is that until just recently, the ideal female body type has grown smaller and smaller with the passage of time. You may wonder if the body type itself sends a message, or if it's what women have done with their figures throughout the ages that's more important. Actually, it's a little of both.

Bigger Was Better

If you've ever been to a major art gallery or museum, you've no doubt come across paintings depicting rotund women just lying around their boudoirs. Prior to the 20th century, the most desirable females were considerably overweight, at least by today's standards. The super-skinny woman, by contrast, was thought to have fallen on hard times. In those days, any woman without an ounce of extra fat was most likely some type of manual worker, probably desperately poor and possibly in poor health – not the kind of girl that the ideal man of the era was hoping to snag for his very own.

Prior to the 20th century, excess fat on a woman was a sign of health and wealth. Thin women were getting lots of exercise as the servants of these 'healthy' ladies.

At this time, the perfect lady was supposed to sit idly and wait for her man to stop by for some intimate relations. (Which is why those paintings depicted relaxed, nude women.) Indolence was admired. Think about this in terms of today's world: if your overweight sister spent the day on the sofa waiting for her boyfriend to come over, you'd take one look at her body language and think, 'She is the laziest person I've ever known.' And as laziness isn't considered a good thing in today's society, you'd be making quite a negative judgment about her. Had your sister been born 200 years ago, not only would you approve of her behaviour, you'd probably be emulating it.

Workouts for the Wealthy

By the 1920s, fortunes were being made by various barons of industry. These wealthy people started to take up hobbies like tennis, golf and swimming. The exercise gave them a more athletic physique than rich people had had in past generations. Suddenly, thin was in – it was proof that one was well off enough to be engaging in a healthy lifestyle.

At this time, make-up was also becoming widely available. Women could hide their flaws and play up their best assets with cosmetics, making their eyes and lips look innocent or sultry and adding a fake flush of excitement to their cheeks with blusher. Movies were also becoming popular, and women were beginning to mimic the behaviour of Hollywood actresses. And thanks to those films, and to magazines and the excesses of the 'Roaring Twenties', women from all walks of life were interested in dressing fashionably. Even the plainest Jane could now doll herself up and learn to bat her eyelashes and strut like a starlet.

One more development of the early 20th century was the flapper. She was thin, had short hair and displayed wildly flirtatious body language. Average women didn't exactly mimic this behaviour, but the flapper planted the seeds of sexual curiosity in many minds – male and female alike – and probably contributed to a more casual attitude about sex among certain segments of the population.

Magnificent Monroe

By the 1950s, Marilyn Monroe had become the new 'It' girl. Her behaviour set the new standards for the 'ideal' woman – blonde, buxom and very sexual. Monroe's body language was a mixture of innocence and overt sexuality. Just watch one of her films and you'll see her big, wide eyes, her plump pout and her suggestive body movements. What was the message behind Monroe's non-verbal cues? 'I may look innocent, but deep down, I'm all woman.'

Interestingly, by today's standards, Monroe would be a size 16, which would make her a 'plus-size' actress. Her personality and non-verbal gestures were so unique and powerful that if she were around today, she might set a new standard for beauty.

Waif a Minute

In the 1960s, Twiggy was the model du jour and she set a whole new standard for the ideal woman: she was so small, she was almost childlike. In fact, with her big eyes and pouty lips she looked just like a little kid. Twiggy was so thin and tiny, she completed defied the ideal female body types that went before her.

Unlike the previous 'ideal' women, Twiggy wasn't chesty and she didn't have curves. She was clearly very pretty, yet tomboyish – hence, the androgynous look was born. Suddenly, women wanted to have a masculine body that looked somewhat feminine – like a little boy's body.

So what was the underlying unspoken message of the Twiggy-like body? It was a statement somewhere along the lines of 'I'm a woman-child. Maybe I'm innocent, maybe I'm not.'

Thin Today

The androgynous, you-can-never-be-too-thin body type took hold in the 1970s. Women would starve themselves to achieve skeletal frames. What did their body language say to others? 'I care so much about my appearance, I'm willing to forgo the basic elements of survival.' As with every 'ideal' body type, the super-thin woman was viewed as being sexual, even though she was completely devoid of curves of any type.

In the 1980s, fitness gurus decided that women shouldn't simply be thin – they should also be fit. An aerobics craze was born and the ideal body type conveyed the message, 'I'm totally into my health.'

Despite supermodels and celebrities often striving for a 'size-zero' figure, nowadays there's a definite swing back towards the naturally feminine body type – curves, breasts and plump bottoms are desirable once again. But more importantly, women are starting to demand acceptance of their bodies just as they are. That's an important step in the right direction, and every cultural group has its own definition of beauty. A European and an African-American woman, for example, have different ideas of what constitutes the 'ideal' body. For the most part, they don't aspire to achieve each other's goals in that regard, which takes some of the pressure off of trying to reach physically impossible standards.

Today, the ideal androgynous body has evolved to include large breasts. The skinny body with a huge bosom almost screams, 'I have achieved what is almost physically impossible. I'm perfect!' Of course, the popularity of breast implants has played a big role in the development of this ideal body type.

The Ideal Attitude

The ideal body type is a thing of beauty, but there's more to it than that. There really are advantages to being almost physically perfect. Attractive, slender women are given attention every time they leave the house: men and women alike can't take their eyes off of these ladies. This, in turn, leads to the 'ideal' woman feeling confident and expressing that confidence in her body language. She stands tall, she makes eye contact and she smiles. Because of her self-assuredness, she's likely to have many positive interactions every day, which increases her sense of confidence, which in turn leads to more positive interactions.

But wait. Go back and read the last part of that sentence again. Confidence is what allows a person to take charge of any situation. Having a nice body can certainly give someone an initial advantage (especially in our beauty-saturated culture), but if you don't have the drive to back up the body, you're going to stall before long. Standing tall, making eye contact, perfecting your handshake, knowing the signals that indicate that you're listening (a head-tilt to the side or a well-timed nod) and showing signs of friendliness (sharing small touches, smiling) are far more important in the long run than having a perfect body. And that's a great thing, as you often can't do a lot to completely change your body type, but you do have absolute control over your body language.

Because the 'ideal' body eludes so many women, slender women are sometimes viewed as a threat and scorned by their peers. If this has been a problem for you, make sure you use friendly body-language cues (like smiling and angling your body towards whoever you're speaking to) to defuse the situation.

Mr Perfect

The ideal male body hardly has as interesting a history as the evolution of the 'perfect' woman's body. In British culture, men have always admired other men who are tall and muscular. Simply put, the ideal male body exudes strength. In this day and age, his physique is perhaps a bit more sculpted than in previous decades, but the general image is the same.

Like the female form, the ideal male body is not the average male body. The middle-of-the-road British male is 5ft 9in – but most men measuring in at this height would describe themselves as short. That's because they're comparing themselves to the ideal of male perfection, which in this culture includes standing at least 6ft tall.

So what advantages does the above-average man have over the others? People take notice of him because of his height. After all, you can't help but notice when a 6ft 3in person walks into a room. And if he happens to be well groomed and fit, he stands out among the masses all the more.

Let's say you are this man. How might your appearance help your body language? Tall men are already considered powerful, so you're way ahead of the game compared to your average peers, whether you're in a dating or a business situation. People will expect confident body language from you – a firm handshake, a killer smile, lots of eye contact – so give it to them. Just be careful not to cross into arrogant territory (don't offer your hand for a palm-down shake, which is a domineering move; don't smirk; and don't overdo the eye contact).

If you're actually a tall shy guy and exhibit meek non-verbal cues – slouching, avoiding eye contact, lots of self-touches – you'll come across as either humble or conceited. Remember: confidence matters far more than your physical appearance. So even though your height may give you an initial leg up on your competition, your non-verbal cues have to be ready to step in and close the deal.

Studies have shown that tall people earn more and are more respected in the workplace than their shorter peers. This could be a cause-and-effect issue, though: the respect that a tall man is given, for example, could result in him being very confident and willing to take risks that earn him a big salary.

Weight and Body Language

You read a little bit about weight in the section on women's body types, but since some reports estimate that 75 percent of Britons are overweight (and 22 percent actually qualify as obese), this section will deal specifically with the issue of weight and non-verbal cues.

Inhibited Interaction

Countless studies have confirmed what heavy people have long suspected: overweight people are perceived as being lazier, less attractive, less intelligent, less healthy and more likely to be in financial straits than their thinner peers. Why are overweight people held in such low esteem, though, when at one time being heavy was considered a sign of status and your ability to keep your pantry stocked?

People simply know more about keeping themselves fit and healthy nowadays. Those who appear not to put any effort into their health – and in fact, seem to be bent on becoming as unhealthy as possible – are perceived as indolent and stupid. And as bad as these judgments are for overweight people, they're ten times worse for obese men and women. What this means in terms of body language is multifold:

- Overweight/obese people are more likely to be ignored in social situations, making eye contact and friendly gestures all but impossible for them to send and receive.
- Because overweight/obese people are often thought of as unintelligent and lazy, any non-verbal gestures they make are often seen through this filter.
- Because overweight/obese people often face insults and indifference every day, they may exhibit non-verbal cues of low self-esteem and low confidence levels, like averted eye contact and slouching.

If your weight has made you feel like the subject of ridicule and nastiness, it's understandable to shy away from other people. You can't control other people, but you can control your non-verbal cues. Act confident (fake it if you have to) and your interactions with most people will improve as they'll think you are sure of yourself.

Average Brits

The average British man weighs about 13 stone (83kg) and the average British woman weighs in at about 11 stone (70kg). What does it mean to be of average weight, in terms of feeling accepted and comfortable enough with other people to send and receive non-verbal cues?

Well, it means a lot. You just read about the problems that seriously overweight people face in our society. Not only are their non-verbal cues often misinterpreted, they're often left out of group activities altogether, so there are no meaningful exchanges, non-verbal or otherwise. To be of average weight means that others see you as one of them. They're more likely to accept you, to trust you, to assume that you're of average intelligence, unless you prove otherwise.

Take this scenario, for example: you have to present your ideas to a board of trustees in order to secure funding for your project. You're a man of average weight, and you're relieved to see that the members of the board are as middle-of-the-road, physically speaking, as you are. You've already overcome one hurdle: you're probably just what they were expecting. Now all you have to do is use your confident body language to show them that you're better than average, and you'll secure your funding in no time.

Skinny Minnies

Super-thin isn't the hot look it used to be. Bony women and men are often suspected of suffering from some sort of eating disorder. Average-sized people wonder if rail-thin men and women are terminally ill. If a thin person is also somewhat dishevelled, friends start to wonder if he or she has a drug or alcohol problem.

What if you just happen to be a naturally very thin person? What if you can't gain weight, no matter how hard you try? Sorry to say, the perception is the same. Women have spent so many years fighting against the ultra-thin model of perfection – on the grounds that for most females, it's just not achievable – that people tend to think that no one is naturally very thin. Very thin men, meanwhile, are often thought of as physically weak and insignificant.

What can very skinny people (men, in particular) do to improve their perception among their peers?
Do your best to look healthy and hardy, whether that means wearing make-up or standing tall and proud. Using confident body language will make others take note of your abilities and personality.

Presenting yourself as a confident person – with good posture, adequate eye contact and appropriate hand gestures – will help to dispel the misperception that you're inconsequential because of your low weight.

Does Fitness Improve Body Language?

Do fit people really have better luck than average people with their body language? It depends on which areas of body language you're talking about. Things like eye contact and smiling aren't really affected by a person's level of fitness. But certainly, a fit person has an advantage when it comes to cues like posture, stance and angling. Simply put, the muscular body looks more powerful, ready to face a fight and win (an important criteria of the fight-or-flight response you read about in Chapter 1). In comparison, the overweight body doesn't look as 'ready to rumble'.

Fitness is a sign of health – and a sign that you're trying to keep yourself healthy. Whether or not others outwardly acknowledge this, it's in the back of their mind when they come face to face with someone who obviously spends a lot of time in the gym or running laps around the track. The very fit body says, 'I care about my appearance and my physical well-being.' The general perception is that these people are a little better than the rest, even if they don't behave that way.

Too Fit?

Is there such a thing as being too in shape? There is; it's when someone crosses the line between taking a healthy interest in exercise and being obsessed with it. When men's muscles appear ready to burst at the seams and women are walking bands of sinew, other people start to take notice in a bad way, questioning whether the super-fit are using steroids or other performance-enhancing drugs. Once this enters into the conversation, it's not such a huge leap for someone to consider that the ultra-muscular are somehow cheating nature. (And if they're cheating nature, they're cheaters, full stop.) Add some overly confident body language to this picture (imagine a body builder strutting his stuff like a peacock, only he's at the post office, not at a competition) and people are bound to conclude that the muscle-bound person in question is arrogant.

Toning Your Body Language

The super-muscular body type says, 'My body is my life.' People may start to wonder if you have your priorities right, if you're capable of caring for anything or anyone as much as you care for your body. Overcoming that kind of judgment can be very difficult. You can't prove you're a decent person unless you get to know someone, but a person who's already decided that you're cocky isn't going to want to get to know you.

To prove your humility, you have to go out of your way to be Mr Nice Guy. Use those friendly cues, go out of your way to talk to other people and, above all, don't do anything to affirm the judgment that you're arrogant. It's all right to be confident, but don't spend your day looking into reflective surfaces, don't flex your muscles while you're talking to other people and don't use your size to dominate other people. Beating others into submission is not the kind of body language that makes you look like a decent person.

Sheldon's Somatypes

In the 1940s, Dr William Sheldon, a physiobiologist, came up with a theory stating that criminals came from a biologically inferior gene pool; therefore, you should be able to identify troublemakers just by looking at them. Sheldon classified humans into three groups:

- Mesomorph: strong, athletic, can build muscle easily.
- Endomorph: chubby, round, can build muscle with effort.
- Ectomorph: thin, frail looking, not able to build muscle easily.

Sheldon assigned certain personality traits to each of the three somatypes: mesomorphs were hard working, aggressive and extroverted, but not necessarily clever; endomorphs were relaxed (almost lazy), sociable people; ectomorphs were likely to be introverted, sensitive and most often found with their head in a book. According to Sheldon, the mesomorph was most likely to end up behind bars.

Sheldon's theory didn't pan out – after all, criminals come in all shapes and sizes. His theories have been debunked as an attempt to prove what he expected to see (in other words, he judged people by their appearance and viewed their body language from that clouded perspective).

The lesson to be learned here is that even educated people make judgments (and mistakes) about how body types relate to behaviour. The fallout from this includes hurt feelings, misunderstandings and unwarranted advantages and disadvantages (depending on one's body type). You can't ignore the body sending non-verbal cues, but you can learn to separate the body language from the body type. In other words, do your best to evaluate and judge the gestures instead of the physique behind them.

Trust Me: How to Spot a Liar

One of the main reasons people want to learn how to decipher body language is to defend themselves against dishonesty. Whether you're trying to read the true intentions of your romantic partner, looking to tap into the mind of a seemingly upstanding salesman, or simply attempting to read your best friend's true thoughts, it's helpful to know the cues that liars display. As always, it's best to look for patterns of non-verbal behaviour in order to get a feel for the other person's objectives.

Chapter 15

Eye Spy

As you read in Chapter 7, the eyes are one of the most expressive regions of the body. Learning to read the non-verbal message contained in ocular behaviour can give you a head start on evaluating the rest of a person's body language. So what, exactly, are you looking for in terms of eyes that reveal a deceptive nature?

Eyebrows

Imagine that you've just arrived at work, early as usual. You say hello to the other regular early birds, Dick and Jane. There are no other employees in the building at the moment. You set up your workstation with your coffee and doughnut before remembering that you left your phone in your car. You rush down to retrieve it. On returning, you notice that someone has taken a big bite out of your doughnut. You immediately call Dick and Jane on the intercom and ask them to report to you, pronto.

Although you're not a detective, you've watched plenty of Morse and A Touch of Frost, so you know how to get to the bottom of this mystery. Your first instinct tells you to look for signs of powdered sugar on the culprit, but it appears that both Dick and Jane have been wiped clean. You throw the accusation out there and wait for a confession.

Of course, they both deny pilfering your cake. Dick's denial is accompanied by two raised eyebrows; Jane, meanwhile, is frowning. Which set of eyebrows is telling you the truth and which is lying? Remember, the eyebrows are just the beginning of this process. Dick's raised eyebrows are telling you that he wants you to believe him; Jane's eyebrows are telling you that she's highly irritated with you. You can't make a judgment of guilt based on this one feature, so you'll have to move on and assess some other non-verbal cues.

Eye Contact

Eye contact is a skill that compulsive liars almost always take the time to perfect. In fact, body language in general is something that a lot of major fibbers know a lot about, so you may fall for someone's tall tale even if you're looking for signs of untruthfulness. (And just to be clear on the issue, this says a lot more about the liar than it does about you – you just can't always defend yourself against someone who is determined to deceive others and who does so on a regular basis.)

For people who aren't professional-grade liars, eye contact can be a bit of a tricky thing. Many of these people – the particularly defiant ones who know they're at fault but also know you can't prove it – will hold your gaze far too long, as though staring into your eyes will break your concentration and convince you of their innocence. It's their way of deflecting guilt by turning the tables on you and saying, 'How dare you doubt me!' A liar who feels ashamed of himself will do just the opposite – he won't be able to look at you for more than a second or two.

Excessive blinking is a sign of anxiety and can indicate lying. The next time you're suspicious that someone is telling you a fib, take note of whether their eyes are fluttering like deceptive little wings.

Take a look at Dick and Jane now: Jane won't look at you and Dick has his eyes fixed on yours. As these are equally incriminating non-verbal cues, you'll have to keep assessing other non-verbal cues to get to the bottom of the mystery.

Pupils

Lying does interesting things to the body. When a person knows he's being deceitful (and he feels bad about it or is worried he'll be caught), his body reacts with increased heart rate, increased respiration and increased blood pressure – all of which are human reactions to fear, or the fight-or- flight response discussed in Chapter 1.

The physical changes that accompany lying prepare the person to make a run for it or to fight to the death, and they date back to when your ancestors were living in caves, defending themselves against saber-toothed tigers. How does this information relate to the eyes? Well, in an effort to make your eyesight as sharp as possible (so that you can theoretically spot potential trouble) your pupils dilate during the fight-or-flight response. Liars may appear to have dinner-plate–sized pupils – that is, if you can see those pupils at all. (As you've already read, many fibbers will refuse to make eye contact with you.)

At the moment, Dick's pupils appear to be larger than Jane's, but as this can also be a reaction to being accused of misdoings, you'll have to dig a little deeper.

Positioning of the Eyes

Do liars hold their eyes wide open or half-closed? This seems to be based on the personality of the liar and whether he thinks he's going to get away with fibbing to you. Professional half-truth tellers (like salesmen) are very careful to keep their eyelids steady, lest they appear too eager (wide-eyed) or suspicious (squinty-eyed). Someone who's less skilled at lying is more likely to widen his eyes to emphasise his point and convince you of his innocence. Unfortunately, this can also be a sign of anger or nervousness, so it's not the most reliable way to catch out a fibber.

Squinty eyes might give you a good indication of a person who's being deceptive, especially if you know this person doesn't usually scrunch up his eyes. Hiding the eyes in this way could be a subconscious attempt to minimise eye contact and/or hide the widened pupils that usually accompany a bold-faced lie.

Hmmm … you see that Jane's eyes appear to be opened to a normal degree; Dick's are opened extra-wide. It appears that you're starting to crack this case wide open.

It's Written All Over Your Face

After taking stock of the eyes, take note of what's happening with the rest of the face of the potential non-truth teller. There are several key signs to watch for in a liar, and the bigger the lie, the more obvious these signs may be. But again, it usually depends on how often this person lies, how comfortable he is at doing it, and whether he thinks he's close to getting caught.

Flushing and Blushing

For starters, a flushed face is a sign of nervousness or embarrassment, and something that unskilled liars are especially prone to. This response is also tied into the chemistry of the fight-or-flight reaction, and exhibits itself in red patches on the cheeks, neck, back and even the torso. This blotchiness is usually more visible in fair-skinned people, so if Dick happens to be of Mediterranean descent and Jane has just returned home all tanned after a Caribbean cruise, it's not likely that you'll be able to see either one of them blushing from anxiety.

There's the Rub!

You might think that flared nostrils would be a clear indication of someone's guilt, but you'd be wrong. While flared nostrils can indicate anxiety or anger and defiance, all of which might be experienced by someone who's hiding the truth from you, these emotions might also be the legitimate reaction to being accused by you. So should you discount the nose in its entirety when you're deciding about someone's veracity, or does it hold other secrets regarding the truth?

If you ask someone a point-blank question and she answers by rubbing her nose, that's actually a fairly good indication that she isn't being truthful. In fact, any sort of self-touch to the face shows that a person is feeling a little anxious (self-touches are designed to soothe the nerves, remember).

A rub to or around the mouth – especially one that lingers as the person gives you his answer – is a big old red flag. This is an attempt to block the untrue words coming out of the mouth.

Have a look at your doughnut suspects now. Dick is rubbing the hell out of his nose while Jane is simply chewing her gum.

Head Issues

A liar uses his head in very particular ways. For example, if Dick stands before you proclaiming his innocence and shaking his head excessively while he speaks, that's a sign of anxiety and an indication that all is not well with him. If he remains silent and tilts his head down or to the side, he's either trying to avoid eye contact or he's thinking of a way to choose his words very carefully, both of which indicate that something's up with him. If he raises a hand to the back of his head or neck

– another self-touch – that also signals nervousness.

If Dick is displaying any of these characteristics while he's under the bright light of your doughnut interrogation, it looks as though you may be closing in on your suspect – especially if Jane is standing by with a rather level, steady head on her shoulders.

Under- and Overstatements

Because untruths come flying from the mouth, you might wonder if this orifice has some instinctual reaction to being the instrument of deception. Do the lips curl at the edges, for example, when an untruth is forced from the mouth? Does the tongue shrivel up or hang out slightly? Do the liar's teeth instantly turn an unflattering shade of yellow? Unfortunately, the non-verbal mouth cues that indicate lying aren't that easy to spot, but if you know what to look for, you might just be able to hone in on a few subtle movements.

If a person shakes his head 'yes' while he's saying 'no', or shakes his head 'no' while he's saying 'yes', he's fibbing to you – or at least he's trying to. His conscience is fighting his best attempts to deceive you by allowing the movement of his head to let you in on the truth.

Loose Lips

One of the most interesting things liars do is let their mouths run wild. This is actually a verbal cue, but it's worth mentioning. Shakespeare wrote, 'The lady doth protest too much, methinks' – and that pretty much says it all. When someone reacts to a relatively small inquiry by prattling on and on and on, it's obviously an attempt to convince you of his innocence, the rationale being that anyone who takes the time to defend himself vigorously against a minor accusation must be full of moral character and therefore deeply offended by the suggestion that he's done anything wrong.

How might this play itself out? If Dick escapes your office without being forced to admit his guilt, he might bring up the incident later in the day in an attempt to showcase the ridiculousness of the situation. Why, he doesn't even like doughnuts! You know, the last time he had a doughnut was in 1995, and he hasn't had the urge to even taste one since. In fact, he refuses to buy doughnuts for his kids. And it's not just doughnuts. Dick doesn't like sweet things in general. He won't eat cake, ice cream, chocolate, anything with refined sugar and, certainly, he's sworn off fried foods, which totally precludes him from the list of doughnut-biting suspects. He still can't believe you thought it was him, but he's got to hand it to you – it was pretty funny, especially as he's the last person in the world who would bite into a pastry. You think Dick doth protest too much?

Pitch Imperfect

There are other vocal cues that indicate a person isn't being totally forthcoming, and they're all side effects of tension. The tone of his voice might be off – usually, nervous pitch is somewhat higher than his normal timbre.

Another little tic that plagues liars is excessive throat clearing or coughing. If the accused is suffering from some sort of respiratory infection, this cue is obviously not very helpful for determining his state of anxiety, but if he's been healthy right up to the moment when you asked him whether he took a big bite out of your doughnut and then he's suddenly seized by an attack of a dry throat, one of two things may be happening. Either his anxiety has actually caused his throat to feel tight and dry or he's using this as a sort of diversion. If he can't talk, he can't really answer you, now can he?

In his attempt to get the lie out of his mouth quickly and correctly, he might trip over the words. Sometimes his spoken words will be out of order, an indication that he's been practising his lie and his nervousness made him get it all wrong.

Keeping the Lie In

Liars are anxious underneath their calm exteriors. They don't want to be found out, and the size of the lie doesn't really matter. Getting caught in a small lie is almost worse than being apprehended for a major untruth because it's those tiny fibs that make people wonder why you'd lie about such a silly thing in the first place. Meanwhile, the big lies (about whether, say, you misplaced four million pounds of the company's money) actually have a purpose – you're protecting yourself from major consequences. That's not to say that you should lie in these situations. The truth will set you free – if not from prison time, then from the anxiety that will haunt you and display itself in your behaviour.

Nervous behaviour can exhibit itself in the areas in and around the mouth. Compressing or biting the lips may be a subconscious attempt to keep the words in the mouth. The tongue-show (a little peek of the tongue, which almost looks as though the speaker is licking his lips) is a sign of uncertainty, a way of indicating that the person doesn't really know if what he's saying is true or untrue. Some liars will smack their lips repeatedly, which is just another exhibition of the nervous energy they're trying so hard to hide from you.

Suspicious Positioning

It would be so easy if liars lived up to their names – if deception caused people to pose in a horizontal position. Unfortunately, this isn't the way the universe works, so you're left to find other ways of determining whether someone is telling you the truth or handing you a load of rubbish. Reading the body positioning of the person in question is another helpful tool in your detective kit.

Level of Confidence

The posture of a liar is one of those things that's completely dependent on the liar and how skilled he is. That means you have to look for patterns of behaviour. If you don't know the person well enough to determine whether he's a nervous sloucher or whether he always has bad posture, then it leaves you to make a judgment call based on the non-verbal cues he's exhibiting at the time.

Right now, Dick is looking less than confident, with his hands jammed into his pockets, his shoulders slouched as he stares at his shoes. Jane is standing in the doorway looking relaxed, but not overly so. Dick's posture is saying, 'I want to run back to my office,' while Jane's is saying, 'Have we finished yet?'

There is one more posture cue that might tip you off to someone's deceptive nature. Unskilled liars (again, those who don't lie out of habit or because their income depends on telling untruths) may cross their arms or legs in an attempt to shield themselves from you (or, in the case of the liar who feels guilty, to shield you from himself). Although Dick has his hands in his pockets right now, it's just as likely that he'll decide to cross those arms over his chest at any moment.

You'll recall from Chapter 3 that hidden hands (hands in the pockets, for example) are a sign of deception. Hands kept on display usually have nothing to hide. Politicians, for example, make sure they always keep their hands where everyone can see them.

Anxious arms cross themselves tightly, which makes sense, as this is a gesture designed to soothe the liar's nerves. He's actually giving himself a little hug as a means of telling himself that everything's going to be just fine.

Angling for the Truth

As you would expect, the occasional liar often angles himself away from the person he's fibbing to. It's as though he can't bring himself to face you, so he turns himself away from you, either slightly or completely.

As you continue to wait for an answer from your colleagues, Dick turns to play with the paper clip dispenser located on your windowsill, which necessitates him turning away from you. At this point, he may muster up the courage to deny his guilt. Remember: it's easier for someone to lie to you if he doesn't have to look you in the eye. If he turns himself away from you, he doesn't have to bother with attempting to make awkward (and unsuccessful) eye contact, and there's less of a chance you'll catch on to his deception.

Dick's your man. He owes you breakfast.

Is Everyone Dishonest?

It would be nice if liars were relegated to certain professions. You'd know when to have your guard up and when to let it down. Unfortunately, the reason people miss a lot of lies is because you just don't expect them, and it's not easy to protect yourself against a sneaky enemy. How many spouses, for example, are shocked to learn of their mate's infidelities and then count the lies they've been told? These people aren't stupid; they just weren't looking for signs of deception in their loved ones. And because taken separately, most non-verbal signs of lying also do double-time as indicators of anxiety, it's easy to give a fibber the benefit of the doubt by saying to yourself, 'Wow, he's really insulted by my accusations. I must be way off the mark.'

Which brings us to the closing point of this chapter. Knowing the non-verbal cues that indicate lying is a helpful tool in some situations. However, if you're a pessimistic person by nature, you could start to see signs of deception in everyone you know. Remind yourself that body language is a study of patterns of behaviour. And when you're talking about body language and lying, it's especially important to look for a combination of cues. In other words, don't assign guilt based on a random cue (someone walking past you with his hands in his pockets isn't necessarily hiding the truth from anyone; he just may have cold hands). You're looking for out-of-the-ordinary patterns and reactions to a specific situation. If something about your friend's reaction to a simple question is obviously amiss, then you may have stumbled on to something – and that's the kind of situation where your knowledge of body language can help determine which direction to take that conversation in.

Last but not least, remember that even though you may be able to determine within reasonable parameters whether someone's being untruthful with you, you can't force him or her to tell you the truth. Experts in the field believe that non-verbal cues override the spoken word, so use your body language deciphering skills, and then sit back and trust your gut feeling.

Love at first Eye Contact?

Does love at first sight really exist, or is that a myth perpetuated on physical attraction? While the statistics are hazy on how many long-term relationships began with a single glance across a crowded room, body language can certainly add or detract from the message you're sending out to potential mates. Whether you appear approachable or stand-offish, for example, can matter far more than whether you're the most beautiful person on the face of the earth. In this chapter, you'll read what attracts the sexes to one another.

Chapter 16

Beauty Is in the Eye of the Beholder

Wait, didn't you just read that there's more to attraction than empirical beauty? Yes, you did, but you can't deny the fact that a good-looking human being attracts a lot of attention – at least initially. Some people have their specific 'types' (you prefer blondes while your friend likes dark hair), but a symmetrical, youthful face without flaws (more on those in a minute) is generally believed to be attractive.

However, obviously no one is perfect and 'flawed' people of all ages manage to find love. How do they do it? Is beauty really more than skin deep, or do they simply settle for what they get and make the most of it?

Beauty and the Beast Within

Think about someone who you couldn't live without and then think about another person who drives you out of your mind on a regular basis. Would you feel any differently about them if their appearances suddenly changed? If your boyfriend gained weight or lost all of his hair overnight, for example, would that affect the way you 'see' him?

If you want to go further with this thought process, imagine that you're blind. How in tune are you with the personalities that surround you every day? Is there a chance that you haven't given someone a fair chance because he or she doesn't live up to your standard of beauty?

This isn't a lecture about learning to value intrinsic beauty. Just consider whether you're limiting your life by associating only with people who meet a certain standard of physical beauty.

You've no doubt seen at least one couple in your lifetime who don't seem to be an equal physical match – in other words, one of them appears to be way out of the league of the other. How did these people come together, you wonder? Well, one of them was open to the possibility that a soulmate isn't always physically perfect – and chances are, the other one displayed a stunning amount of charm and confidence through non-verbal cues.

Playing the Confidence Card

Not everyone is born with model-like features. Then again, model-like features don't automatically bestow sparkling personality on a person (which is not to say that extraordinarily good looks and a great personality are mutually exclusive). What do men and women find sexiest about one another? Confidence. (Note that that doesn't say cockiness.) A sense of being self-assured in who you are and what you have to offer someone else is something everyone needs to bring to any relationship, regardless of looks.

When someone is good at projecting confidence, he or she is very good at it, and is usually the belle (or beau) of the ball. Whatever imperfections they have obviously aren't holding these people back. They have a joie de vivre that's infectious.

Confidence Personified

Let's say you know someone who isn't a classic beauty, but men love her anyway. What is she doing that you're not? She's simply projecting her confidence and enjoyment of others through her body language. At a party, for example, she:

- Places herself near the centre of activity instead of hiding in the corner.
- Stands tall, projecting confidence.
- Smiles, laughs and makes eye contact when she speaks to others.
- Uses small touches to convey the message, 'Hey, we're friends'.
- Angles herself and her head towards whoever she's speaking to.

She's not doing anything outrageous or even out of the ordinary; what she is doing is showing a genuine interest in the people around her and welcoming people into her world. Most people will respond to this kind of solicitous behaviour in a positive way – that is, they'll want to get to know her. Depending on how brilliant a conversationalist she is or how funny she may be, she may have men eating out of her hand by the end of the night. (Oh, and by the way, she's ten pounds overweight and has a zit on her chin. She's just the kind of girl others would look at and say, 'What's she doing with that great-looking guy?' Maybe that chap was powerless to defend himself against her charms, and – just as importantly – she never doubted for one second that the two of them belonged together.)

Setting is Crucial

Many average-looking men feel as though the deck is stacked against them. They wander out to the nightclubs where they spot women who are dressed to kill – none of whom will speak to them. This is a valid complaint, so step one is to expand your horizons and look beyond the nightclubs. It's hard to break into a pack of girls, and chances are if you've spotted a real beauty at the bar, someone else has his eye on her, too.

This is not to say that you should adopt an attitude of defeatism – it's just best to know when and where to put forth your best efforts. Parties are often a much better setting for meeting someone because you can actually talk to each other in more than three-word phrases (and without shouting). This set-up makes it much easier to put your confident body language into action.

So what kind of body language do women look for in the standard good guy (in other words, the man who will treat them well and not make them wait by the phone for a call that never comes)?

- Eye contact.
- Smiling.
- A confident posture.
- Some sign of humility (perhaps a hand in the pocket, or the occasional shrug).

Now, there's an entire subset of women who prefer the bad boy to the good guy and there's a huge difference in non-verbal cues between these two men. Where the good guy's entire presence is based in showing his interest in the woman, the bad boy is cocky beyond belief and woos one woman while checking out the other 'talent'. If you're trying to quit your bad-boy ways, reread the above list and practise your body language skills. Eye contact is especially important when it comes to convincing a woman that you're more than a player.

The Purpose Behind the Pick-Up

If you've heard it once, you've heard it a hundred times: men play at love to get sex; women play at sex to get love. These words are never truer than in the initial moments of the chat-up. Even in this age of sexually liberated women and sensitive men, the roles are more often than not the same as always: the guy is looking for a sexual encounter and the girl is looking for more.

Some women don't mind when a man views them as a sex object; other women do. In any event, it's good to be aware of where his head is at before you spend (or waste) time with him. Read his body language and you'll know what you're in for.

Can you tell a person's true intention about where this is all going from his or her body language? Actually, often you can. Some body-language rules of thumb for women who are looking for a potential mate are:

- Don't go home with a guy who hasn't looked you in the eye for more than one second all night long.
- Don't go home with a guy who has been rubbing up against you all night.
- Don't go home with a guy who's been checking out ten other girls during the course of the night.

In other words, if he hasn't given you good reason to believe that he actually wants to get to know you at some point – if he hasn't made eye contact, if sex is first and foremost on his mind (i.e. he's been groping you all night), and, most of all, if you suspect you're interchangeable with a number of other females – then he's not into you, at least not specifically.

What Did That Mean?

Men often feel they get mixed messages from women. Many women often flirt outrageously but at the end of the night want to be left alone. So how does a man decipher the difference between a woman out for a relationship and one out for sex?

A man should not live his life based on assumptions, but it is fair to assume that a girl who's flashing her unmentionables might be interested in sex, whereas it's also fair to assume that a girl who's keeping things under wraps might be a bit more conservative and traditional in her expectations.

A woman who is interested in more than a one-night stand with you will:

- Make eye contact with you.
- Actually listen to you talk; she'll angle her body and head in a way that shows she's interested in what you're saying.
- Give you lots of little friendly touches.
- Laugh and smile a lot.

A girl who's interested in sex, pure and simple, will behave much in the same way a man in the same situation does, except maybe in a more overt manner. She'll have her hands all over you and conversation and eye contact won't be an issue – she'll be scanning the room for other prospects. If you left the room for ten minutes, another guy would be in your place when you returned.

So there you have it: the key to determining what you're in for with a girl is whether her body language tells you, 'It's only you for me,' (in which case, if you're not looking for a relationship, leave her alone) or, 'You'll do for tonight.'

Signals for Singles

Wouldn't it be great if there were an easy way to tell if someone were single and looking? Perhaps a little sign on the forehead, something along the lines of, 'Ask me about my relationship status!' Alas, life is more complicated than this. So how do single men and women make themselves known to potential mates? There is an array of non-verbal cues that singles (and not-so-singles) use to put themselves out there and assess who might be out there with them.

Roving Eyes

People who are interested in other people are natural eye-contact makers. It's not that they put a lot of thought or effort into it; they can't not look into other people's eyes. Every person they pass, every stranger on the street is subject to a glance and a friendly, 'How's it going?'

'Now wait,' you're thinking. 'Some people just do that. It doesn't mean that they're looking for love. They're just friendly.' That might be true in some cases, but try your own experiment. Walk into a crowded café or bookshop and take note of how many people actually make eye contact with you beyond a fleeting glance. The number will inevitably be small. Anyone who does look at you for more than a second will probably smile or offer you a greeting. If this person isn't an employee, there's a reasonable chance that he or she is open to conversation, and possibly more.

Unlike holding doors and offering seats to women and old people, friendly eye contact isn't something that's usually ingrained in children as a polite measure. Many adults struggle with appropriate eye contact, especially with strangers.

Snuggling Up

Later in this chapter, you'll read about how to use personal space to your advantage when you're looking to get to know someone better. For now, you need to know that when someone comes into your personal space (which is a 12- to 18-inch perimeter surrounding you), he's getting friendly with you. Obviously, this doesn't apply on a crowded bus or even in a jam-packed nightclub, but let's say you have a colleague who's always standing a little too close to you – and it's not only when you're both reading the same document or constructing a model of some sort; it's when the two of you are waiting in line at the cafeteria, and when you take the lift together in the morning (even though there's plenty of room to spread out), and when he comes into your office to see what you're up to.

This very situation happened to Katie, an overworked architect who, like her co-workers, had little time to date and even less time to evaluate the close proximity between herself and her colleague Alan – until friends in the office pointed it out to her. 'I assumed he thought of me as his sister,' Katie says. 'We didn't have a flirtatious relationship at all, so when my friends started noticing how close he always stood to me, I laughed at them. But then I started to notice it, too. They were right. He asked me to dinner, and the rest is history.' (Katie and Alan have been married for four years.)

Most people have an innate sense of personal space. Women are more likely to stand too close to other people than men, who tend to be especially protective of their perimeters. If a man is creeping ever closer to you, there's a reason for it: he likes you.

Lip Service

In Chapter 6, you read all about the body language of the mouth, including that licking the lips isn't always a sign of sexual interest – but sometimes it is. You have to take the situation and the environment into consideration. Men are more likely to misinterpret the language of the lips than women are. A common myth is that a girl who chews her ice or straw is looking for action. It could be that she's a very tense person and this is her way of releasing some of that pent-up energy. It's more important to take stock of her eye contact, body angling and whether she's using friendly touches. If she's staring into your eyes, turning her body to face you and placing her hand on your forearm, these cues suggests that she's interested in more than friendly conversation.

Someone who's working hard on a project at his desk and biting and licking his lips is doing this as a means of soothing his nerves and/ or expressing his frustration. But someone who's staring at you in a restaurant and biting his lips is expressing his interest in you.

Things to Avoid

This section will examine a couple of body-language cues that hurt and help your chances of attracting the right person. Perhaps you'll find a pearl of wisdom here, something that makes you gasp and say, 'So that's what I'm doing wrong!'

No Public Grooming

As the study of body language links human behaviour to that of primates, you'd think that just about anything goes. Monkeys groom themselves in public, so that must mean that you can too! Stop yourself right there. No one of either gender wants to see a public display of personal hygiene. This includes picking at the ears, rubbing the nose and clearing spittle from the corners of the lips. These are non-verbal gestures that say, 'I don't really care about keeping my germs all to myself. Here – have some!' (Don't be surprised if everyone else's body language answers back, 'Eewww!')

There's one exception to this rule: women and their hair can get away with a light grooming in public – say, a twirl or a push behind the ear. This doesn't mean that you can pull out your brush and spray and refresh your locks in the middle of a date. That kind of behaviour shows an obliviousness that's beyond compare. Keep a little mystery alive – excuse yourself and groom in private.

No Leering

In the realm of body language, keeping things simple is often the key to winning over the person you have your eye on. You've read about eye contact, angling your body, using friendly touches and invading someone's personal space in order to express your interest. Don't cross the line into leering, groping and hanging on someone who clearly isn't on board with this behaviour.

How will you know if you're being a little too outgoing? Read the other person's body language. If your behaviour is unacceptable, you'll see some of the following cues:

- A fake smile, one where the lips pull back towards the ears and the muscles around the eyes don't crinkle.
- A glare, which shouldn't be mistaken for prolonged, positive eye contact. The glare is usually accompanied by flaring nostrils and a jaw set in stone.
- An increase of space between the two of you, as the other person steps back or angles her body away from you.
- A lack of eye contact, where the other person is doing her best to pretend you aren't there.

If you're picking up on these behaviours, you've probably already blown your chances. You can scale back your non-verbal behaviour considerably or you can call it a night and excuse yourself from the scene.

He Loves Me, He Loves Me Not

All right, maybe we're not talking about love here. Perhaps the title of this section should be more along the lines of, 'He's interested … wait, no, he isn't … is he?' How can you tell if someone is being friendly or if he is enthralled with you? Ideally, everyone would follow the same body-language protocol and make things easy on society in general. In reality, people have their own quirks and emotional baggage affecting how they view the world and express their intentions, even when it comes to simple physical attraction. The information that follows is the low-down on interested versus non-interested body language.

Insecurity

Have you ever spotted someone who instantly intrigued and intimidated you? Despite your best efforts, you can't look away. You feel compelled to get to know this person, but you know you won't make the first move because you lack the confidence. This is a punch to the ego that manifests itself in a voice in your head which says, 'Don't waste your time. He's way too good looking/wealthy/successful/tall/young/old for you. You'll be shot down inside of one second.'

Unfortunately, it doesn't stop there. Your insecurity also expresses itself in your body language, like so:

- Lack of eye contact.
- Angling away from a person.
- Angling the head down.
- Slouching.

In short, you try to make yourself as invisible as possible. You reinforce your own insecurities because no one is going to take notice of someone who's intentionally keeping a low profile. It's a vicious, self-perpetuating cycle. And for all you know, that person you have your eye on might think you're attractive, but your behaviour is saying that you could not possibly be less interested in him or her.

Is there any way to improve this scenario? There is. Go back and reread the beginning of this chapter. You don't have to be a supermodel to win the affections of others, but you do have to show others that you're worth getting to know. And the way to do this is by using confident body language.

We Have (Eye) Contact!

Aside from laying your hands on someone and verbally telling her that you're falling head over heels for her, eye contact is the easiest way to send out the positive vibe to someone – or to receive it from someone else. Jake is a painfully shy graduate living in Exeter; his family lives in Edinburgh. During a cross-country trip several years ago, Jake's connecting train was cancelled due to a blizzard. Local hotels were full and he was looking at spending the night on the station floor surrounded by strangers.

Hold your head up high, smile and make eye contact with other people. You might be surprised to learn that just by acting secure, you'll feel at least a little confident – and that will also express itself in your body language. Call it a self-fulfilling prophecy: 'I think I'm sexy and worthwhile, therefore I am.'

Now, Jake isn't one to make conversation with people he doesn't know well. In fact, Jake isn't one to look up from his books long enough to give other people the chance to be friendly to him, but as luck would have it, he'd done a fair amount of reading on the first leg of his journey. Fatigued, he sat and surveyed the other stranded passengers. He caught the eye of a redhead girl as she walked by and remembered her from his first train. Perhaps she remembered him, too, because she smiled at him as she kept walking, trailing her suitcase behind her. Jake was so pleasantly surprised by her simple friendly gesture, he smiled back at her before he knew what he was doing. (Jake is also not one to take chances, socially speaking.)

Eventually, a bored Jake pulled out a book and continued with his reading – until he heard a voice asking if the space on the floor next to him was taken.

It was the redhead, who had just spent an hour waiting to hear the status of her own train, which had also been cancelled. The two spent the evening talking and discovered that they had similar interests and lived just a few streets away from each other. Before their respective trains departed the following morning, the two had exchanged phone numbers. It was a match made in a station – and it all started with a little eye contact.

Get a Little Closer

Edging in on someone else's territory sends the unmistakable message that you want to be closer to her. People often base personal space on specific relationships, so the amount of space that exists between you and your girlfriend is less than the amount of space you keep between yourself and a shop assistant. (More on the subject of personal space in Chapter 17).

When you're interested in getting better acquainted with a man or woman, is it a good idea to attach yourself to his or her hip, figuratively speaking?
While this may be effective in some cases, it might be seen as overly aggressive in others. It's best to leave about a foot of space between you until you're invited to get closer.

When someone who doesn't belong there enters into your personal space, take that as a sign of interest. At a social gathering, you can show increasing signs of interest by:

- Angling your body towards him.
- Tilting your head as he speaks.
- Employing lingering, friendly touches.
- Using prolonged eye contact.

Just keep in mind that no matter how good you are at working these tactics into your interaction, they'll do you little good if you insist on maintaining more than a foot of distance between you and the target of your attention. Getting closer is the first step to securing a successful outcome.

Move It Along

So what kinds of non-verbal cues will you be getting if someone's just not interested in you? Fleeting eye contact, or a complete lack thereof, is a good tip-off. Even though some people are unskilled at the art of appropriately timed gazes, if someone is interested in you, she should want to look your way. Not doing so is an indication that she is polite enough to tolerate you for the moment, but has no intention of carrying things any further.

Angling away from you is another sign of lack of interest. If you're speaking to someone and she doesn't bother to turn to face you, that's not good. If she actually turns her head away as you speak, or keeps taking little steps away from you, that's also not good. Take your own steps towards someone who'll give you the time and attention you deserve.

Skills for Single Girls

When you're wandering the streets of your city looking for true love, it helps to know what to watch for. More importantly, it helps to send out the right vibe just in case you cross paths with someone who's searching for you. In this chapter, we'll cover the basic moves women need to know in order to land that someone special.

Chapter **17**

Eye Love You

OK, you don't love the guy you've just spotted across the fruit and veg aisle, but you'd definitely like to get to know him better. Yet you're not the type to walk over and ask him how to choose a pineapple. How can you get him to come to you? Start with your eyes.

Open Up Those Windows to Your Soul

Some women are blessed with gorgeous eyes – big, beautifully hued peepers adorned with long lashes. But you – you have small, swollen, squinty or crinkly eyes, and you're convinced that your chances of meeting a man will increase if your wear sunglasses. Wrong! It doesn't matter if your eyes aren't perfect; what matters most is putting what you've got to good use. To that end, it can't hurt to learn how to dress up your eyes.

If you have no idea how to make use of eyeliner and mascara, it might be worth your while to make an appointment with a beautician or make-up artist. She'll be able to give you some valuable tips on the best eye looks for you, as well as showing you how to achieve them.

You may be wondering why this is important. You don't particularly like make-up; in fact, you've never worn it and you don't plan on starting now. Just sit tight for a minute and keep reading. When men are looking for a mate, they instinctively try to find someone who can bear their children. This instinct dates back to the cavemen days, where procreation meant the difference between the survival of the human species and the end of it. Supposedly, men are looking for young, fertile mates.

Here's where your eyes come in: big, bright eyes make you look young – youthful enough to have a child – and harmless, much like a baby or a child yourself. Using make-up to accentuate these features works in your favour – as long as you don't overdo it. If you hate make-up, just hit the basic trouble spots around your orbital areas. Camouflaging dark circles with concealer is a start; adding lash-lengthening mascara gives your eyes a 3D boost. You'll read about other ways to play up your eyes throughout this section.

Work It!

Once you've hidden your flaws and played up your eyes' assets, it's time to put them to work. Making eye contact is your first move, but it's not as easy as it sounds, as anyone who's ever felt awkward making eye contact will attest to. Eye contact is a subtlety of flirting that can easily go awry.

Too much eye contact can scare the other person away ('Why is she staring at me?'); too little can lead the other person to believe that you aren't interested, either in meeting him or in listening to him, depending on the situation.

So what's the right way to make that initial flirty eye contact? Use the one-two-three rule:

- One: a brief meeting of the eyes, no more than three seconds.
- Two: a look back at the person, this time with a little smile.
- Three: After a brief interlude (a couple of minutes at least), a sure and steady glance accompanied by a wider smile.

After Three, you have to make a decision: either get up and go talk to this guy or wait for him to approach you. But cool it with the eyes for a while. You can't spend the entire night stealing little glances at him without parlaying that into actual conversation. That just shows a lack of effort on your part.

Of course, every situation is different. If you're sitting in a conference and you happen to catch his eye, you obviously aren't going to strike up a conversation right then and there, but the same rule applies: don't continue to stare or glance over at him too often. While some men find it incredibly appealing when a stranger can't take her eyes off of him, others find it disconcerting. As you're making a first impression with your eye contact, play it safe until you actually know him.

Briefly Breaking the Connection

Although people don't actually speak with their eyeballs, eye contact is a huge factor in everyday communication. You've already read about giving someone the eye across a crowded room; what are you going to do with your eyes when you're face to face with this man?

Keep in mind that prolonged eye contact sends a very definite message that isn't always appropriate in everyday conversation. The polite version of this communication says, 'I can't stop looking at you. I'm very interested in getting to know you better.' So even though it's all right to hold eye contact longer than you would if you were, say, talking to your neighbour (assuming you're not interested in bagging your neighbour for a romantic interlude), too much is still too much. You have to break eye contact once in a while or your interaction with this person will amount to little more than a staring contest.

Widening your eyes when you're talking to a man mimics the wide-eyed innocence of youth. Since men are instinctively programmed to find a mate to bear their children, they respond to body language that makes a woman look young.

So where do you look – and how often? If you're in a club, restaurant or other social setting, there should be plenty of things that will naturally catch your eye. Look down at your glass, look at the people standing next to you, look off to the side of your date's head. The break from eye contact shouldn't be more than a few seconds. You shouldn't be holding eye contact for more than five to ten seconds at a time, which doesn't sound like very long, but try it out on yourself in the mirror. Ten seconds seems to span a much longer period of time in an intense situation.

Be careful to look to different areas when you break eye contact. If you look towards the same spot every time, your date might wonder who's catching your eye while you're flirting with him.

Get on the Eye Express

There are a few basic eye expressions that come in handy in the dating world:

- The wide eye.
- The wink.
- The eyelash-bat.
- The demure look upwards.

Some of these gestures were discussed in Chapter 7, but here they'll be discussed in the specific context of flirting.

When you widen your eyes, you make yourself look youthful and interested – as long as you don't overdo it. If you pop your eyes open as wide as they'll go, you look frightened. Combine a slightly widened eye with a smile and you're good to go.

Winking is a bold move, of course, because in our culture it's a means of saying 'You're quite a hottie. Come over here and talk to me.' Work on your wink before using it in a public place. Make sure you've got it down pat: it should be a quick blink of one eye. And a smile always sweetens the deal.

If you can't wink without closing both eyes, then don't do it! People will wonder if you've lost a contact lens or if you're suffering from chronic dry eyes. Either way, you won't be landing a date with this move.

Batting the eyelashes is something that requires natural ability and practice – it's not a move for amateurs! If you spend your Sunday afternoons watching old black-and-white movies, you've no doubt seen this tactic employed – and probably not in the most subtle manner. It should be such a natural move that no one notices anything other than your beautiful, innocent eyes.

Here's the move: preferably no more than two quick blinks at once and then cool it. The eyelash-bat combined with a coy smile is a game-winning play, but again, you need to practise this in the privacy of your own home before displaying it in public. And remember: less is more. Overusing the lash-bat will only make you look like you have some sort of eye disorder. That may in and of itself gain you some sympathy from the chap in question, but that's about as far as things will go.

Angling your head downwards and looking upwards at your date sends the message that you're harmless and he's powerful, even if he happens to be shorter than you are. It's also one of those moves that's undeniable in its message: basically, it's sex in a glance.

Lips Don't Lie ... or Do They?

As many women already know, the lips can be a powerful tool in your body language arsenal. When you display them correctly, all your date can think of is kissing you. Contorting the lips, meanwhile, usually makes you look crabby, elderly or just plain strange. You don't have to have a naturally full and luscious mouth in order to make men take notice. Like the eyes, you just have to know how to make the best of what nature's given you.

Don't rush out and fill your skinny lips with collagen! Despite the prevalence of cosmetic surgery, most men still prefer a natural appearance to an overtly fake one. If you have a very thin mouth, lip liner and gloss or lipstick can give your lips a fuller appearance.

Your Words Say One Thing, Your Mouth Says Another

In Chapter 6, you read about the non-verbal messages that the mouth can send. This may be one of the most confusing aspects of decoding body language, since the very instrument that's spouting words can simultaneously contradict itself with its movements. So, when you're speaking to someone you'd like to get to know better, it's important that your words and your lips are in agreement, so to speak.

Let's take a look at a situation where this kind of contradiction clouds the conversation. You're late for a dinner date (again) and are apologizing profusely to your significant other when you finally arrive. She insists that she isn't angry – after all, you didn't cause that three-car accident on the motorway – and yet, when you take a peek at her from your menu, you notice that her lips are pursed and her jaw appears to be set in concrete.

There's always the possibility that she's angry about something else entirely, but there's also a fairly good chance that you're in her line of fire at the moment. Perhaps she's not the confrontational type; maybe she just wants you to fix her car without any further discussion. Whatever the case, her clenched mouth clearly conveys the message that all is not well with her at the moment.

Obviously, this is far from a romantic situation, where it's even more important that your words and mouth motions match one another. If the guy you've been pining over for the last six months finally asks you to go to dinner with him, which response from you is going to leave him confused?

- 'I'd love to!' spoken with a big, wide grin.
- 'I'd love to,' spoken with lips that purse immediately after the words are spoken.

The first response will have him feeling like this might be a fun date; the second will make him wonder if you're really into him or if you're just going for the free food.

The Pout

You've seen the pout; you've done the pout; you've watched others put it to use. Depending on who's doing it, it can look rather natural or completely ridiculous.

What's the point of the pout? It's another one of those facial gestures that makes a person look young, helpless and innocent. (And very annoying, at least in some cases.) In the classic move, the pout shows sadness combined with disappointment or even anger. When women use it during the flirting process, it's usually meant as a cute way to show disappointment without crossing into anger territory (that comes later in a relationship, after all).

Let's say you see a girl pouting at her dinner date. Perhaps he's told her that she can't accompany him on the trip to Rio with his buddies that he's planned. Since this isn't exactly a committed relationship (in fact, this is only their second date), she can't really be angry about it, but she's going to show her displeasure anyway. She might not change his mind, but she's made her feelings clear.

Licking and Biting the Lips

This section covers the unspoken messages behind biting and licking your own lips – not someone else's. (If those signals aren't getting through loudly and clearly, there's nothing this book can do to help you!)

Pouting is harmless – as long as it isn't a chronic condition. But be forewarned: it gets old fast, and the cuter you try to be while sticking your bottom lip out, the faster your date will want to hightail it away from you. As a general rule for anyone over the age of six, pouting should be a definite rarity.

Licking and biting the lips are two moves that are touted as having overt sexual overtones. The truth is, it depends on the situation. If you pass your cute colleague who's hard at work at his desk and you notice he's biting his lips, you can be fairly sure it's a sign of frustration and not an invitation for you to pull up a chair. But if you find yourself in a social setting with this same guy and he's smiling and biting his lips, you can take that as a sign that he likes what he sees standing in front of him. (That would be you.)

The same thing goes for licking the lips, except men are more likely to misinterpret this move than women are. (And who can blame them? When a female character in a film wants to catch the hero's attention, what does she do? She starts licking her lips.) The bottom line is that if you want to give a man a definite signal that you're interested in him, you can't miss with this move. You can roll the tip of your tongue all the way around your top and bottom lip, or you can just give the top lip a good lick.

Be aware that provocative lip-licking sends a very strong message about what you're interested in. (This is worlds away from the wide-eyed harmless approach.) He'll think you're up for much more than a casual, get-to-know-you-better conversation.

Want to Win Him Over?

One really easy way to show a man you're interested is to smile at him while you're speaking to him. A genuine smile, one that shows happiness or joy, curves your lips upwards and crinkles the corners of your eyes. A fake smile simply pulls the corners of the lips to the side and doesn't rise up through the face to engage the eye muscles.

People usually can't help but like people who like them – and smiling is a simple way to say, 'I find you really interesting. I want to know more about you.' So go on and grin at him, but don't overdo it. People who wear perpetual smiles on their faces tend to appear nervous or as though they're faking it.

Move Over

Once you've mastered the art of flirting with your facial features, it's time to pull out the big guns: the personal-space–invading tactic. When executed carefully and correctly, he won't know what hit him – he'll only know that he likes it (and you). Again, these are gestures that are best practised at home first, and even once you've perfected them, use them sparingly. Crowding someone for a short time is all right; bumping into him all night long will only make him think you have vertigo.

Defining Personal Space

So what do people mean when they say 'personal space', anyway? Are there set measurements that prevent men and women from occupying a given amount of the same square footage? No, there are no laws (at least not yet), only general recommendations, which include:

- Professional areas: if you work in an office, take a look around and estimate the amount of space between desks. Most offices try to put at least six feet between work areas.
- Common areas: if you're at the supermarket or walking down the street, you should have at least three feet between yourself and the person nearest to you. This advice also carries over to certain meetings and formal gatherings, especially where the people you're chatting with are merely acquaintances.

- Friendly interactions: when you're hanging out with your friends, maintain a space of one to three feet, depending on how well you know them.
- Intimate interactions: 12 inches are all you need between you and the one you love (or the one you think you might love).

Obviously, the better you know someone, the less personal space you need to maintain between the two of you. But when you want to get to know someone, the trick is to cut down on that space without making it insanely obvious.

Generally speaking, men need more personal space than women do. For example, it's not unusual to see two female friends sitting or standing less than a foot apart, but you'll rarely see two men positioned this closely to each other.

Moving in Closer

Stealing someone's personal space is easy, given the right set of circumstances. A standing room only meeting, a crowded party, a packed club … these are all great spots for sidling up to someone. Still, you can't just attach yourself to his hip. Are there any ways to sidle in a sneaky manner?

Here's a move that allows you to get into his personal space without making him feel as though you've taken up residence on the front of his body. You'll need to have about a foot of air between the two of you. As you're talking, slowly angle your body to the side, towards him. (Pretend you're shifting your weight on to that leg.) Now take the arm that's closest to him and put it on your hip, letting it bump up against him. Bingo. Your torso is all of six inches from him now, you're actually touching him with the arm on your hip, the pressure of eye contact has been reduced (because you're on an angle now, you can naturally look off to his side without appearing to be uninterested in him), and he doesn't feel walled off by your presence. The angle has opened up some space in front of him while eliminating it in another area. So you're close – and yet, he doesn't realise how close. (Smooth move, sister.)

Tiny Touches

Touching is a definite intrusion of personal space. Men tend to accept touches from women; women tend to be less accepting of touches from casual male acquaintances. Touches are usually viewed as a sort of nurturing move, so they simply seem to be more natural and genuine if they come from a woman.

Nurturing is fine, but what if you want your touches to say, 'Hey, this touching business is fun! Let's do more of it!' What's the secret? Well, you can go two ways here: you can shoot for subtlety or you can go for broke. There is no in-between.

Subtle Touches

If time isn't of the essence, subtle touches are a good way of breaking the ice between yourself and the chap you've set your sights on. If you're sitting next to each other, let your leg bump his. Once you start getting really comfortable, let your leg rest right up against his. If you're standing, reach out and touch his arm while you tell him about the most incredible thing that's ever happened to you.

Touches on the arm or leg are one thing; touching his face is moving into fairly intimate territory, which is a great way to get your point across – but only if you have a legitimate reason to put a hand on his head. You can pretend to brush an eyelash off his cheek or ask to have a closer look at the diamond stud in his ear. Just make sure to use a gentle, feminine touch (which, again, shows him you're harmless).

Going for Broke

Once you've sworn off subtlety, any touch will do. Rubbing your hands all over his body sends a very obvious message. And if you know without a doubt this guy is completely into you, you're venturing into safe territory. If you have any reservations, though, it's best to start off with something a little less obvious. There's nothing more humiliating than being reprimanded for crossing the line.

Play Up Your Assets

Women who are looking to woo men do well to show off their assets, and not just the obvious ones. Take stock of your other feminine features, like your neck, shoulders, back and arms. Well, this might not be all it takes, but most men find toned arms attractive, even if they don't realise it. The same goes for pretty

THE ONLY BOOK YOU'LL EVER NEED Body Language

shoulders, a flawless back and a graceful neck. These features accentuate the differences between the sexes: men want to have big arms, big shoulders, big necks and big backs. These features are usually smaller on a woman, which again says to the man, 'I'm little and harmless and I need you to protect me!'

Of course, women don't actually need men to protect them these days, at least not in the same ways that men protected their women (from wild animals and marauders) centuries ago. Still, a lot of body language is based on instinct, so many men are drawn to women who are smaller and (supposedly) weaker than they are.

Now, not every woman is blessed with toned arms and shoulders, a graceful-looking back, and a swanlike neck. But take a good look at these upper-body areas in your mirror and find a way to show off what you do have. Display your lovely arms in sleeveless tops; wear a backless dress on your next date; show off your neck if it rivals Audrey Hepburn's.

Full of Grace

Earlier in this chapter, you read about playing up your most feminine features (eyes, mouth, shoulders, arms – whatever you've got, use it!) to land the man you're after. This includes learning to be graceful in areas where you may not be – like walking. Pigeon-toed adults tend to look childish, sloppy and weak. People who walk with their toes pointing out to the side look uptight. You want those toes to be straight ahead when you walk (if they point outwards a little bit, that's fine), and don't scuff your shoes along the ground. Again, that makes you look childish and sloppy.

What about those women who walk around looking like they're playing pinball with their hips? Do men like this move, or do they see it as a flirtatious ploy? Well, most men seem to take notice of swaying hips because it's an instinctual reaction. You see, because men are biologically programmed to find a fertile woman, they're also programmed to check out the woman's pelvis (which is where she'll be carrying his children) to make sure it's up to scratch, so to speak. Women, meanwhile, are biologically programmed to show off their pelvic region. Learning to shake it can't hurt your chances, but don't go crazy with it – a little shimmy goes a long way.

That's good advice in general for when you begin using your body-language tricks to land yourself a date: take it easy at first. Using overly coy (or just too much) body language doesn't guarantee that you'll bag yourself a quality man. Think of this as training. You're in the first division of flirting right now, working on the moves that suit you best. When you're ready, you'll get that call and can move up into the premiership.

Move On

Knowing how to work your body language won't guarantee that the guy you're interested in will fall madly in love with you – or even ask you out. Using effective body language simply puts your message out there and gets you noticed. There are many other factors – personalities, schedules, influences of other people – that can affect how and if a relationship will proceed. There are some body language cues that let you know that he's just not interested, including:

- Really bad eye contact: poor eye contact can sometimes be chalked up to poor social skills. An avoidance of eye contact (i.e. he doesn't even bother to look your way while you're speaking to him) is bad news in any relationship.
- The blank face: you're talking to him and there isn't any sign of life on his face – no smile, no frown, no eye contact.
- The step-back: if he takes a step back when you approach him, he may not want you inside his personal space.
- The flinch: you try to sneak a peek at his earring and he quickly pulls away from you. Again, he's defending his personal space.

Some men are just plain shy, which can make it difficult to tell whether he's uninterested or simply nervous. But even a timid man will look your way now and again if he finds you charming, and more importantly, he won't react to your touch as though it were a chemical burn.

Now, the opposite actions are, of course, good news for you. In other words, if he's making an effort to smile and maintain eye contact or he's accepting of your invasion into his personal space, there's a good chance he's into you. Cross your fingers, remember what you've learned in this chapter, and proceed with cautious optimism.

Guidance for Guys

When it comes to luring a woman into your lair, are there certain rules of protocol – or worse, etiquette – that must be followed? Is behaving like Mr Nice Guy the way to a girl's heart or, deep down, do all chicks want a rebel for a boyfriend? Well, it may sound complicated, but all women are different. Some like the good guys, some like the bad boys, some like 'em somewhere in-between. The first step to winning her over is convincing her that you have a few social skills – something that's easy to do with your non-verbal communication.

Chapter 18

Eye Saw You First

If you've read any of the chapters in this book dealing directly with eye contact (most notably Chapter 7), then you already know how important it is to maintain an appropriate level of ocular interaction with whoever you're speaking to. The rule of thumb is that you look into the person's eyes for a few seconds before looking off to the side or down towards the ground for a few seconds; then you repeat the pattern. By staring non-stop into someone else's eyes, you may come across as intimidating (or slightly crazy); by seldom looking into her eyes, you appear uninterested.

These are the rules for polite conversation. Do they apply when you're trying to secure a date with a girl you've just met? Yes – and no.

The Art of the Chat Up

There's one theory that the early stages of flirting and dating are no time to be polite. There's a lot of competition and little time to spare, you believe, and the more eye contact you can make – with as many girls as possible – the better. It's like deep-sea fishing: If you put out enough lines, you're bound to make a catch. (Such a romantic you are!)

Different women are attracted to different personality types. If you're a nice guy who's trying to attract a woman who likes bad boys, you may not be able to win her over, no matter how skilled you are at wielding your 'come to me' body language.

While this theory will probably prove to be successful, it's probably not as successful as you think, at least percentage-wise. If you spend the night making eyes at 20 different girls and your friend spends the evening concentrating his efforts on only two or three and you both go home with one phone number, you've done seven times the amount of work he's done.

'Hey! That's not fair!' you're thinking. Why was he as successful as you when he's obviously not as dedicated to the craft as you are? He was showing genuine interest in a chosen few, while you were putting yourself out there as some sort of gift to any female who might glance your way.

Call it a study in subtlety, but women tend to pick up on this type of thing. Girls don't like to feel as though they're expendable, that they could be replaced by any other female. So if you're making flirty eye contact with every woman you see and still going home alone, that could be why. Slow down, pick a couple of candidates from the crowd, and concentrate your efforts there.

The Stare-Down

There's polite eye contact, there's more-than-polite eye contact – and then there's crossing-the-line eye contact, which will be discussed a little later. As you've read, polite eye contact involves looking into her eyes for a few seconds before looking away and repeating the process. This is fine and well in casual conversations, but if you want to express a romantic interest in a woman, you're going to have to use more eye power. That's right – pull out the prolonged eye contact.

Perhaps you're the kind of person who despises the awkwardness of eye contact, so you regularly look at your shoes or at the top of a person's head when you're speaking to her. This isn't going to cut it in the dating world. You need to look into her eyes and hold that gaze. Count to ten before you look away. If you're really enamoured of this woman, keep on looking, but do be conscious of taking a break every now and then. Look down or off to the side and then bring your eyes back up to hers.

Continuous, unbroken eye contact is something that makes most people feel uncomfortable. If she looks frightened or as though she's planning an escape route, that's a pretty good indication that you should cut back on the eye contact a bit.

Holding eye contact for more than just a few seconds tells her two things: you can't take your eyes off of her, and you're genuinely interested in what she has to say. Now, in the event you're using extended eye contact to draw her towards you – in other words, you haven't met her, but you're giving her the eye across the room – the former message still applies. You're showing your interest in her. Once you make your way over to her, remember to use eye contact that says, 'I made the right decision by coming to talk to you.'

Put Those Eyes Away!

It's fine to use more eye contact than usual when you're talking to someone you find particularly interesting, as long as you don't overdo it and scare the poor girl. There's another instance in which prolonged eye contact crosses the line – when you're so focused on her body that you don't bother looking at her face when you're talking.

Staring at a woman's chest from across the room is probably not going to win you many points. And looking at her chest while you're actually speaking to her is going to get you downgraded into her pile of 'not a chance' men in a hurry.

The lesson to be learned here: take a quick look; then bring your eyes up to eye level – and keep them there.

Shaping Your Eyes

Eye contact is important in any conversation, but so is the shape of the eye. Squinting, drooping eyes simply don't look interested. An open eye shows that you're into the conversation and not daydreaming about your golf outing tomorrow afternoon.

At the very least, use a polite amount of eye contact when you're talking to the object of your affection. If you're truly smitten, use prolonged eye contact. What you don't want to do is look everywhere but into her eyes. This says 'I'm biding my time till someone more interesting comes along.'

Do the eyebrows communicate anything worthwhile in the area of love and romance? They work as a unit with the eyes. Raised eyebrows are used to drive a message home – it's almost like saying, 'Please believe what I'm saying.' Furrowed brows make you appear tense or angry, so if you have a habit of knitting your eyebrows together, relax them.

A wide-open eye paired with a relaxed or raised brow line makes you appear interested in the other person. Practise this look in the mirror; you'll be surprised how making little adjustments (opening the eye just a bit more than you usually do, for example) can make your entire face look more awake and alert.

The Best You

Finding a way into a woman's good graces begins with presenting yourself in the right light. While some women are naturally drawn to timid men, many women like to see some show of confidence. You don't have to be 6ft tall to look sure of yourself. You just have to know how to pull yourself up – literally – and put your best assets on display.

Attention!

First things first: how's your posture? If you're a natural sloucher, you're going to have to work on standing straight. Put your shoulders back and hold your chest slightly out. Now walk. Have a look at your feet. Are they moving in a straightforward fashion or are your toes pointing inwards (making you look weak) – or outwards (making you look feminine)? Work on setting them straight. When you're talking with a girl, should you stand to attention to show you're paying attention, with your shoulders thrown back, or should you act a little more relaxed by, say, sticking one hand in your pocket? The choice is yours and it depends on how comfortable you are in the situation. Just know that while it's a good idea to walk with a straight spine, maintaining that stance all night could make you look too sure of yourself. It's all right to slouch every now and then, as long as this isn't your main posture.

Limbs

When you're talking to a woman, what are you supposed to do with your arms and legs? Is it ok to get really comfortable by crossing the legs at the knee or by spreading them wide so you can stretch your back? It's best not to get too comfortable while you're trying to cosy up to a girl. Sloppy posture implies you're not on your best behaviour, which in turn implies this attempted pick-up isn't that meaningful to you.

As for the arms, it's all right to make them comfy during a long conversation. You can cross them loosely, hang on to your drink with one, whatever strikes your fancy. Just don't hold your arms off to the side too much while you're talking, no matter how wild the story is. That's a sign of aggression, which can be a real turn-off for some women.

Getting Friendly

Man cannot date by eye contact alone. There's obviously much more to winning over the woman you have in your sights. Women use friendly little gestures to show their interest in other people. Men are much less likely to do this, perhaps for fear of seeming too friendly. But is there a way to pull this off without becoming known as the creepy geezer who's always touching all the women? There is, but before you learn it, you must dedicate yourself to repeating the mantra, 'Less is more, less is more, less is more …'

There's a very fine line between friendly, barely there touches and inappropriate touches, so pay attention here and keep yourself on the dateable side of that line.

Touching Basics

Women almost always initiate friendly touches by lightly smacking your arm as you speak or admiring your shirt as they rub the fabric. How can you possibly turn the tables here without coming on too strong? Very carefully. Men really have to have a reason – a good reason – to initiate the friendly touch.

Buy her a drink and let your hand rub hers as you hand it over. Sit next to her and let your knee or your foot touch hers. If you're both non-dancers watching everyone else shake their things on the dance floor, give her a little nudge now and then to point out what a fool your best friend is making of himself.

Until you know a woman well, keep your friendly touches to a minimum. Men who touch too much are often thought of as a little creepy and predatory. She'll understand the intention behind your reserved contact.

It's these seemingly meaningless touches that carry a lot of weight. Obviously, this can't be your only move – you have to pair it with eye contact, proper body positioning, the right stance (all of which you'll read about in this chapter) – but a well-placed touch or two could be the thing that makes her really take notice of your attempts.

In the Workplace

Is there ever an appropriate way to extend a friendly touch at work? Not in this age of harassment accusations and industrial tribunals. If there's a woman in your workplace who drives you crazy, refrain from touching her except in the most necessary ways – handing her the stapler, passing her important documents, helping her up after she's broken her heel and taken a tumble. Otherwise, keep those hands to yourself. And don't try to sneak touches in – don't give her a hug when she looks blue; no neck-rubs when she feels tense. Even if she doesn't mind, your boss might. And if she does mind the unsolicited massages, you're going to find yourself in a world of trouble.

You might be disappointed, because you just read that friendly little touches are the way to cross the line from friend to potential mate. How can you be successful if you can't use every tool at your disposal? You'll have to do it with your eye contact and your body angling, and by using your winning personality. Take her on a date and then put your nudges and lingering touches to work.

Turn, Turn, Turn

It'll do you no good to make friendly chitchat with a girl if you're facing in the opposite direction. But even if you're facing her, putting four feet of space between the two of you will send the wrong kind of message – one that says, 'I'm kind of particular about having a lot of personal space.' How is she supposed to imagine herself in any sort of situation with you if you're doing your best to keep your distance?

Find Your Angle

Angling the body simply means positioning it in a certain direction. When you want to show your interest in another person, you angle your body towards her. For example, let's say you're in a bookshop perusing the cookbooks. When you pick one up, the girl standing next to you says, 'You'll love that one – it's perfect for single guys.' You ask how she would know this, as she's obviously not a bachelor, and she tells you that she wrote the book. You're immediately interested in what this girl does for a living, and without even realizing it, you've turned to face her and are chitchatting away about slow cookers and silicone spatulas. If you hadn't been interested, you might have turned your head briefly to acknowledge her input, but you would have kept your body angled towards the bookshelf.

Tilting your head to the side when someone else is talking is a form of angling. This shows that you're listening intently. Combining the angling of the body with the tilt of the head sends a powerful message: 'I am completely enthralled by you. Please date me.'

You can angle your legs, your shoulders and your head – and yes, you can use them all at the same time, but let's start off slowly here by talking about just one body part. Imagine you're at a casual get-together, sitting with a group in the living room. The girl you're interested in is seated to your right, but you can't really turn your entire body her way, because it would shut out the rest of the group. Remain facing forwards, but let your lower body wander over towards the right. If you're comfortable crossing your legs, that's an easy way to accomplish this move. If you're not a leg-crosser, then allow your right leg to stretch over towards her.

Space Case

In general, strangers try to keep about three feet of personal space between one another. Friends maintain about 18 inches of personal space between them. At these distances, people can be near one another without feeling as though they're being crowded. When someone steps into your personal space, you feel it. Depending on the person who's just crossed your imaginary line, you might feel pretty excited about the whole thing or you might have the urge to establish a new area of personal space – far, far away.

You need to know how to enter a girl's personal space without coming across as overly aggressive. If you're in a crowded club or party, your circumstances have pretty much taken care of this for you. In fact, you could argue that plenty of couples end up dating not because they went looking for each other, but because they were forced to be near one another in a crowded space. Proximity is a powerful thing.

Once you find yourself within 18 inches of your woman, work that body language. This is your opportunity, and you may not get it again. Make eye contact. Smile. Strike up a conversation. Tilt your head to show you're listening. If she uses friendly touches (even if she hits your arm when you tell a joke), you're doing all right. Keep it up.

If you're working in an area that's relatively uncrowded, like a dinner party, you're dealing with a whole different ball game. You have to be a real artist to move into her personal space under these conditions without being too obvious about it. A good way to accomplish this is to time your trip to the bar or the hors d'oeuvres tray so that you cross paths with her.

Space Invaders

What if you're on the receiving end of an invasion of space? Should you automatically take that to mean that this girl is dying to get to know you? Usually, it's a good sign when a girl wants to get close to you, but there may be extenuating circumstances – such as in the crowded club, where she can't be anywhere except where she's standing. She's physically stuck, so you'll have to take stock of her other non-verbal cues to determine whether she's interested or simply tolerating you until a path to the ladies opens up. You know what to look for – eye contact, body angling, a genuine smile, friendly little touches, wide eyes, tilting of the head. If she's working two or three of these moves, things are looking pretty good for you. Even if she does follow that open path to the powder room – she'll be back.

It's easy to find yourself in close quarters with someone else when you're both pouring a drink or filling a plate. Be natural in your approach – ask her to pass you a lime or a napkin – before you launch into small talk. Use your charming body language to show her your interest and to keep her interested in talking to you.

Bust a Move, Not Your Ankle

You've been in this situation more times than you care to count: you're working your body language on a girl, you're making some headway, you're feeling pretty confident, and then she goes off to dance with her girlfriends. And while she's dancing, some stud moves in on her, grooving left and right, and before you know what's happened, she's sitting with him, suddenly looking very attached.

If you hate to dance, are your chances of meeting a girl so seriously diminished that you should hang it up right now and devote your life to your dog? Relax. All hope is not lost. You don't have to imitate a pop star on the dance floor just to score a date with someone. But maybe you need to understand the concept behind dancing.

Dancing actually dates back to primitive rituals, when people would dance to express emotion or as an offering to their gods. These days, dance is a way of putting yourself on display, of saying, 'I'm here, I'm moving it, and – wow! Look at how virile I am!' (Important note: do not repeat those words on the dance floor.) Prospective mates are looking on, evaluating your fitness, the execution of your routine (no, not really), and your potential as a partner.

So again you ask, 'Must I dance?' Let's take a look at the facts here: a lot of girls love to dance. Dancing is a great way to move into a girl's personal space in a legitimate manner, thus opening up a whole new avenue for apres-dance conversation.

Dancing can't hurt your chances of meeting someone – unless you dance in such a terrible manner that you stand out for all the wrong reasons. Dance in front of the mirror before you debut your moves in a club, or consider taking a class or two of hip-hop or street dance.

When to Give It Up

Even when you're armed with this sort of knowledge, things aren't always going to work out between you and certain girls. If you're a real Casanova, this might only happen to you occasionally; if you're like most men, it happens more often. You just can't create attraction where there isn't any, no matter how hard you try. What are the signs that a girl just isn't into you and you should pack it in and move on?

Bad Eye Contact

When a girl is interested, she'll use her eyes to let you know. She'll make lots of eye contact, bat her lashes and look at you while she angles her head in different ways. When you talk, she'll be focusing on you, not on the people walking by, nor on the guy over by the door. If her eyes aren't into the conversation, she isn't either.

Keeping Her Distance

If you take a step closer and she takes a step back, that's not a good sign. If you move over a seat to be closer to her and she asks you to move back, that's not a good sign. If she could sit down in the empty seat next to you but chooses to sit much farther away, that's not good. Basically, if this girl is doing everything in her power to keep you out of her personal space, she either hasn't noticed you and your intentions or she wants nothing to do with you.

Reserved Body Language

Some girls are naturally more reserved than others, so you can't always depend on her using lots of friendly touches to let you know she likes you. Still, there should be an element of relaxation between the two of you. If she has her arms and legs tightly crossed as you're trying to break the ice and those limbs aren't budging even after you've used your funniest lines on her, then she's probably not interested. Keep trying if you must, but if she doesn't loosen up, you're not going to get her number (not her real number, anyway). And really, why would you want it? Think about it: you've gone a step beyond the efforts of other men by taking the time to learn about non-verbal communication. That's actually quite respectful – it certainly beats trying to draw a girl's attention by acting the fool, and it's also far better than standing around trying to look cool when you're actually bored out of your mind.

If you're not getting anywhere with your target girl, don't lose hope. Use your body-language reading skills to determine which woman might be a better prospect (remember – look beyond the clothing). You should be able to pick out a live wire, a shy type, or a tall, cool one just by watching her interact with other people. Your body language will tell her what she needs to know – whether it's that you're sincere, a little nutty, or the strong, silent type. If she's really a good match, you have nothing to worry about by simply being yourself.

Body Language Online

Meeting people online can be a boon for many reasons – it's easy to find like-minded people; you can log on at any time; you can narrow your options by filling out a simple questionnaire. There's another reason some people like to use the internet to initiate relationships: if you're a victim of your own body language (i.e. people tend to see you as shy or insecure, even though you feel like a confident, stable person), sometimes it's easier to get to know other people via electronic means.

Chapter 19

The Talkative Type

Most people go looking for online friends who share an interest, like an undying devotion to a specific band or the desire to find a soulmate. Websites like Facebook and Twitter have made online socializing commonplace, but they're far from the only forums out there. No matter what your intent, no matter what your interest, you'll be able to find some type of message board on which to post your thoughts and interact with friends and strangers alike. The qualifying factor here, of course, is that once you chat with someone online, she becomes an instant friend – for as long as neither of you displays any off-putting behaviours.

Safety First

First, a word of warning: for the sake of this discussion, we're going to assume that you're an adult presenting yourself as an adult in your online discussions. Why the disclaimer? Adult internet predators often use texting shorthand and online lingo either to present themselves as children or to seem 'cool' to the teens and kids they're talking to online. Adolescents are at highest risk for being lured by a predator. Adults are usually less impulsive, wiser and more cautious than teens – in other words, less trusting and more wary of strangers – so are at a fairly low risk. Of course, it's always good to keep your personal information (real name, address, credit card and pin numbers) to yourself, especially when you're talking to someone you don't know well or haven't met in person.

What Your Typing Says about You

What does online communication say about personality? Let's say you're chatting with two friends, Maria and Emily. Maria's messages are always very simply written – in fact, you get a lot of one- or two-word answers, almost always in texting shorthand. (CUL8R is her favourite sign-off.) Emily, on the other hand, writes long messages with every single word spelled out in its entirety. (She prefers to end her messages, 'See you later.') If you had never met these two in person, what conclusions would you draw from their typed messages?

- Maria is young, more into the instant-message jargon, and is probably talking to three other people while she's online with you.

- Emily seems to be over 30. She's either less in tune with the texting shortcuts or such a purist in her writing that she refuses to use them.

Of course, these are generalizations. Emily might be a brainy 22-year-old who thinks shorthand text is immature. Maria, meanwhile, could be a 45-year-old mum whose teenagers have taught her all about texting shorthand. However, the generalizations tend to be true in this case: aside from the predators you read about earlier, older people usually type it all out; younger people use shortcuts because that's how they've learned to communicate online.

Finding a GR8 M8

So what does this mean to you? Should you use more or fewer shortcuts, and why does it matter in the end? Let's say you're a thirty-something lady looking for a mate in his mid-to-late twenties. It wouldn't hurt you to incorporate a few abbreviations into your online communications, like:

- LOL: Laughing out loud
- OMG: Oh my goodness!
- BM&Y: Between me and you
- CYO: See you online
- F2F: Face to face
- BF: Boyfriend
- GF: Girlfriend
- :-x : Kiss

There are literally hundreds of abbreviations making the rounds in cyberspace. Feel free to use a few, but just don't go crazy.

And what's the danger of not using any shortcuts? You might appear uptight, out of the loop – in other words, old. (Don't panic – this is merely a perception of your non-verbal communication, one that you can easily change.)

Now let's flip this situation around: if you're a younger guy looking for a slightly older mate, play up your maturity factor and start typing some of your words out. The danger of using too many shortcuts is that your message may be nothing more than a source of confusion to your reader. If she can't decode your message, your relationship will be over before it has begun. One word of warning: if you're not known for your ability at spelling, use your spell checker or dictionary. Consistent misspellings scream, 'I'm really 12.'

Many secondary school teachers and university professors have recently complained about the amount of online lingo students are using in essays, though some progressive educators believe that this is simply an adaptation of the language and no cause for concern.

So what have you learned from this section? The mode of communication – shorthand or longhand – along with correct spelling tells people more about you than you might think. If you find you're not attracting the kind of people you'd hoped to at the onset of your journey into online dating, change your typing.

Keyboard Cronies

You might recall from earlier chapters that experts estimate that about two-thirds of face-to-face communication is non-verbal. As online friendships blossom and strengthen every day, perhaps you're thinking that there must be something to eliminating most of those confusing and conflicting non-verbal gestures and simply dealing with words. Is this the way of future relationships?

Turn-Ons, Turn-Offs

When you're working within the parameters of online communication, what types of non-verbal behaviour draw people to you and what types of behaviour send people straight to the 'Block User' button? Online chatters:

- Tend to search out people with some common interest, whether it's the same profession, living in the same area or participating in a particular activity.
- Respond well to posters who show compassion and/or 'listening' skills.
- React negatively to posters who dominate the conversation and/or consistently throw out nasty or negative comments.

- Tend to respond negatively to rude or inappropriate suggestions or questions (such as someone asking 'What's your bra size?' on a political message board).

What do you notice here? These are the same behaviours that tend to attract – and repel – people when they meet face to face. If you tend to dominate the conversation in real life, for example, that can carry over into your cyberspace relationships. The same goes for someone who tends to be quiet and meek. (You might be called a 'lurker' online, for example, if the only posts you contribute to a message board are comments to the moderator. This is a sign of someone who likes to be on the edge of a conversation but not in it.) The good news is that because you're not dealing with eye contact and posturing, you can easily fix your personality flaws. If you talk way too much in real life, try holding your tongue (in other words, sit on your hands) once in a while when you're online. If you tend to keep other people at a distance, try jumping into the conversation and voicing your opinions. The positive feedback you get from trying something new online might just inspire you to make similar changes in your face-to-face relationships.

You Win Some, You Lose Some

People who are into networking on message boards and chat rooms swear that they develop online relationships faster and more easily than in person, perhaps because the very things that might make initial meetings awkward – personal space, uncomfortable eye contact, long pauses in conversation – are absent from the picture. The problem is that without body language, you might have a hard time determining if someone is truly sincere or if she's just presenting a very carefully edited version of herself. It's easier to tell in person, for example, if someone is lying or being manipulative because you can evaluate her eye contact, her stance, the angle of her body and even the tone of her voice.

While meeting online can be a great starting point for a new relationship, your actual meeting with this person could be very different if that person behaves in unexpected ways.

Meeting an online friend in person may not be the experience you expect, for many different (and unanticipated) reasons. Ali is a woman in her 40s who regularly checks in with her online groups and has many internet friends. Last year, Ali started chatting with a woman named Tara, whose husband was terminally ill. Since Ali's husband had suffered through a terminal illness just a couple of years earlier, she and Tara formed an instant and intense bond.

Several months after Tara's husband died, the women planned to meet for a golf weekend (it was their interest in the sport that had brought them together in the first place). Ali says, 'Things just seemed to change. She was distant and guarded. The whole weekend was just awkward, nothing like our conversations had been up to that point.'

Ali thinks that she was a flesh-and-blood reminder of the saddest time in Tara's life, something Tara may have begun to realise before their trip together. Looking back, Ali realises that there were chats where Tara was very blunt, using just one- or two-word replies instead of her usual paragraph-long responses. There were also stretches of several days when Tara wasn't online at all (a big change from her previous habits). Had they been neighbours instead of online friends, Ali probably would have seen a big difference in Tara's non-verbal gestures and sensed her friend's change of heart before their ill-fated holiday. But this hasn't changed Ali's view of cyber friendships. 'It would have played out this way no matter what,' she says. 'I just would have realised it sooner if she lived down the street from me.'

Picture Perfect

Earlier in this chapter, you read about how your personality comes through in your typed messages. Now you'll learn how to present the best image of yourself online, which is especially important if you're considering using an internet dating service.

It's true that you don't have to post your picture on dating websites, but if you don't put your mug up on the screen, then you aren't going to attract a lot of attention. In this case, it makes sense to let the world see you. But what if you aren't very photogenic and you're afraid that posting your photo or video clip will only do more harm than good?

There are plenty of ways to adjust the controls on the pictures, and still come out looking like yourself. Angle, lighting and the colour of the room around you can all play a part in making you look fab or freakish.

People with pale skin, prominent features, or very thin or very round faces tend to suffer the heartbreak of bad pictures. If you're terrified of how your image might turn out, consider hiring a professional to take your picture. If you don't want to spend the money on headshots, there are a few precautions you can take at home:

- Choose clothing that complements your complexion, giving you a glow. Whether it's red, purple or green, wear it in your picture or video clip.
- Find the right angle. If you have a large nose, for example, have your picture taken at a downward angle. Film your clip from a straight-on angle. This won't eliminate it, but it will help to de-emphasise it.
- Use natural light if possible. It's flattering to most skin types. (Pale people, especially, don't photograph well in fluorescent lighting.)
- Smile. A genuine grin is your best asset when trying to attract quality attention.

Once you've got the angle and lighting covered, you can focus on putting a little body language on display. Do you want to appear:

- Sultry? Pout those lips a bit and angle your head down or to the side.
- Innocent? Widen your eyes and show off your great big smile.
- Cool? Tilt your head back a little, lower your eyelids a smidgen and pout your lips.
- Fun? Big, open-mouthed smile, as though you're laughing.

No matter which direction you go in, try to keep your expression as natural as possible. The camera will catch your vibe; there's no need to overdo it. Ta-da! You've produced an image that captures the essence of who you truly are, and whether your potential suitors realise it or not, what they'll be responding to is your non-verbal gestures.

Video Star

Video-sharing websites (like YouTube) are hugely popular because they allow you to share clips with friends and family who can be next door or halfway around the world. After you upload your own video, you can click around and watch the presentations submitted by complete strangers. Some are amusing, some are disturbing, but there's one thing they all have in common: they're out there – for the rest of eternity, as far as anyone knows. The moral of the story: before you post any video (or picture, for that matter) online, make sure you're OK with the idea of its never-ending circulation – even if you're not putting it in a public domain.

Sneak Peek for Employers

Video CVs are sometimes used to screen candidates for job openings before a company invites them for a sit-down interview. In this type of video, you have a great opportunity to express your confidence and enthusiasm for the position. Follow the tips you read earlier for perfecting your image, and then bring your business body language into the picture: make eye contact with the camera, sit up straight, smile every now and then, and make sure you're not displaying any signs of nervousness (nervous shifting in your seat, for example, or clasping your hands too tightly, or touching your face).

Digital videos are a wonderful way to show your body language to someone you're interested in, but they're easily copied and forwarded around the internet. Don't put anything out there that you want kept private.

If you have the chance to send this type of CV to a prospective employer, think of it as a gift – you have the chance to edit your first impression! Once you get that invitation for a real interview, you can feel confident that someone in Human Resources liked what she saw in your video, and that will help you project your self-assurance in person.

Reading Minds Online

Throughout this chapter you've read about the benefits and drawbacks of online communication. The lack of face-to-face interaction can be a good thing (when it helps to lower your inhibitions) or a bad thing (when you can't tell if someone's being untruthful or manipulative). Modern technology may be able to rectify this situation once and for all. Researchers at the University of Cambridge have developed what they call 'mind-reading machines'. Don't worry – no one's going to come up behind you, point a ray gun in your direction and read your thoughts. This 'machine' is actually software that analyses facial expressions in order to gather information about a person's state of mind.

This could open a whole new door in the world of computer interactions! Imagine you're talking to a friend on a web cam. She's backing out of the plans the two of you had made for the evening, claiming she has a sinus infection. She doesn't appear to be ill, so you'll just have to take her word for it – or will you? The mind-reading software would allow you to analyse her facial expressions – and her sincerity – in the comfort of your own home.

The main goal of the University of Cambridge's 'mind-reading' software development is to help parents and caretakers understand the intent of autistic individuals, who are often unable to express themselves verbally (and are also often limited in their non-verbal expressions).

In trials, the software has proven to be fairly accurate, which is good news for anyone who's concerned with how we're all going to connect with each other in this increasingly technological world. Further research is going into developing a system to analyse the rest of the body's non-verbal communication. The goal is to develop a program that can link into avatars (an internet user's representation of himself in the form of an icon or model), which will then show how you're sitting, standing, angling and so on, while chatting online.

The increasing use of technology leads many people to fear that we're all going to end up isolated, staring at our computer screens instead of interacting with other people. But things certainly don't seem to be going that way. According to the Millenials (also known as Gen Y, YGen or the Internet Generation – anyone born between 1981 and 1995), meeting new friends and keeping up with old ones (not to mention making and changing plans) is much easier done online than by calling or seeking them out in person. Cyberspace is a virtual playground where you can meet new best friends, love interests or someone who may turn into an instant regret. Do log on and be yourself, but also be careful and remember that certain personality traits can make the long trip through cyberspace.

Minimizing Body Language Mistakes

By now you know that it's important to view body language in a certain context; that is, you can't pick out one gesture and use it to pin an underlying motive on someone. And since many non-verbal cues indicate different messages depending on the circumstances, it's unwise to paint everyone's behaviour with the same brush. However, try as you might, it's often difficult to recognise, let alone decipher, a confusing verbal/non-verbal combination in real life. This chapter will cover some major areas of misunderstanding in the hope of heading them off at the pass.

Chapter **20**

Content and Context

Environment plays a huge role in how body language is expressed and interpreted. When people feel free to express themselves without reserve, you can get a great 'read' on their non-verbal gestures. For the most part, when those same people are forced into a more conservative setting, their behaviour adapts to the surroundings. But this isn't always the case. (Picture the colleague who takes his fresher-party behaviour into the conference room, for example.) What are you supposed to make of people who don't adjust their behaviour to their surroundings?

Letting Loose

When you head out for a night on the town with your friends, it's a good bet that your body language is as relaxed and as uninhibited as it's ever going to be. You're touching people, invading their personal space, smiling, angling your head to look coy, batting your eyelashes and puckering up – in a friendly way, of course.

When you head back to work on Monday, most of these behaviours won't be coming with you. There's simply a time and a place for wild displays of giddiness and enthusiasm, and then there are settings that are far more reserved. Granted, some workplaces are more relaxed than others, but for the most part, there's an expectation for employees to behave in a professional manner.

Rein It In

But let's say you're one of those people who doesn't believe in toning yourself down for anyone. What other people see is what they get, and you're not ashamed to be loud, brash and very expressive, no matter where you are. There's certainly something to be celebrated about having a free spirit, and if your lack of inhibition has served you well, then more power to you. However, many people who refuse to adjust their body language to their environment find themselves on the outside looking in.

Bosses expect employees to conform to a certain standard. Colleagues want to know that the people they're in the trenches with are professional enough to get the job done. Everyone in the company wants to avoid offending clients. These types of relationships rely on successful verbal and non-verbal behaviour.

When it comes time for promotions and pay rises, everything about you is up for evaluation, including your body language. If you're making people uncomfortable with your non-verbal cues or if your behaviour is a huge distraction to the staff, then you're a liability to the company.

Some examples of distracting or offensive body language in the workplace:

- Ogling members of the opposite sex, which is just plain lecherous.
- Standing too close to colleagues or clients invades their personal space and makes them uncomfortable.
- Constantly touching other people is also an invasion of personal space.
- Continuous yawning or sighing makes you appear bored. These are also 'contagious' behaviours. (Before you know it, everyone in the office is half-asleep.)
- Foot tapping or finger drumming can be very distracting to others around you.
- Lots of self-touches – to the nose, to the eyes, to the mouth – make people queasy. No one wants to touch your hand when it's been all over your mucous membranes.
- Constant throat clearing or loud, booming laughter can also be highly irritating, especially in close quarters.

So should you sell your soul to the corporation and become an unmoving, unfeeling zombie? Not necessarily; just consider toning down any inappropriate behaviour – and then note if others are responding to you in a more positive manner. A small change in your non-verbal cues may be all it takes to move the spotlight off of your behaviour and on to your work, where it rightly belongs.

Duelling Gestures

As you've read throughout this book, there are several non-verbal cues that can send more than one message. You know by now that it's important to assess an entire group of behaviours before drawing conclusions about a person's intended message, but this is often easier said than done. Your own emotions can play a powerful role in interpreting – and misinterpreting – someone else's body language. Be aware of this possibility and proceed with caution.

Arm-Crossing

You're discussing holiday plans with your girlfriend. You want to head to the beach; she's holding out for the mountains. You've had a long day at work, you're grumpy, and you just want this settled. She's standing there, her head tilted to the side, lips in a straight line, arms crossed. You seem to recall that the arm-cross is sometimes a sign of hostility: maybe she's trying to block you out of her world. You also seem to recall that the arm-cross can be a sign of insecurity, an indication that she's trying to protect herself from you. You don't know whether to argue or apologise for scaring her.

Both of these interpretations of the arms can be correct, but you're still off the mark here, probably due to your own rotten mood. If she were frowning, raising her voice and flatly refusing to go to the beach, then you might interpret the arm-cross as a sign of hostility. If she were acting pouty, then you'd be right on the money thinking that her crossed arms were an attempt to shield herself in some manner. But as the rest of her body language is rather neutral, it's probably safe to say that she's simply getting comfortable. That's the third interpretation of this gesture: sometimes those crossed arms just feel good.

Nose-Rubs

You've just asked your brother to lend you his car for the weekend. You wouldn't ask if it weren't an emergency, but your best friend who lives 100 miles away is going through some tough times and you need to help him out. As you say this, you rub the tip of your nose. Your brother looks right at you and tells you he needs his car to deliver meals to the elderly. And then he takes a swipe at his own nose.

You're immediately suspicious. You've never known your brother to do anything out of the goodness of his heart. He rubs his nose again, a gesture that you know can indicate untruthfulness. You're very sure of yourself as you yell, 'Liar!' And then he sneezes. And sneezes again. And then you notice the nasal spray and the tissues on the table.

Considering you were rubbing your own nose – not because you're suffering from allergies like your poor brother, but because you were lying about your own intentions (you really wanted the car so you could spend the weekend with your latest squeeze) – you shouldn't be so quick to throw stones. The fact that you were fibbing to him is probably what made you see dishonesty in his behaviour.

Lying has an entire set of non-verbal cues. Rubbing the nose can be one of them, but there's also the averted (or prolonged, dominating) eye contact, crossing the arms tightly, hiding the hands, flushing of the face and angling the body away from the other person.

As your brother was angled towards you and wasn't over- or under-doing his eye contact, his nose-rub was left standing on its own, and you took it out of context. Next time, be careful to assess the entire scene before hurling an accusation of dishonesty.

Looking for Trouble

Eye contact is something that a lot of people struggle with. For this reason, it's easy to misinterpret what someone else's eyes are saying, even if you're armed with the facts.

Let's say you've met an interesting man at a book signing. You seem to have a lot to talk about, so you agree to grab a cup of coffee with him afterwards. As you sit sipping your latte, working your way through the abridged story of your life, you notice that he has his chin in his hand, a little grin on his face and he's looking at you – too much. He hardly looks down at the table, or around the restaurant, or at his coffee cup. You're starting to get a little freaked out.

People who try to intimidate others display arrogant gestures, like using prolonged eye contact, raising the chin and making themselves look as big as possible. One of these gestures in the absence of the others doesn't necessarily mean a person is domineering.

Extended eye contact can certainly be a sign of domination, but it can also be a lack of awareness – this guy might have trouble with the whole glancing-off-to-the-side concept. Dominant personalities usually display themselves with a whole set of unmistakable cues. This guy isn't doing these things; in fact, he's fairly relaxed. It could be that he never learned when and how to break eye contact. Or it could be that he's smitten with you. Try telling him that he's making you uncomfortable – his non-verbal reaction to this comment will give you an indication of whether or not he's a decent chap.

Voyages of Discovery

In the last 20 years or so, a global economy has developed, along with a sense that the world isn't the big, mysterious place our forefathers believed it was. Not only are you likely to cross international borders at some point, you're very likely to know at least one person who has relocated to this country from some far-flung place. The desire to accept and understand each other is admirable, but it can be a difficult – if not impossible – task to accomplish if people from different cultures don't understand one another's body language.

Chapter 12 covered a lot of territory on this topic. The crux of the issue is that many non-verbal cues reveal a culture's underlying value system. For example, you don't go around touching heads in India, because the top of the head is believed to be the dwelling place of the soul. You don't rely on eye contact in Japan, because staring into the eyes is a sign of disrespect, and the Japanese culture is, in many ways, based on reverence. Even our own culture has its rules, believe it or not. British men are supposed to refrain from openly leering and shouting suggestive comments to women walking down the street. But this kind of behaviour is common in many South American countries and isn't intended to be degrading to women.

Knowing what to expect in terms of body language from another culture helps to eliminate countless misunderstandings, some of which can lead to serious issues like bigotry and/or ethnocentricity.

Whether you're travelling for business or pleasure, take the time to find out what kind of body language is acceptable and what's deemed wildly inappropriate in the region you're heading to. You'll have a better trip if you make an effort to behave like a native instead of making the conscious decision to stand out like a sore thumb.

Non-Verbal Tricks

There are some men and women who are well schooled in the art of using non-verbal cues to their advantage in almost any given situation, and then there are some people who have concentrated their attention on just a couple of winning efforts. It's not only business people who work confident, friendly body language into their everyday dealings. Your friends, your spouse and your neighbours also have some favourite tricks for turning situations to their advantage. What are they up to?

High Eyes

In any given argument, the person who is physically higher is subconsciously deemed to be in the position of power. So let's say your spouse is trying to convince you to invest in her brother's business. You tell her it's a bad idea. Her brother is a certified nutcase as far as you're concerned, and you wouldn't trust him with a ten-pound note, never mind half your life's savings. You sit yourself on the sofa, turn on the cricket, and consider the conversation over. Suddenly, your wife is in front of you, peering down into your eyes, informing you that the savings account belongs to her, too, and she's entering into this deal with or without your approval. In addition to the browbeating she's giving you, she's probably using several other domineering non-verbal cues here – crossed arms, wide-legged stance, a set jaw, furrowed eyebrows – but it's her position of being above you that gives her an added boost of power. When she walks away, the case seems closed.

The high-eye position is reminiscent of a parent scolding a child, which is why humans tend to either cower in reaction or rebel with everything they've got.

Queen Bee

It has long been theorised that women will use their female assets to get what they want from men. Is this true, or is this belief a throwback to pre-feminist days of male chauvinism?

It's fair to say that some women are very skilled at this practice, while others would never dream of flirting to get ahead in life. Women who do view their femininity as a tool tend to be equal opportunists – that is, they use their body language to charm men and women. Friendly touches, smiling, intense eye contact, angling the body and closing in on personal space are all tricks of the trade here. The difference, of course, is that men will fantasise about sleeping with this woman, where other women will consider including her in their lunch plans. The touchy-feely woman, of course, knows all of this beforehand and doesn't seem deterred when some people react negatively to her behaviour. The law of averages, she figures, is on her side. And judging by her success rate, she's right.

Alpha Male

Men have their own set of behaviours designed to intimidate one another and snare the most coveted females, the most profitable clients and the best seats at any given game. A man who's the head honcho in any given situation – whether it's business or pleasure – is known as the alpha male. He's usually taller than the other men (but not always – Napoleon Bonaparte was an alpha male who, contrary to common belief, was of average height) but he's not necessarily more intelligent or better looking. So how does he intimidate men, woo women and win business contracts?

The alpha male refers to the leader of a wolf pack. His female counterpart, not surprisingly, is the alpha female. The rest of the wolves are beta males and females. Their lot in life is to follow behind the alphas.

Simple. He acts confident. He uses the classic confident posturing – shoulders back, head up, straight spine – but at the same time, he looks content and relaxed. He's very sure that he's going to get whatever he wants, whether it's a seat at the bar or a date with the waitress. So what do you do with a man like this? If you're a woman attempting to date him, you have to let him come to you so he thinks he's made the conquest.

If you're a man dealing with an alpha male, don't be afraid to use your own confident body language in response to his domineering behaviour. Because this guy can be intimidating, he makes a lot of average guys feel badly about themselves. Just remember, he doesn't have anything that you can't achieve with confidence and persistence (two of his best tricks).

Patterns of Behaviour

What's normal behaviour for one person may be completely out of kilter for someone else. Some people are naturally smiley; others show their happiness with a peaceful look on their face. There are people who use touch to establish relationships, and then there are people who recoil when strangers lay an innocent hand on their forearm. If you know someone well enough, you know how she acts and perceives the world. In fact, you're probably already aware of her pattern of body language. When you notice changes in her behaviour, do you jump to the wrong conclusions or wait for the situation to play itself out?

Tune In to Others

Any radical change in behaviour – for better or worse – can indicate that something big is going on in a person's life. You've seen this before: your normally glum sister was all smiles in the weeks before she announced her pregnancy. Your always-cheerful grandmother was down in the dumps before she told you she'd been diagnosed with a serious illness. In each case, you pressed her for information – you just felt there was something to know. Once you heard the news, you said to yourself, 'I knew something was up! I could tell by the way she was acting!' Part of what you were noting was a change in body language. If your sister were normally a giddy person and your grandmother suffered from chronic depression, their secrets might have been safe forever (or at least for several more months).

Losing Touch

Knowing how to read patterns and changes in body language is a useful tool. Even if the other person is trying to hide his or her feelings, you can often pick up on the smallest non-verbal cues – your outgoing friend has been avoiding your eyes, for example, or your normally happy husband hasn't been smiling lately – and instantly know that something in this person's life is amiss.

A change in non-verbal cues is simply someone's way of letting the world know that all is not well with her. Making mention of it is your way of saying that you care.

One thing you don't want to do is let your observations get ahead of you. In other words, don't start looking for signs of love – or deception – in everyone you meet. That's the fastest way to go from leading a sane life to living a completely miserable existence. Take people as they are and learn to read their non-verbal cues as they appear. Once you know individuals fairly well and are used to their patterns of behaviour, you'll know what's normal and what isn't.

Symptoms of Illness

Last but not least, there are a number of physical ailments that affect the movement of the body. Even if you're aware that someone is suffering from one of these conditions, it can be hard to overlook gestures that don't fit into the context of the situation or conversation. And when you aren't aware of someone's ailment, confusion is the order of the day. This is just the type of thing that leads to social isolation for these people.

Neurological Disorders

When someone has a condition that affects the nervous system, he can have all sorts of behavioural symptoms – far too many to get into here, so let's talk about one specific condition that can wreak havoc on the body: Parkinson's disease. Sufferers may experience:

- Uncontrollable shaking.
- Stiffness.
- A shuffling walk.
- Unclear speech.
- A 'flat affect' of the face.

In the earliest stages of the disease, these symptoms can easily be mistaken as signs of aloofness or jitteriness, which may drive other people away, which only makes the situation worse. Understandably, many sufferers also deal with depression, which comes with its own set of physical symptoms.

So are you supposed to ask everyone who trembles if he has some sort of neurological problem? Of course not. It just helps to be aware that when someone's non-verbal cues are somewhat unusual, they may be out of his control. Try to give him a fair chance through verbal communication before you write him off as being uninterested or too nervous for your liking.

Specific body parts can be affected by illnesses. For example, Graves' disease often results in bulging eyes. Kyphosis is the medical term for a hunched back. Rosacea causes flushed cheeks. Consciously looking beyond these physical conditions can help eliminate misunderstandings in non-verbal comunication.

Depression

It's estimated that one in five people suffer from some sort of depression at some time in their life, which makes it very likely that you know at least one person who's in the throes of some serious blues. The physical signs of depression can include:

- Lack of facial expressions.
- Poor posture.
- Angling the body away from others.
- Anxious behaviours, like tightly crossing the arms.

Basically, a depressed person will often appear to have no interest in the people and the world around him, which leads other people to stay away from him, which can lead to a deepening of the depression. It's not your job to diagnose emotions or act as a therapist; however, acknowledging that body language isn't always sending the message it appears to (it's easy to mistake depression for aloofness, for example) might lead to a better understanding of the people around you.

It's human nature to reject the people who seem to be rejecting you. But if you open the door to meaningful communication – by simply saying hello, for example – you might see an instant change in the depressed person's demeanour (a smile, eye contact, a straightening of the spine and so on).

It's All Human Nature

Speaking of human nature – at this point you know that non-verbal communication is based on instinct, and so are many of our reactions to unspoken messages. As you read in the opening chapters of this book, experts estimate that two-thirds of all face-to-face interactions are non-verbal. The person who learns the basics of body language has a distinct advantage over the person who thinks non-verbal cues are random and unimportant.

Even if you're not able to completely decode every person you know, reading non-verbal gestures can provide you with a gut feeling about another person's true intentions. And what are gut feelings? Instinctive reactions. People often find themselves confused by their spouses, friends and colleagues because they ignore these innate responses to non-verbal cues and rely on the spoken word instead. For example, you can probably sense when a friend is lying to you (because you can see his anxious body language), but because he verbally insists he's being truthful, you believe him. (Or at least you would have believed him before you realised the power of body language.)

You now have enough knowledge about non-verbal cues to project your most confident self, protect yourself from liars and create meaningful connections with the people around you. In short, knowing how to read and express non-verbal gestures has the power to greatly improve your life. So don't be shy – get out there and start using what you've learned. Just let your body do the talking.

Appendix
Some Important Body-Language Signs

Ten Signs Your Date Is Interested in You

1. Prolonged eye contact.
2. Angling the body towards you.
3. Lip-licking.
4. Confident posture.
5. Tilting the head to the side.
6. Hair-twirling (females only).
7. Widening of the eyes.
8. Invading your personal space.
9. Friendly little touches.
10. Smiling.

Ten Non-Verbal Cues to Display in a Job Interview

1. Eye contact.
2. Angling the body towards the interviewer.
3. Confident posture.
4. Mirroring the interviewer's body language.
5. Keeping the hands in sight and relaxed.
6. Steady feet on the floor.
7. Avoiding self-touches.
8. Occasionally tilting the head to the side to show that you're listening.
9. Smiling.
10. Firm handshake.

Ten Non-Verbal Signs of Liars

1. Wide eyes.
2. Flushed face.
3. Self-touches (touching the back of the neck, the face, the nose).

4. Lack of eye contact.

5. Excessive eye contact.

6. Excessive blinking.

7. Angling the body away from the accuser.

8. Hiding the hands.

9. Biting the lips or covering the mouth.

10. Exaggerated movement of arms and legs.

Ten Non-Verbal Cues That Could Get You into Trouble in Other Countries

1. The 'peace' or 'V for victory' sign.

2. The 'OK' sign.

3. The 'thumbs up' sign.

4. Eye contact.

5. Kissing.

6. Invading personal space.

7. Showing the sole of your foot.

8. Touching the top of the head.

9. Blowing your nose at a social function.

10. Excessive display of emotion.

Index

accessories (clothing) 170
adaptors 18
affect displays 18
    see also emotions
aggressive behaviour,
    children's 139–40
aging
    and clothing 174–5
    eyes 94–5
alpha males 258–9
ambiguous body language
    253–6
androgyny 182–3
anger, signs of 80, 83, 87–8,
    97, 103, 108–9, 132, 147, 220–1
angling 32, 65–6, 122, 144–5,
    213, 235–6
    and dating 213, 235–6
    heads 71–4, 236
    and lying 199
animal behaviour 14–15,
    59–60
anxiety
    redirecting the energy of
        127–8
    signs of 47, 48, 118–25, 147
    see also nervousness
appearance 20–1, 70–1, 94,
    176–7, 200–1
arms 30, 63–4
    arm-crossing 47, 64, 198–9,
        239, 254
    male positioning 233–4
    positioning and cultural
        difference 162
arrogance
    shyness masked as 31,
        32–3

signs of 31–3, 73–4, 188
assessing your body
    language 33–7
attractiveness, physical 70–1,
    176–7, 201–2
authority, positions of 66–7
autism 135, 249
avatars 249

babies 130–2
`bad boys' 204
baldness 77
big, making yourself look
    58–9, 60–4, 77, 122
Birdwhistell, Ray 17–18
biting 90
    lips 198, 208, 222
    nails 143
Blair, Tony 52
blank faces 21–2, 131, 227, 261
blinking, excessive 193
body parts 29–30
    see also specific body
        parts
body types (physique)
    179–89
    and body weight 180–3,
        185–7
    ideal female 180–3
    ideal male 184
    and physical fitness 187–8
    Sheldon's somatypes
        188–9
body weight 20–1, 180–3,
    185–7
boredom, signs of 47–8, 56,
    99–100, 103, 117, 253
Botox 94, 97

bouncing 124
Bow, Clara 82
bows 164–5
Brazil 163–4
breasts 183
`broadside display' 122
bullying, relational 135–6
Bush, George W 52
business cards 163–4
business-oriented body
    language 28, 141–53
    appropriate body
        language 252–3
    conformity 142–3, 252
    facial expressions 147–8
    hands 145–7
    inappropriate body
        language 152–3
    job interviews 141–51, 168,
        263
    posture 143–5
    promotion 151–2, 253
    touching others 235

Castro, Fidel 46
charms, false 22–3
chewing 89–90
children 118, 125, 129–40
    aggressive behaviour
        139–40
    babies 130–2
    extreme body language
        138–40
    lying 136–8
    manipulative body
        language 134–5
    nature-nurture debate
        130–4

preschoolers 132–3
relational bullying 135–6
tantrums 132, 133, 138
chin tilt 71
China 159, 164
chopping motions 42
Clinton, Bill 52
clothing 167–78, 247
accessories 170
and age 174–5
colour wheels 177–8
and common sense 168–9
and dating 176–7
defying dress codes 172–3
dressing the part 169–73
errors in judgment 173–5
feeling uncomfortable
with your 170–1
powering up 171–2, 178
Collins, Phil 62
colour wheels 177–8
compulsive skin picking
(CSP) 120
confidence 62, 73, 183, 203–4,
258–9
conformity 142–3, 252
confusion, signs of 88–9,
96, 97
context 252–3
cosmetic work 82, 83
coughing 197
court 169
'critical distance' 60
crow's feet 94–5
Cruise, Tom 62
CSP see compulsive skin
picking
culture 19, 37, 155–66, 256–7,
264
curricula vitae (CVs), video
248

da Vinci, Leonardo 18–19
dancing 238
Darwin, Charles 14, 17, 18
dating 35, 201–13
and clothing 176–7
and confidence 203–4
and eye contact 102,
206–7, 211–12, 216–20, 227,
230–3, 240
and mouths 208, 220–3
online 241–50
and personal space 207–9,
212–13, 223–5, 227, 236–9
and physical
attractiveness 201–2
signs of indifference 213,
227, 238–40
signs of interest 206–8,
210–13, 263
signs people are only
interested in sex 205–6
skills for single guys
229–40
skills for single women
215–27
things to avoid 208–10
women's mixed messages
205–6
depression 101–2, 131–2, 261–2
dermatillomania 120
development, oral phase 89
disagreement, signals of 87,
112–13
disguises 30–3
disgust, signs of 109
displeasure, signs of 112–13,
221
dominating body language
73–4, 255–9
alpha males and 258–9
eyes 101

hand gestures 44–5,
49–50, 51
handshakes 146
head gestures 80
duel interpretations 253–6

ectomorphs 188–9
elbow-grab 51
emblems 17, 42
emotions
and arm movements 162
and the eyes 104–5
and flared nostrils 108–10
'flat affect' 21–2, 131, 227,
261
and the hands 118–19
inability to express 21–2
and the mouth 161
see also affect displays;
specific emotions
empathy 72
endomorphs 188–9
endorphins 127
environment, and body
language 252–3
errant body language,
correcting 37–9, 251–62
evolution of body language
13–24
excitement, signs of 80, 117,
124
eye contact 100–4
breaking 102–4
cultural influences on
157–9
and dating 102, 206–7,
211–12, 216–20, 227, 230–3,
240
and lying 136, 192–3
minimal 28–9, 32, 37, 71,
136, 158, 209, 213, 227, 239

misinterpreting 255–6
eyebrows 95–8
    frowns 97–8, 192, 232
    and lying 192
    positioning and cultural
        difference 159
    raised 28–9, 96–7, 159, 192,
        232–3
eyelashes 98
    eyelash-bat 219–20
eyes 93–105
    aging 94–5
    appearance 94–5
    demure look upwards 103,
        219, 220
    and emotion 104–5
    'eye roll' 103
    half-closed 99–100, 194
    and lying 136, 192–4
    make-up 94–5, 98, 216
    male 95
    positioning 194, 257
    shifty 103–5
    squinting 99, 194, 232
    wide 100, 194, 218, 219,
        232–3
    winks 219
    women's 94–5

fabric 169
faces 30
    attractiveness 70–1
    babies and 131–2
    blank 21–2, 131, 227, 261
    and business body
        language 147–8
    distorted expressions 21–2
    flushed 137, 194–5
    and lying 194–5
    and mind-reading
        software 249

rubbing 48
    see also eyebrows; eyes;
        mouths; noses
false charms 22–3
fear, signs of 14, 16, 88–9, 109
feet
    movements 123–5, 253
    positioning and cultural
        difference 165–6
fertility 94–5, 174–5, 216
fidgeting 117–28, 138
'fight-or-flight' reaction
    14–16, 108, 193, 195
fingers 46
    drumming 48, 121–2, 253
first impressions 175
fists 45–6, 53
flappers 181
'flat affect' 21–2, 131, 227, 261
flinching 227
flushing 137, 194–5
friendliness, signs of 31
frowning 97–8, 192, 232

gaze
    aversion 131
    'gaze down' 102, 103
    'gaze up' 103, 219, 220
gender stereotypes 62
glaring 209
'go away', indications of 122
Graves' disease 261
Greece 156–7, 163–4
grooming, public 78, 209
gut feelings 262

hair
    flicking 77
    hairstyles 74–6
    self-grooming 78
    twirling 78–9

hands 30, 41–54
    and business body
        language 145–7
    fingers 46
    fists 45–6, 53
    handwringing 38
    to the heart 42
    hiding 36, 52, 137, 198–9
    hyped-up 46–8
    indicators of happiness
        126
    nervous 118–22
    palms-down gestures
        44–5, 46, 53
    palms-in gestures 44
    palms-out gestures 45
    palms-up gestures 43–4,
        53
    'patting' gestures 53
    placement 52–3, 146–7
    positioning and cultural
        difference 162–5
    and self-touches 47
    signing 54
handshakes 36, 48–51
    for business 145, 149
    and cultural difference
        164–5
    the grip 48–9
    limp 48–9
    palms-down 49–50, 146
    palms-up 49, 50
    the shake 50
happiness, signs of 90–2,
    109–10, 125–7
heads 30, 69–80
    angling 71–4
    chin tilt 71
    faces 70–1
    hair 74–9
    levelling 73

and lying 195–6
nodding 80, 156–7
positioning and cultural
    difference 156–7
shaking 79, 196
tossing 157
height 184
    making yourself appear
        bigger 77, 122
    making yourself appear
        smaller 28–9, 57, 59, 60–1,
        123
    standing tall 62–3
highly animated people
    138–40
`hip' body language 26
hips
    hands on 64
    swaying 226

illness 21–2, 260–2
illustrators 17–18
impression making 101, 153,
    175
inappropriate body
    language 152–3
indecision 84
India 156, 157, 163, 166, 256
indifference, signs of 56, 213,
    227, 238–40
innate body language 16,
    46, 130
innocence, appearance of
    72, 73
insecurity 62
    regarding appearance 21
    signs of 21, 31, 56–7, 62,
        210–11
instinct 262
interest
    lack of 66, 99–100, 213, 227,

238–40
showing 65–6, 100, 206–8,
    210–13, 263
Iran 157
Italy 161, 162

Japan 158, 159, 162–5, 256
jaws 87–90
    chewing 89–90
    jaw-drop 88–9
    locked 87–8, 221
    size and shape 88
job interviews 141–51, 168, 263
judging others 20–2

Kennedy, JF 52
kinesics 17–18
kissing 85, 161
knuckle cracking 48
kyphosis 261

Laos 157
laughter 91–2
learning body language 16
leering 209–10
legs 30
    leg-crossing 61, 124, 198–9,
        236, 239
    male dating position 233
    wide-legged stance 60–1
lips 81–5
    biting 198, 208, 222
    compressed 83, 88, 198
    and dating 208, 220
    fillers 220
    licking 86, 208, 222
    lip-purse 83–4
    positioning and cultural
        difference 160–1
    pouts 84–5, 221, 222
    puckers 84

listening skills 72, 102
love see dating
lying, signs of 27–9, 47, 87, 96,
    112, 120–1, 136–8, 191–200,
    254–5, 263–4

MacArthur, General Douglas
    49
make-up 94–5, 98, 181, 216
management 27–8, 49–51
manipulative use of body
    language 22–3, 32–3, 52–3,
    134, 257–9
medical conditions 21–2,
    260–2
meeting others 34–6, 58
men
    alpha males 258–9
    dating skills for single
        229–40
    eyes 95
    gender stereotypes 62
    ideal body types 184
    signs he is only interested
        in sex 205
mesomorphs 188–9
Mexico 161, 164
Millenials 250
mind reading, online 249–50
mirroring 145
mistakes, minimizing 37–9,
    251–62
Monroe, Marilyn 181
mouths 81–92
    expressing happiness
        with 90–2
    jaws 87–90, 221
    kissing 85, 161
    laughter 91–2
    and love 208, 220–3
    mouth chewing 90

mouth-rubbing 195
positioning and cultural difference 160–1
smiling 90–1, 209, 223, 247
tongues 85–7, 198
see also lips

nail biting 143
nature-nurture debate 130–4
neck rub 38–9
nervousness 117
see also anxiety
neurological disorders 260–1
'no', signalling 79, 156–7, 196
noses 107–15
blowing 160
and cultural difference 160
flared nostrils 108–10, 195
nose-crinkle 112–13
nose-rubbing 112, 195, 254–5
nose-tapping 111, 160
nose-touches 110–11
sneezing 113–14
snorting 114–15
nurses 21

obesity 185
'OK' sign 42, 163–4
O'Leary, Dermot 62
online dating 241–50
photographs 246–7
predators 242
reading minds online 249–50
safety issues 242
spelling 244
texting shortcuts 242–4
turn-ons/turn-offs 244–5
video-sharing websites 248

openness, signs of 31
oral phase of development 89
over-statements 196–8
overweight 20–1, 185–7
ovulation, indicators of 175

Pakistan 157
panic attacks 118
Parkinson's disease 260–1
patterns of behaviour 259–60
personal body language, what it says about you 25–39
personal hygiene 146
personal space 33
and cultural difference 165–6
and dating 207–9, 212–13, 223–5, 227, 236–9
defining 223–4
at work 253
Philippines 157, 159
Phoenix, Joaquin 62
photographs 246–7
physical attractiveness 70–1, 176–7, 201–2
physical exercise 127–8, 181, 182
physical fitness 187–8
physique see body types
politicians 52–3
positioning
authoritative 66–7
and lying 198–9
postnatal depression 101–2
posture 37, 55–67
angle 65–6
arms 63–4
and authority 66–7

in the business world 143–5
hands on hips 64
leg language 61
and lying 198–9
making yourself appear bigger 58–9, 60–4, 77, 122
making yourself appear smaller 28–9, 57, 59, 60–1, 123
and male dating 233–4
perfecting 58–61
perils of poor 56–8
standing tall 62–3
and work 58
pouts 84–5, 221, 222
power suits 168, 171
preschoolers 132–3
promotion 151–2, 253
puckers 84
pupils 193

Queen Bees 258
quizzes, body language assessment 33–7

regulators 18
relational bullying 135–6
Roberts, Julia 91
rosacea 261
Russia 163

sadness, signs of 97
salespeople 23
Saudi Arabia 158–9
self soothing 78, 111–12, 119–21, 123–5, 199
self-protective body language 28–9, 64
self-touches 29, 47, 111–12,

119–21, 137, 147, 195–6, 253
Sheldon, William 188–9
shoes 172
shoulders 30
     shoulder-smack 51
     squaring 65
shrugging 37
shyness 31, 56
sign language 54
'size-zero' 182
slouching 37, 56–7, 60, 143
small, making yourself
     appear 28–9, 57, 59, 60–1,
     123
smiling 90–1, 247
     fake 91, 209, 223
     zygomatic 91
smirks 32
sneezing 113–14
snorting 114–15
somatypes 188–9
spine, shifting away 122, 123
spoken word
     matching to body
        language 27
     mismatched with body
        language 15, 27–9, 37–9
squinting 99, 194, 232
staring 35, 217, 231–2
startling 130
stress 127–8
submissive body language
     34, 36, 49, 101–2
sucking 130
suits, power 168, 171
surprise, signs of 88–9, 110
swaggering 32

tantrums 132, 133, 138
'templing' 42
Thailand 156, 157, 159, 165

thinness 182–3, 186–7
throat clearing 197, 253
thumbs up 42, 163–4
Tibet 156
tongues 85–7
     tongue-show 87, 198
touch
     self-touches 29, 47, 111–12,
        119–21, 137, 147, 195–6, 253
     sense of 119
     touching others 225,
        234–5, 253
trends 26
Truman, Harry S. 49
Trump, Donald 76
tuning in 259
Twiggy 182

under-statements 196–8

'V' for victory sign 42
verbal/non-verbal confusion
     15, 27–9, 37–9
video CVs 248
video-sharing websites 248
vision, poor 98, 99
vocal tone 197

waifs 182
walks 32, 226
waving 42
winks 219
women
     dating skills for single
        215–27
     displaying your assets
        225–6
     eyes 94–5
     gender stereotypes 62
     ideal body types 180–3
     mixed messages in love

205–6
     Queen Bees 258

yawning 253
'yes', signalling 157, 159, 196

Acknowledgments

Many, many thanks to Jessica Faust at Bookends, for keeping me knee-deep in work and seeing me through the rough spots; Dave Givens (quite possibly the fastest technical editor in the world), for your insight and suggestions; Tricia Dinunzio and Fay Leff, for connecting me to your web of internet pals; Kerry Smith, for your patience; Jennifer Lata Rung and Helen Edelman, for your combined encouragement; and last but not least, to my family and friends, for continuously giving me an audience to play to and loads of observational material to work with.

For my brother, Mark

LOVED THIS BOOK?

Tell us what you think and you could win another fantastic book from David & Charles in our monthly prize draw.

www.lovethisbook.co.uk

The Only Book You'll Ever Need Running
Art Liberman
978-1-4463-0140-1

From gentle jogs to intense marathons this is your complete guide to fulfilling your running goals. Covers everything from training safely to choosing the right equipment, and increasing physical and mental strength.

The Only Book You'll Ever Need Guitar
Ernie Jackson
978-1-4463-0138-8

The perfect introduction to playing the acoustic or electric guitar, with clear step-by-step instructions, diagrams and practice tips. Features playing your first songs, reading music and tablature, and even forming your own band.

The Only Book You'll Ever Need Meditation
David B. Dillard-Wright and Ravinder Jerath
978-1-4463-0139-5

Features everything you need to know about this ancient tradition – proven to relieve stress, ease an ailment, and enhance concentration. Covers posture and breathing techniques, creative visualisation, and the various cultural and religious approaches to meditation.